I0518623

FROM NAPTOWN TO RED CARPETS

LIFETREK

ANTHONY MONTGOMERY

A Memoir

For my children, Meghan and Aiden.

Written by Anthony Montgomery

Edited by Andrew E.C. Gaska with Eric Thomas
Production by Chris Northrop
Cover Art Design by Myke Smith

www.AnthonyMontgomery.com

*Trek Life

FOREWORD

In my salad days - to the extent I ever had salad days - I understudied a theatrical production of a musical called '*Working*', based verrrrry loosely on a book of interviews of blue-collar people, conducted by the late great Chicago journalist Studs Terkel. I can't get the damned earwig tunes out of my brain to this day, a testament to the potency of cheap music, as Noel Coward once said, and too bad, because it was a fairly execrable production, and stirs bad memories of a time when I couldn't sing and dance my way *into* a paper bag, much less out of one . . . But what has also stayed with me, even more than my inability to hit my high notes (or my low notes, or my in-between notes), is the source work itself, a fascinating collection of recorded conversations with Americans about the work they did, and the lives they led. It was my first exposure to what Terkel called 'oral history', a form of story-telling, revelatory to me then, that I have subsequently come to deeply cherish.

People talking about their lives, people sharing their stories, people speaking clearly in their own unaffected and unpolished voices, is an entirely different kind of genre than memoir or autobiography. In further books (about the Great Depression, for instance), Terkel refined his craft as an interviewer, and laid the groundwork for a slew of other journalists who followed in his wake, awakened to the possibility of publishing 'the people gabbing' opuses of their own (notably, of late, the magnificent '*Secondhand Time: The Last of the Soviets,* a symphony of Soviet citizens speaking about the disintegration of the Soviet Union, compiled by Svetlana Alexievich).

(Anthony should have known, when asking me to write a preface, that I'd be long-winded about it: my nature, and if I were him I'd have made fun of me about that in this, *his* marvelous oral history of *his* own 'life and times'. . . . he spares me, the damned fool, although thank God he teases Dominic Keating a bit.)

Anthony is very candid with us in his book, letting us know on page one that he is not a writer, he is a person with an impassioned soul that he'd like to share with us, a person with a story he thinks we should hear, a story that he doesn't want to entrust to somebody else to tell on his behalf, and who - consequently - is prepared to risk some roughness and some rawness in the telling to ensure that it comes out the way he thinks it should.

In this book, you'll hear Anthony speak directly to you, in a voice at times enraged, embittered, chastened, exultant, fumbling, reflective, bemused. It's a voice with a million colors, reflecting Anthony's many, many talents (that bastard, he CAN sing and dance) and his many, many interests. It's the voice of a man who has led a fascinating and difficult life, and who is brave enough, dare I say foolhardy enough, to try and tell us what it was like to be him, in a direct, simple and unadorned way: what it was like to be treated harshly by a physically abusive parent, abused by neighborhood creeps, reviled by heartland bigots; what it was like to be a talented but directionless young man who wasn't sure whether he should be a dancer, an actor, or a thief; what it was like to be a prideful person in Hollywood having to learn how to navigate an industry that asks you, over and over again, to check your ego at the door, in ways that are not often kind. Rarely kind.

It is, most importantly, Anthony's *voice* you'll hear. A voice I know, and love, well.

This isn't the artfully nuanced memoir of a professional writer, or a careful and clever autobiography ghosted by a professional ventriloquist - it's raw, as I said, and unshaped at times - I give you permission to skip the parts about swimming, sorry Anthony - but what it mostly is, and why I think you should read it, is bracing, and honest.

It's honest about what it means to grapple with pain and loss, insecurity and trauma, all the dark stuff of life, but it also has much to say about what it is to develop poise, what it is to find a growth of confidence, and grace, in spite of - perhaps because of - all that dark stuff. Real dark stuff. Anthony's journey is an inspiriting journey, finally, and that's the kind of story that never gets old.

Anthony alludes to the fact that I used to call him 'Force of Nature' Montgomery, when we worked together on *Star Trek: Enterprise.* This

5

because, when I was in the make-up chair very early in the AM, getting my rubber head glued on, quietly listening to classical music, enjoying the calm of an empty backlot, Anthony would show up for work (earlier than he had to be there, no surprise for this over-achiever). Jesus, nobody's around, who's he yelling at, you'd think, but Anthony would somehow find the few peeps about to holler his greetings to. The security guard, the janitor. Stray cats. Always boisterous, exuberant, and joyful (I also called him The Human Car Alarm, but he didn't like that nickname as much), Anthony had then, has now, always will have an unquenchable thirst for life and a deep appreciation of the need to celebrate existence itself. This 'oral history', told by Anthony Montgomery to Anthony Montgomery (he saved a buck on this tome by cutting that Terkelesque cat out of the process) is about a man undaunted, and the nature of what it took to be able to lay claim to that state of undauntedness. It's a celebratory book, and one I'm very, very proud to have been asked to give my smooches to.

Foreword by John Billingsley

INTRODUCTION

I resisted the idea of writing a book because the concept of actually revisiting some of the major events that shaped my past is an overwhelming thought. I've also never cared about being famous. Fame has come to me as a by-product of doing what I love and doing that to the best of my ability.

More than any job I've ever had, I love acting. I love to perform. I used to say, "I'm just an actor," but after more than thirty years of performing in various capacities, I've realized that I'm much more than just that. I am an entertainer. I can act, dance, rap, emcee, host, sing (not the best, but I can carry a tune), perform stand-up comedy, and I've become a writer and graphic novelist. I've found a true passion and love for those other creative art forms (all save for writing—the only one that I've yet to become completely comfortable with. I find it challenging and it doesn't come easy to me. But without writing, we wouldn't be here, would we?).

Each creative endeavor I start off on provides me a way to distinctively display different aspects of myself, allowing me to express my entire being. Entertaining gives me opportunities to interact with diverse and amazing people around the world. I've learned that if done successfully, each form of artistic expression comes with its own degree of recognition and fulfillment, and bringing it back around to fame—that's the point. Whether fame is achieved or not, entertainment is in my blood and I do it because I love it. I love to affect people on the deepest level… a soul level… and authentically make a sincere bond. Entertainment gives me a way to do that, gives me a platform to connect with the masses. And hopefully, I can make a difference.

Thanks to Gene Roddenberry's vision, I've already been blessed with celebrity and success on a global scale. Decades of compelling storytelling from the *Star Trek* producers and writing staff combined with my being a member of the best crew in Starfleet (yes, I'm biased), my crew… my *Trek* family – Scott Bakula, John Billingsley, Jolene Blalock, Dominic Keating, Linda Park and Connor Trinneer—and the most loyal fan following on the planet (Trekkies worldwide)—has made a difference in my life. The moment I was added to the cast of *Star Trek: Enterprise* as Ensign Travis Mayweather and joined such a storied franchise, I instantly gained fans and celebrity around the world in places I didn't know existed.

Though I initially resisted writing, I also understand that I have connected with a lot of people and that many of them want to know more about me. That's hard for me because I'm not big on sharing my personal life.

I have overcome some major challenges and wanted to write a book that could offer hope to readers. I wanted to make sure the book would be engaging, moving and inspiring. With a bunch of thoughts swirling around my head, I decided to give a look inside my mind, heart and soul. I could easily have gone down the same dark roads as some of the people I knew growing up, but I have such a love for life and zest for living that maintaining the life of a criminal is not an option for me. I choose to control the negative energy in me and redirect it into something positive. But I wasn't always this way.

I have done *a lot* of dumb things that I wish I could undo. I have also done some incredible things that give me pride. This book is my truth. This is my life. This is my trek.

Here we go.

SENSITIVITY WARNING: Some of what you are about to read in the following pages may contain sensitive subject matter that could be triggering to some readers. I have written this book from a place of love and being healed, but some of the roads that lead me here may be uncomfortable for some people out there.

CHAPTER ONE
HOME

On one of the best days of my life I was living in a two bedroom, two bathroom apartment. Not far from Universal Studios, my home was in an area of North Hollywood that was eventually rezoned and renamed to West Toluca Lake. It wasn't a fancy spot and it wasn't very big—only 864 square feet—but it was big enough for me. I had an oversized, puffy, cream colored leather chair, an Earth tone-colored couch that was custom constructed for me, and a quality set of rustic furniture (armoire, two end tables, coffee table, DVD/CD case that I paid the company to build), along with all new electronics (TV and DVD player, surround sound stereo system). But the apartment unit itself was basic. There were no vaulted ceilings or marble countertops, no hardwood floors or crown moldings, no glamorous features of any kind, save for a balcony. The building was so old that the letters spelling its name on the front were falling off and looked rundown. None of that mattered to me because that was the longest period I had lived anywhere besides my mother's house. The neighborhood was safe, my place was clean, and it was my home. There wasn't anything particularly special about that day but it was one of the best because I was at peace with everything in my life. All of my bills were paid and I had excellent credit (my FICO score was over 800). During that time I was paying my rent months in advance, my child support and responsibilities for my daughter were taken care of, and I had my mother on an allowance that paid her bills and kept a little money in her pocket. I was able to help friends out financially whenever I could. I lived beneath my means so I was able to travel whenever and wherever I wanted. My life was good. I was blessed and filled with gratitude. I worked hard to get to that point. It was one of those good days that Ice Cube rapped about.

I mentioned how my life was at that time because no one knew that the same guy who was excited for a simple thing like being able to pay my bills on time, was also successfully working in one of the most coveted fields in the world. I was part of one of the biggest franchises in Hollywood history, working as an actor on a pretty popular science fiction series. For me, it was a wonderful day at the office.

It was a beautiful LA day, about 70 degrees, blue skies, the thin layer of smog that blankets the city was barely visible. There was a moderate amount of traffic, nothing to get bothered by. I made it to the studio in no time, which was normally only about 20 minutes from my front door (with no traffic). I smiled brightly and pulled up to the Paramount gates where I was greeted with a smile and a wave from the security guard as I flashed my badge to gain entry. I got a rush (as always) driving onto the Paramount Lot, going past the giant blue backdrop that greeted everyone, on my way to the set of Enterprise. I felt a rush because I was living my dream, knowing I was one of the chosen few who was actually able to make a living at an acting career, knowing that I probably beat more odds than I would ever know about. I knew how incredibly fortunate and blessed I was to be a working actor in Hollywood, to be a part of the elusive 1% of actors who get to support themselves as artists. I found a space among the rows of cars, parked and walked towards our sound stages. Stage 18 will always be special to me because that's where our bridge set was housed.

When I got to our trailers, I checked in with my castmates, stopping by their trailers after leaving my personal belongings in my own.

"Hey, Dom, good morning," I called out to Dominic, who was usually the first person I saw.

"Morning, T," he called back, in his cool British accent.

"What's the word, Con?" I said to Connor, "Morning."

"Hey, Anthony, mornin'," he pleasantly responded.

"Morning, sis," I greeted Linda.

"Hey, good morning," Linda warmly called back.

"What up, Ma?" I called out as I knocked on Jolene's door, per our usual fun banter.

"What's up, Pops?" she replied, opening her door with a bright smile.

As was often the case, John was off that day and he was missed when he wasn't there.

I stopped by Scott's trailer last. I knocked on his door and waited. He opened the door and in his normal fashion, greeted me with a big smile and warm hug.

"Good morning, Anthony," he beamed.

"Good morning, Scott," I smiled.

I asked each of them if they wanted or needed anything for breakfast and they all declined, so I headed to the caterer to grab something for myself before going back to my trailer.

I checked the sides (small versions of the script) that were left for me to make sure nothing had changed from what I studied the night before, then tackled the day's work while I ate and listened to music in the background - Sting ("Seven Days" stayed on repeat) and Lenny Kravitz ("Fly Away" always took me away). After a while, a production assistant knocked on my door and said they were ready for us to rehearse the first scene. I downed the last of my juice, gathered my sides and went to set. I was overjoyed with the state of my world.

But I didn't start that way. I didn't come from that world. I survived my life to earn the life I wanted.

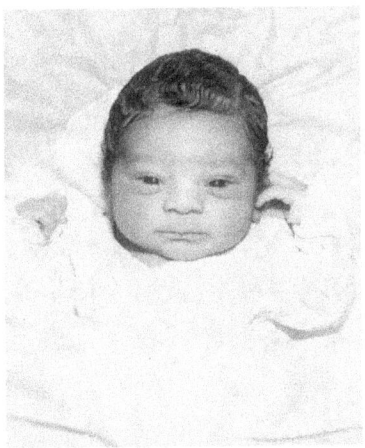

Baby Anthony

I was born Anthony Dwayne Montgomery on June 2, 1971 in Indianapolis, Indiana. My mother's name is Sandra and my father's is Harold (he wasn't part of my life growing up so I just referred to him as "my biological"). My parents met while they were in high school. My mother had me when she was sixteen and I was her second kid. She had my sister, Nicole (who I call "Nikki") at fifteen—one year and one week before I came into the world.

Growing up I was a scrawny, rambunctious, hyperactive, animated kid with a lot of energy. I was always getting into something and ran my mouth too much. I was a wild boy and rarely controlled what I said. I'm sure

Little Anthony

I got on a lot of people's nerves as a child and teenager. I talked so much, I may have made myself a target to be picked on, at least to some degree. I was bullied a lot growing up. By bullied I mean I was chased home after school almost everyday—mainly at one elementary school I attended, most times having to scramble over 8-9 foot fences, and only then getting away because I was faster than them. When I wasn't faster I'd have to hide in abandoned houses until the bullies were gone. When I couldn't run or hide I'd sometimes be surrounded and taunted by three or four boys while the nastiest one kept punking me and punching me. It would have been way worse for me if not for my sister Nikki.

Nikki was my first friend. When I was little she was my protector.

Left: *Three years old*
Above right: *Nikki and me*

Nikki is the nicest person you could ever meet but would also be really tough and she never let anybody mess with me. I acted like I wasn't afraid, but I was scared of fighting, although I would still huff and puff and stick my chest out and talk a lot of trash. Nikki showed up like the older brother I never had. Even though she was tiny, she fought with the heart of a lion. She got into a lot of fights with different boys for picking on me. When I was taught to fight as a kid, I never really learned to defend myself. I was shown how to punch and told to "keep swinging" and if they were bigger than me, to "pick up something and bust 'em up side the head." My life would have been miserable if Nikki hadn't been there for me. Nikki was my defender, my guardian angel in the flesh. I love you, Nikki.

As a kid, I never knew why my father, or Harold as I came to call him, wasn't in my life and we never talked about him. I cried to myself for years wishing he was around. I have a large family (aunts, uncles, cousins, etc.) but most of my relatives weren't open about discussing family matters unless information was coming from the parent of whichever child had questions. I didn't learn much about Harold until I was an adult and about to move to California. I only remember seeing him a total of three times in my life before moving across the country: I saw him once when I was between 11-13 years old when he stopped by where we were living and drove mom and me around the block in his truck. I remember feeling anxious sitting between my mom and my dad for the first time. I don't remember saying much, I was too nervous and surprised that he was there. I don't remember him being very talkative either. I remember just smiling nervously. What I wanted was for him to stay in my life and be my dad, teach me. Teach me what I didn't know. Help me grow. Help me learn how to be a man. I didn't know how to communicate that as a kid. He didn't stay around.; I saw him a second time when I was about 21 and home from college for the weekend - I was at an auto body shop owned by a man who I had recently learned was my grandfather, Harold's father, my grandpa Earnest. I was walking into the shop and Harold walked right past me out the door. I spoke (like most Black men speak to each other, even if they don't know each other) but I didn't realize he was my father until grandpa Earnest pointed it out to me after Harold had gone. I walked back to the entrance and looked out toward where his car was just as he drove away. I didn't show it but I felt completely insignificant, like I didn't matter. He knew who I was and he couldn't even say he was my dad? That really hurt me to my core; The third time I saw Harold I was 25 and moving away from Indiana in a couple days. He came to my mom's house. That time we had a powerful interaction. Because of the circumstances surrounding our meeting (and me not wanting to be there because he initially dismissed my request to meet him), he was fairly quiet and didn't really know what to say. On the other hand, I spoke excitedly and pretty aggressively (I think I started with, "So where the hell have you been my whole life?"). I gave him a barrage of questions he wasn't able to answer. He eventually offered an explanation that he couldn't deal with my grandmother (or she made it really difficult, something along those lines). Wrong thing to say. I understood because I know how my family can be, but I had already gone through my own parenting tribulations by that time, so I didn't want to hear any excuses. I fought to be in my daughter's life and I believed he should have fought to be in mine. Whatever his reasonings, I wasn't receptive and my responses turned into me yelling at him with all the years of pain I had stored up. My mom had to calm me down. I released a lot of negative energy. That was the day I forgave him.

As a boy and young man, I carried years of sadness and resentment towards Harold for not being there for me. No one ever saw it and I never told anyone, but I felt worthless because I felt like my dad didn't want me. I was embarrassed and jealous of other kids I knew who did have dads. I wanted to meet my dad so bad that I used to complain to my mom about meeting him (which is what prompted him to come around when I was between 11-13). I didn't know what was so wrong with me that would make Harold not want to be my father. I couldn't understand it, but for years I thought it was my fault he wasn't part of my life. I hid my true feelings about Harold not being there because I couldn't talk to my mom or anyone else about it. Instead, I acted out a lot and consistently got in trouble. Because of where I grew up, what I showed on the outside about Harold was "If he doesn't want me, then to hell with him. His loss. I'm gonna do something with my life and he'll *wish* he was my dad." Having that mentality was easier than dealing with my actual feelings. It was more than just missing a father to teach me how to walk or ride a bike, or how to play ball, or talk to a girl. As I got older, my unhappiness and resentment turned to bitterness and anger that Harold didn't help get me ready to go out into the world, he didn't prepare me for the obstacles I would face as a man. Not-to-mention being honest and upfront about some of the brutal truths I would be forced to endure as a Black man in America—a Black man in the world. Not so that I would walk and live in fear, but so that I would walk and live aware. I was hurt and angry that he never gave me "the talk" that most African American families have. I didn't even know what "the talk" was until a buddy of mine told me about it. But, after I became a young dad with a child out of wedlock and dealt with my own parenting dramas, having that perspective gave me a better understanding and level of empathy for Harold and some of the obstacles he may have faced when I was younger. He missed key opportunities to have a positive impact in my life, but I got it. Life happens.

Besides not having him in my life, the largest feeling of loss I carried regarding Harold was that I didn't get to grow up knowing other members of his family – Aunt Brenda (the kindest, sweetest woman who I love dearly- Rest in Paradise), Aunt Valerie (before she transitioned-Rest In Paradise), my cousins Anthony P. and Judge Mike M., both incredibly successful legal professionals who've inspired me immensely as they fight for the rights of the less fortunate, especially the youth, and fight for justice in Ohio – and all the other wonderful people who I've come to know over the years from Harold's family. Years ago, I learned he has two other children, a son and daughter. I've been able to build a relationship with his son, my brother Kevin, but not yet his daughter, my sister Kendra. With a lack of influence and guidance from my biological father, my life was shaped by my mom, grandma, aunts and uncles, the few positive mentors I had, and the many hard lessons I learned in the streets.

Helping my mom raise Nikki and me was my grandmother, Serene. Grandma was not a well-educated woman herself but she didn't play when it came to school and to the best of her ability, made sure all her children got their education. So even though mom had Nikki and me at a young age, it was not an option for her not to graduate from high school, kids or no kids. And graduate she did, on time and with the rest of her high school class.

As a kid I spent a lot of my time with grandma which gave me a very special connection and bond with her. I love my grandmother more than I can put into words. She was a very frank and no-nonsense type of woman and while she was not a very big woman, to me she seemed like a giant. She was a simple woman from Canton, Mississippi, stern, loving, but not in the "Clair Huxtable" kind of way. Grandma didn't give a lot of hugs and I don't remember grandma ever saying "I love you" to me when I was a kid. Whenever I would say, "I love you, grandma," she would say, "Okay, baby."

I always felt sadness when she didn't say it back. Looking back, grandma wasn't overly or outwardly affectionate… but I always knew she loved me. It wasn't until I learned that a possible reason behind her lack of an emotional connection in the traditional maternal way was because grandma lost her own mother when she was a little girl—about 7 years old. She was raised by her father, who had to raise three daughters by himself in the 1930's.

Aunt Frances once told me that my great grandfather was a quiet man who didn't show a lot of emotion. He protected his girls and taught them how to take care of themselves and take care of their home. That's it. The "I love yous" weren't part of his character.

Aunt Frances also told me grandma not only faced racism from the outside world, but because she was the darkest of all her siblings, she also dealt with colorism from her own sisters. When they got mad at her, they called her "blacky." These things made grandma a very guarded woman, but she was also incredibly kind. Grandma was always giving with her family and friends. She was fiercely protective of her family, even going as far as to carry a pistol in her purse—I think it was a .32 caliber—and I'm told she wasn't afraid to use it.

Grandma usually gave me whatever I wanted—within reason, and she would discipline me when I needed it. That discipline was never spanking because, as she put it, "I don't like putting my hands on other people's kids," even if those other people were her own children. I was definitely not raised in the "time out" generation. Grandma's slightly gruff, country tone and words were always loving and educational. I always felt like what she said was knowledge for me to be a better person. She didn't talk a lot, but when she spoke, I felt what she said.

Grandma was a terrific cook. She passed those cooking skills to my mom, who is a fantastic cook, who passed those skills to my younger sister, Gayla, who's also a great cook. Grandma was such a wiz in the kitchen that she was even featured in the local Indianapolis newspaper. The article had a nice picture of her holding some of her delicious fried chicken. Thinking of grandma's cooking made me remember different Thanksgivings. That holiday was always memorable at grandma's house. She would get several turkeys and chop the heads off of them herself. It was disgusting. The bodies of the birds would keep running around. I learned as I got older that's where the phrase "running around like a chicken with its head cut off" came from. I was always grossed out by the headless birds but grandma wasn't fazed. That was just grandma and I loved her.

Never overly ambitious, all grandma wanted to do was care for her seven children and give them the best life she could provide. She raised the family while her husband Wes (who she married when they were both 19

*L-R: Grandpa Wes' step-brother Lee, Grandpa Wes,
Grandma Serene, Grandma's sister Woolimae*

years old) worked to establish himself as a force in the jazz music world, an extremely daunting task for a Black man in the 40's, 50's and 60's. They grinded through the ups and downs of life together until Grandpa Wes died of a heart attack in my grandmother's arms on June 15, 1968. The house on 44th Street where Grandpa Wes died was the first house I ever lived in. Grandma stayed a widow until she married the only grandfather I've ever known - Grandpa Perry - when I was 10 years old and they stayed married until Grandpa Perry passed.

L-R: My cousin Nicole, Grandma Serene and me

The memories I have of my early years living at grandma's house on 44th Street across from Butler University are some of the best memories I have of my childhood. I used to love playing with some of the neighborhood kids in the field right across the street. Sometimes the college students would go out there and throw the football with us or let us play frisbee with them. We would explore the cool grounds of the campus and walk around amazed at how manicured the lawns were.

I remember there being a really cool wooded area with a small waterfall that opened into a small lake. We would sit and look at the scenery for what seemed like hours, or we would jump on the rocks that were lined across forming a make-shift bridge and try not to fall into the water. We'd run around all day playing, until the campus security eventually kicked us off the grounds because we weren't supposed to be playing in the area. It didn't matter. We would just find the next thing to get into. We stayed outside all day, from sunrise to sunset. I just had to be back in the house before the streetlights came on. When I didn't make it back, there was hell to pay and some sort of corporal punishment ensued. Once, I made the mistake of not being home by curfew, (I was maybe 11 years old and we lived in a different place) and my mother found where I was playing and tried to punish me while I was with my friends on the football field. I ran home and she walked behind me, calling out "Go on and run. I know where ya live." She finished what she tried starting on the football field when she made it back. The kids I played with clowned me for that until we moved away from that area.

At home, there were always people around. My mom is one of seven kids: Aunt Charlene, Aunt Sharon, Uncle John, Aunt Frances, my mom-Sandra, Aunt Toni and Uncle Robert (who I called Uncle Bobby). When I was born, only mom, Aunt Toni and Uncle Bobby were left in the house, my older aunts and uncle had already moved out. I was closest with Aunt Toni because I spent the most time with her. I remember laughing a lot when we lived on 44th street. We would have a blast playing Yahtzee or Tänk. Spades games got out of hand. Monopoly games were always extra crazy and fun, people always talking over everybody else so they could be heard. Constant arguments, of course, but they were fun family moments. And people had each other's backs. If anything ever happened, like someone from outside the family attacking one of my family members, everyone who was available went to fight.

Of course, our family had our crazy moments like every family does. There were times where I thought everyone was gonna kill everyone else, especially when they started physically fighting one another - hands, feet, furniture moving, kind of fighting. But even with all that craziness, we were happy. I was happy.

There were also very painful memories in that house. I was happy but there was also misery because my mom was more than tough on me growing up. I don't know how talkative my mom's father was, but as I said, grandma wasn't a big talker when I was growing up. She didn't work on getting you to express your feelings. My mom didn't either. I think because of that we didn't usually have conversations - my mom talked and we listened. As I learned when I went through therapy, it's possible that it's because my mom didn't communicate her feelings well, when I didn't do what I was supposed to do, most of the time when she got angry with me she would express it physically. My mom was fiercely protective of us when it came to others, but like many mothers of her generation, especially protective Black mothers, she had no problem whooping us. She was tough on my sister too, but I got the worst of it. The hitting started when I was really young (2-years-old) and escalated as I got older.

I felt helpless most of my life. My grandma and aunts used to shield me from mom's wrath, but that would send her on a rampage, "That's MY child!" she would scream. I don't remember the reasons for all the beatings, but I remember there were a lot of them, daily and for many, many years to come. I definitely wasn't a perfect kid. I got into things that I had no business getting into, but my actions usually ended with some sort of extreme punishment. I was lucky while we lived with grandma. Mom would start in on me but she would eventually get stopped by my relatives, but because she was also confrontational with a volatile temper, she would flex on my other family members. I inherited that trait from her. I had no problem getting in somebody's face and talking smack, even when I couldn't back it up. As I got older, although I'm a Gemini and my other side lives just beneath the surface, I learned to control the combative side of my nature.

I grew up opinionated and argumentative. It took me until adulthood to learn that my opinion won't matter to most people, so I've learned to keep it to myself for the most part. I don't like to argue for the sake of arguing. When I debate, I argue for what is right, not so I can be right.

My family could be some of the nicest and kindest people you've ever met. They would literally give you the shirts off their backs… if they were in a good mood. Otherwise, to hell with you. I inherited that trait too. I'm an artist and although I'm extremely giving in my craft, I've learned about myself over the years that I'm a creature of opposites: I can be extremely selfish (much more so when I was younger; I've grown more selfless as I've emotionally matured and gotten my ego in check over the years) and I can also be generous to a fault (I've made healthy shifts in that behavior since learning to not try and please everyone). As an adult, I've also learned that I genuinely love humanity, I love people. But I don't always *like* humanity. Sometimes people can be real assholes. I know I can, although I don't like being an asshole. I used to indulge in a lot of bullshit from people but I've learned over time that I don't "suffer fools," as they say. I don't like dealing with unnecessary BS from anybody. I work to be a good person, a fair person, and I'm direct and to the point. I am a "Force of Nature," as my Trek brother John Billingsley told me when we met decades ago. I love to party and can definitely turn up with the best of them. The flip side to that is I have an intensely serious side and can go 0-100, real quick. That's Naptown.

When we moved out of the house on 44th Street, my childhood memories weren't always the happiest. Some were good - we didn't have a lot but we laughed a lot. But other memories were painful. My mom worked hard to provide for us, to make sure we had what we needed (a roof over our head, food to eat and clothes on our backs). I love my mother with all my heart and soul and I honor her sacrifices. I'm forever grateful for everything she did for me and my siblings. I know it wasn't easy. I wasn't easy.

Mom and me.

We grew up poor. There were a lot of times when mom couldn't find work and raising us was incredibly difficult, which forced her on welfare sometimes. Often we didn't have much food and ate that hard government cheese, ramen noodles or whatever mom could afford. There were also times when we had more than enough food, where the refrigerator was overflowing. It was during those times that mom created a Thanksgiving tradition for us where she would make each of us an item that we really wanted, in addition to what she was already cooking. I have a bad sweet tooth and mom would make me a lemon pie. She would make another pie for the family and I would get my own. Gluttonous? Yep. But I loved those times.

After searching for work for a while, mom found a job and worked for ten years at Cold Springs Schools, working with mentally challenged people. It was during that time and interacting with the different kids mom worked with, that I learned to have compassion for people who had different developmental challenges. I'm grateful for those lessons because I gained an empathy for other people that I've carried throughout my life.

Holidays were difficult. I stopped believing in Santa Claus because there were so many holidays that we didn't have anything for Christmas. As an adult, I know how heart-broken mom must have been during those times. She was determined to give us whatever she could. And because of her determination, there were also times when the presents were overflowing. There was one Christmas I hounded mom for weeks, maybe months, to buy me the new Invader From Space game by Epoch. I may have been nine or ten years old. Even though I stayed in trouble, I acted good during that time because I desperately wanted that game. Mom came through as only a committed mother can and made sure she got it for me. That day there were more presents under the Christmas tree than we knew what to do with, presents that were still being opened days later. But those times were short-lived. Unfortunately, I remember much more vividly the majority of the bad times than I do the times when things were good. It felt like most of the time it was hard.

We went through the rough times together, and we were a family, so there was still joy. Even when we didn't have much, I really loved watching mom exercise her skills as a seamstress. She was masterful with her sewing machine. I remember one day she had different kinds of fabric laid out on the floor with five or six patterns nearby. Mom knew what she wanted to make, chose the fabric, picked the patterns and started laying out the pieces. She meticulously pinned all of the patterns to the fabric until there were no patterns left. Then she took some oversized scissors (at least they looked oversized to me) and started cutting out the patterns. As I watched, I remember her being focused and intent that the shapes and sizes had to be exact, every angle extremely precise. She followed the dotted lines on the patterns and cut along the lines. One after another, she cut piece by piece until she had all the patterns cut to the perfect size. As I looked at the different pieces and patterns, my mind kept trying to process how they would connect to make whatever she was constructing. I looked at the pieces like a jigsaw puzzle and imagined how they were supposed to fit. Then mom gathered all the pieces and sat at her sewing machine. I paid close attention as she focused on threading the sewing machine. Once the machine was prepped, she started connecting the pieces, slowly removing the pins that held the patterns to the fabric as she sewed. She worked non-stop for awhile and when she needed a break, she stopped. She left everything where it was, cleaned up her mess and went and did something else. Then she went back to it when she was ready. As mom sewed the different swatches together, I watched as the garment took shape. I was amazed watching mom turn those yards of raw material into a beautiful pants suit. She repeated the same process with all different kinds of wardrobes: blouses, pants, dresses, suits, choir robes, anything she wanted to make. I would just look at the front of the pattern packaging to guess what she was gonna make from the options they had pictured. After watching her do it many times, I knew that even though I was looking at raw fabric, by the time mom was done the fabric would be beautiful pieces of clothing that would look like they were just bought from a store. I was always so proud of mom when she finished making something. She didn't show it much, but I could see she was proud too.

Mom taught me how to use a needle and thread when I was younger and I've been able to do a few things with clothes since I was a kid, but I'm no seamster. I always knew making clothes was a gift mom got from God.

We moved a lot when I was a kid, but the one constant that mom maintained in the middle of moving so much and our turbulent lives was going to church. Mom made sure we kept God first in our lives, no matter how good or bad things got, and she made sure we knew to keep God first throughout our lives, no matter how good or bad things got. I used to get mad back then because we were in church all the time. Sunday school, regular church service, late church service, bible study, vacation bible school, all of it. As a kid I wanted to do other stuff, but that changed as I grew up and spiritually matured. I'm eternally thankful that in addition to the gift of life, the greatest gift I ever received from my mother was making sure I know God and that Jesus Christ is my Lord and Savior. During the great times in my life and all the dark times I've endured (or caused), I've always known that God has me. At my core, I strive to do right by people and do good in the world, so despite my faults, I know that God, the great I AM, loves me for who I am, what I am, and how I am.

THE CUSSING CHRISTIAN

I know God loves me even though I am a "cussing Christian." What that means is that although I keep God first in my life, I'm not a Saint and I've got no problem occasionally using profanity when expressing myself. I do not cuss all the time. I have a college degree, a firm grasp of the English language and a more than adequate vocabulary that I keep expanding, so I know how to communicate intelligently and without vulgarity. I'm also from the block in Indianapolis, where we are how we are and we talk how we talk. You feel me? Because of those factors, I love using all the words at my disposal, including cuss words. I know the Bible teaches that words are important and have a profound impact on others, so I'm also mindful of the environments I'm in and do not use profane language in inappropriate situations. I don't cuss around children, I don't cuss around elderly people, I don't cuss in circumstances that are not suitable for that language. I know how to censor myself. But I don't pretend to be someone I'm not. I'm not perfect and I don't pretend to be. I believe God will always love me through all of my flaws. That's the beauty of God's grace and mercy.

I lived with the feeling of being unsettled when I was young. I went to a bunch of different schools, some because I got in trouble all the time and got kicked out and others because of us moving. I don't recall all the specifics but I remember places we lived on Bond Street, MacPherson Street, a house grandma owned on College Avenue near 38th Street and an apartment off of 38th and High School Road. I went to IPS (Indianapolis Public Schools) #43, #87, #72, #79, Crispus Attucks High School my freshman year, where I went until it was shut down and eventually turned into a Junior High School, and then I was bussed to George Washington High School—where I graduated. I don't remember all the details of the places we lived or all the schools I attended, but I always felt like "the new kid" in every neighborhood and every school. I constantly felt desperate to be liked. Because of that I eagerly attempted to get close to people. I'm sure I was annoying to some kids as I tried to fit in and find my place. Instead of letting kids get to know me for me, I was always "too much" and overcompensated to be liked. My natural energy can be a lot for people, so unfortunately, it often had the opposite effect and turned them off, making them want to distance themselves from me. I didn't catch it as a kid, but I understand it as an adult. It hurt my feelings as a kid, not as an adult.

When I did get close to friends (and there were some awesome people I knew and hung around years ago), it was really hard for me to lose them and their friendships. I worked much too hard to be friends with people, even if they weren't the best people to be friends with. I didn't value my own life like I should have so I ran around Indianapolis like an idiot and did ignorant stuff too often with those same friends. Moving around so much, the bad friends were usually gone before long anyway, so to me it didn't matter if I acted a fool with them. Searching for acceptance in different circles, sometimes I was also the cause of a lot of the stupidity we got into. (As I got older, I realized how warped that mindset was which, understandably, got me into a lot of trouble.) By the time I got to high school, I had already settled into the image of me I was going to show people, no matter what pain was buried. Of course, I was as insecure as any other teen, but I didn't show that. I projected my natural high energy. I was a happy, hyped, silly guy who wanted to party and have fun. I didn't look to start trouble but if I was put in a negative situation,

I was "ready to go" at any time and didn't care what happened. There were many times where I was the hype guy getting everybody geeked to get into some shit, even when secretly I didn't want to do it. My best friend and the guy I was closest to more than anyone was my boy John. During those years I also started meeting some great guys and cool girls who were good people, but I lost touch with most of them over time. I'm grateful for the genuine friendships I've had over the years, no matter how long or short-lived the encounters may have been.

The last house we lived in

The last house I grew up in was off of 27th Street & Dr. Martin Luther King Jr. Street (which was previously named Northwestern Avenue). Too often there was shit jumping off in that area. There were constant fights, people getting shot or robbed and other acts of violence and aggression. I hated the fact that like it is in many urban neighborhoods, there was a liquor store on several of the corners in a fairly close proximity to where I grew up. However, because that was our neighborhood, I managed to find fun sometimes. It was a good time when dozens of cars and motorcycles took over Northwestern and lined the streets for a "car show" every weekend. Souped up Harley Davidson motorcycles, tricked out Cadillacs, Delta 88s, dozens of cars sitting on Trues and Vogues. And everybody was always dressed like they were going to a club. Ladies looked hot and sexy, fellas looked fly in fresh gear. It was the vibe Will Smith rapped about in his classic "Summertime." When I got into doing music, the wonderful nostalgia I feel every time I hear that song, inspired me to write my own summer anthem called "Kick Back." LYRICS 1 I also loved the fact that we lived so close to some of the best barbecue (especially the rib tips, greens, macaroni & cheese and chess pie) you've ever tasted (Bar-B-Q Heaven on 25th and MLK and Pa & Ma's Barbecue, that closed down). Our area was cool until the fighting and shooting started – and it always started. Because I hated being around that energy, I changed my environment and normally met people and became friends with folks on other sides of town from where we lived. I rarely hung out with guys from my block or my immediate neighborhood. I did a little when I was younger, but as I got older and could be further from home, I stayed gone, stayed in the streets.

A major blessing on Earth that I was given was having a mentor we called "Billy." I met Billy at church when we went to Puritan. I didn't understand at the time how much of a God-send Billy was in my life. Billy was a single man who had gone through a painful divorce and was working to keep his own life moving forward. He was a genuinely good human being and wanted the best for others, especially young people. He became a mentor/big brother/father figure to me and many of the kids at church who came from broken homes. He selflessly gave his love, time and resources to all of us and treated me better than people who were close to me. I used to wish Billy would date and marry my mom and become my step-dad, instead of the guy my mom married. Billy was really smart, brilliant, in fact. He was an engineer for the government. He also loved building model airplanes and cars. He tried to get me into them but I never really had the patience to assemble models like he did. He taught me how to make kites from raw materials and once we made one that was as big as the car he drove and we flew it in the Coca Cola fields in Indy. It took three of us to keep the kite from blowing away.

Billy was the first person who ever challenged me to be a critical thinker. I didn't know that's what he was doing. I would implement and then marginally apply many of the lessons he was teaching me, but I'd revert back to my immature and childish ways. But he kept trying to reach me. Billy saw that I was a smart kid, albeit aimless and mischievous, who had potential and needed guidance. Billy always steered me in the right direction. He saw the good in me and tried to cultivate it. He pushed me to make myself smarter and keep gaining knowledge. I wasn't disciplined, though. Billy always guided me to do right and keep myself on the straight-and-narrow. He worked with me on being more confident and believing in myself. He used to try to help me channel my energy so I would focus on a particular task. I was all over the place a lot, but could zero in when motivated. I always felt like a better kid when I spent time with Billy. He made me feel like a better person. Because he was one of the most positive male role models I had in my life for a long time, I was shattered when Billy moved on with his life and was no longer a part of mine. He didn't leave in a negative way or anything, our lives just went different directions, but it still hurt. I never talked to anyone about my sadness but I held on to the pain of losing his mentorship and friendship for a long time. I'll always be grateful to him because without Billy's love and guidance, I would definitely have gotten into even more trouble than I did. I've always wished him love, happiness and prosperity in his life. Thank you, Billy. I love you.

Some of my favorite summers as a kid were going to my Aunt Charlene's house and spending time with her and all my cousins Carla (Cookie), Darryl, Lawrence, Ronald and McKinley (Malik). Aunt Charlene was a beautiful spirit and was always the kindest person to me. I used to love going to the bowling alley and watching her compete on her local bowling team. I think I started liking bowling more because of her. Rest in Paradise, Aunt Charlene. I love you. My cousins' dad, my uncle Sonny, was a motorcycle rider (a Harley Davidson type) and seemed scary to me for some reason, but he was the nicest guy and always really kind to me. I'm closer in age to my younger cousins so I hung out with Malik most, and Ronnie. We didn't usually do much other than play around the house, but I had the best times with them. I used to wish I could play drums like Darryl, who was a fantastic drummer. Being the only boy with my mom, I loved having all my guy cousins to hang around, even when we didn't do anything. I actually used to be jealous of them because they had brothers.

I will always love and cherish the times I had with my cousins during those summers. Looking back, I appreciate that they tried to toughen me up, even though it didn't really work. While there, I did strengthen my resolve in one area. They would tease me that I "sound White." I hated that shit. And they were relentless. But fortunately, those summers prepared me for when random people would say that ridiculous statement throughout my life (and I've heard that idiocy my <u>whole</u> life). I developed a thick skin for the comment. I'm a Black man and I don't sound White, I sound like an educated Black man, one who has the college degree to prove it. One who can also sound country at times because of my Midwest upbringing. That's it. Nothing more, nothing less. Fact is, I'll never be as eloquent an orator as the brilliant Dr. Cornell West and people of his ilk, but I can hold my own in a room full of conversationalists. It's ridiculous to me that so many people associate a well-spoken parlance with only White people, and a broken language with only Black people or other marginalized groups. Even if the stereotype is obviously demonstrated in different instances, it hurts my soul that we as Black people are viewed that way. Regardless of how I'm perceived, I'm grateful that my vernacular allows me to feel comfortable communicating no matter where I am in the world.

When I was between five and six years old, my mom met and married a guy who turned out to be horrendous. He seemed like a good guy at first, but he wasn't. He was an asshole. An abusive, demeaning and morally corrupt asshole. I assume he had some good qualities that mom saw in him, but I don't remember those. I remember how he used to hit my mother.

The memories I have of him punching my mother and beating her down to the ground in the living room, or wherever it happened, are seared into my memories. Trauma I had to work through in therapy. He treated my mother like he was fighting a man, a stranger in the street, not the woman he claimed to love. Even though I was young, I always felt like a coward and powerless because I couldn't protect my mother. One time when I was about eight or nine, I tried to pick up our lazy boy chair to throw at him to make him stop hitting her. I could barely lift it but I was scared and mad and tried with all my strength. He came after me and my mother got an inner-strength and went ballistic. She fought him until he left me alone. That may have been the time she broke a 2-inch thick glass ashtray she owned over his head. I always prayed to be strong enough to fight him back. He used to beat on me too.

I never told my mother because just like the time with the chair, any time he tried to hit me in front of her, she would go off and end up fighting him. She fought with all she had (he knew he had been in a fight), but she would still usually end up beaten down. I didn't want my mother getting hurt because of me, so I kept it to myself and took his abuse.

He got to the point where he would only hit me when my mother wasn't around. I grew up with a hatred for him that bore to the core of my soul. I didn't know how to let it go. And because of what I saw him do to my mother, I wasn't in the space to forgive him. When my mother got pregnant with my younger sister, I was filled with dread because I knew he would always be in our lives, even though I always prayed that he would go away, or just die. It was during that time that I developed more resentment towards my biological father. Although it wasn't his fault, I blamed my "real" dad for not being there to protect me from my step-dad. I didn't know anything about my biological father at the time, but I still had anger towards him for not saving me. I held onto my hatred for my step-dad until my adult years when I eventually put my feelings into a song that I wrote for my mother. I wanted to celebrate my mother and show my love and admiration for her being determined to not let him break her, and for staying so strong while dealing with his horrible ways—and destroy him as an abuser at the same time. I put my sentiment about this into words on a song called "Strongest Ever" on my 2007 album, "A.T". LYRICS 2

I will always thank God for my mother's bravery, strength and courage as a domestic abuse survivor. Because I never wanted to throw my life away by maiming or killing my former step-dad in real life for what he did to my mother (although I did pull my gun on him once), and because I never wanted my younger sister to hate me for hurting her dad, I actually felt better after making that song. I released most of the hate I was bottling up inside, hate that was tainting my spirit. Instead, I chose to focus on the good that came from him – my wonderful younger sister, Gayla. We would have fun but she would also drive me crazy when we were kids, taking my clothes (and cutting my jeans into shorts - even my Z Cavaricci jeans) and being a typical little sister. Honestly, I was a crappy big brother most of the time. But she was also my heart. I would do anything for her and she would do anything for me. She was quiet but really funny and could be the sweetest kid…if she was in the mood. She's a Scorpio after all. I'm told a lot of Scorpios can be that way. Being seven years apart, we weren't always close as kids but, without a doubt, she is the beautiful light and best gift that God blessed our family with, in spite of those ugly times with my step-dad. I'm grateful for my baby sister and couldn't imagine my life without her. Eventually I found forgiveness and, surprisingly, gratitude for my step-dad. Perspective. Without him, I would not have my younger sister. For as much as I hated him, I would endure his abuse all over again if it meant that *not* going through it would take my sister away. I love you, Gayla.

Being gone out of grandma's house, the beatings from my mom only intensified, especially after she married that guy. Day or night, it didn't matter. I caught a lot of hell for not washing dishes when I was supposed to or not keeping my room clean and would periodically get beaten awake from a sound sleep. Those were the worst because I had to orient myself and figure out where I was, only to be in extreme pain and duress the moment I realized what was happening. There were plenty of times I showed up at school with welts on my arms and legs and back, similar to that *Good Times* episode where Penny was being beaten by her mother. Mine felt more severe than what I remember seeing on that episode. My mom never burned me with an iron but that show still stuck with me because of the physical abuse I did suffer. After talking with a lot of different friends and other people who grew up during the same time period, including strangers, I know that what my mom did wasn't anything out of the ordinary. Back in the day, many Black households dispensed discipline through violence, whippings, beatings, etc.

There was one beating in particular that I'll never forget. We were living in the house on College Avenue and mom left me home and in charge of Gayla. I loved my sister but I hated having to watch her. I was being a brat and at the time, I felt like I wasn't getting a chance to have a "fun" childhood. I don't know what I wanted my life to be but I felt like I was too young to be left babysitting (I don't recall exactly how old I was but it was somewhere in the 10-11 years old range). I'm not sure where Nikki was but I remember being mad that I had to be home and responsible for Gayla. I had to make her lunch and I made her a chicken pot pie. I put it in the oven and cooked it like I had learned, but when it was time for me to give it to her, I put Dawn dish liquid in it. I think I wanted to make her sick because she made me sick. She sat at the table and looked at it but she never ate it. Thank God. I didn't really want to hurt my sister, I was just being a brat of a kid. But I didn't throw it away, I just left it on the table. When mom came home, she saw it and went off. I remember her saying, "What the hell is this??"

I told her that I put dish liquid in Gayla's food because I was mad, and after yelling for a couple minutes the beating started. I ran from her and she chased me for a little while and then she said, "I'm not chasing you! Get yo' ass over here!" I had to go back to her and stand close to her while she beat me. I remember it lasted forever. The beating started downstairs and eventually moved upstairs when I did run from her.

My mom was good for hitting me with whatever was close at hand: her hand, shoes, extension cords, switches, whatever. Well, this day she was especially angry and started with a belt, I think, or a switch, something that had a whip to it, and she ended up beating me with some sort of wood board, a solid piece of wood that didn't break and didn't give. She made me stand with my hands on the banister and just waled on me. It progressed from there. I ran wherever I could to get away. I remember being on my bed and mom beating me with that object like she was chopping wood. No matter how hard I screamed, she wouldn't stop. At one point, I blacked out and when I came to, she was still hitting me. And although she didn't usually care where on my body she hit, that particular time, she focused a lot of her rage on my butt.

It was the first time I understood the phrase "beat your butt so bad you can't sit down." I discovered later, the swelling and black and blue marks on my butt were so severe that I literally could not sit down. After a while, mom either got tired of hitting me or realized that she needed to stop because we had choir rehearsal that night. She told me to get cleaned up and get ready for rehearsal. I remember being in the bathroom and crying so hard trying to clean myself with a washcloth that I just used the soap and tried to clean the areas that didn't hurt – under my arms, my penis and hands - everywhere else hurt. When the church van came to pick me up for rehearsal, my mom acted like nothing was wrong and sent me on my way. I think everyone in the van instantly knew what had happened because when I tried to sit down, I immediately started crying again. I couldn't sit. I had to lay on my side. What made it even worse was that the van had a lot of people in it and I had to lean over and into the lap of one of the other choir members. I don't remember his name, but he was a heavy-set guy and he smelled really bad. I cried all the way to the church.

When we got to the church, I cried as I had to lean over while I

Siblings L-R: Nikki, me, Gayla and Keith

was sitting in the choir stands. I remember members of the church (I forget exactly who they were) having a hushed conversation about what to do. I think everyone knew (or at least, suspected) my mom was hard on me but no one had ever seen it get that bad. I remember hearing them debate about whether they should call the police, or child services and report my mom. I never wanted mom to go to jail, I just wanted the beatings to stop. In the end, nothing happened. They didn't do anything. Mom showed up at rehearsal later and rehearsal went on like normal. I channeled the pain inward like I always had and moved on.

After many years, I stopped caring about why I was punished so severely and just focused on getting through it. I felt like I had no control but I knew one day I would be grown and never have to deal with that kind of pain again. In the middle of my circumstances, I looked to the future. Being fully honest, I should have changed my behavior completely and stopped getting in trouble. It would've made my mom's life easier, and my own. But for the longest time I didn't. I wasn't always a degenerate kid, but in addition to the good things I used to do, I also continued making poor choices and brought unnecessary hardships into my life. After taking accountability for my own actions years ago, forgiving myself and giving myself grace, forgiving my mom and giving her grace, and after having had the chance to have lived experiences on my own, I gained perspective. For as much as I disliked the pain of those times, knowing that she had to bear the burden of being both mother and father, I believe my mom did what she thought was right and her firm love helped mold me into the man I am today. If she hadn't stayed on me, I don't know how I would've ended up. Thank you for the tough love, mom. I love you.

Years later, my younger brother, Keith, was born. I was so grateful to have a brother, and to have another boy in the house. There's an eleven-year age difference so our interests were far apart, but I always hoped I would do things in my life that would inspire my brother to be his best in his own life. He's a fantastic artist. I wish I had a fraction of my brother's artistic talent for drawing. I thank God for my younger brother. I love you, Keith.

I didn't know what I wanted to do with my life when I got older. I was unmotivated and didn't like to work. When I was a kid, I got a job delivering newspapers once and got fired. It was freezing cold and I wouldn't deliver the papers. I would wake up and get them from the delivery guy and then throw them behind a bush near where we lived and go back home and back to sleep. Mom would get mad because people would call our home looking for their papers, and she knew I left to go on my routes. I would tell her the truth about where the papers were because I was sleeping and she would make me get up and go deliver them. I would always mess up my collections and my bank, sometimes spend my bank on candy and have to owe the newspaper. I didn't take the responsibility seriously and deserved to be fired.

I never set any major goals for myself. I used to talk about being a doctor or lawyer when I was younger but that was only because I heard those professions made a lot of money. Although I admire and respect doctors and lawyers, I never actually had an interest, passion or calling for either of those fields. Not to mention the fact that I didn't want to be in school for as long as it would take to pursue one of those careers. I didn't really consider a career in acting until I got into college. I just believed there was a good life for me somewhere out there. I assumed at some point I would figure out what I genuinely wanted to do, what I was passionate about. As I imagined what my life would eventually be when I was on my own, the main thing that got me through the turbulent times was reading comic books.

I read everything from Scooby Doo and Archie comics to my favorites – superhero comics: Superman, Batman & Robin, X-Men (especially Wolverine), Green Lantern (I wished I could be the John Stewart Green Lantern), The Amazing Spiderman, The Fantastic Four, all of them. Even when my body was in pain from welts and my skin aching, I was able

Top: *Miles Away*
Bottom: *Junior Outcasts from Outer Space (JOFOS)*

to escape into my imagination and not think about the pain. I used to envision myself as the hero (and sometimes the villain) being powerful enough to never have to deal with being abused by anyone. I would get absorbed in the story of whatever was being overcome in a particular issue. I learned that heroes and villains also went through struggles in their lives. It made them stronger. I knew that whatever I was going through was somehow making me stronger. I didn't know exactly how I was getting stronger, but I knew I was. I grew to love reading comics so I read them all the time. My love of comics carried over when I started watching animation. I watched a lot of cartoons not only to escape, but because I really wanted to see comics that I had read for so many years brought to life as cartoons or movies. Cartoons just made sense to me. I learned a lot of lessons from those shows, even though I didn't call it learning lessons. I was just watching cartoons I liked. But all of the ones I liked most, *He-man and the Masters of the Universe*, *Super Friends* and *Transformers* always had a positive moral message woven into the story and plainly stated at the end of each episode.

I soaked up all those lessons but it would be years before I realized that along with the lessons I got from my mom, the comics and animation were also molding my moral compass. It never occurred to me that I could work in the animation industry. Looking for a way to encourage kids who may experience what I went through as a kid, I set a goal for myself to one day have my own animated series and make sure our shows infuse positive morals and values into our stories. I started the journey to inspire and excite boys with my own graphic novel called Miles Away, which was co-written by Brandon Easton. (More about that creative process later.)

I independently produced *Miles Away*, released it through a small distributor called Antarctic Press and toured with it for five years. After years of pitch meetings and being repeatedly turned down, I was fortunate to secure a licensing deal for it to be shopped (taken around to different animation companies to get someone to partner) to be turned into a series. Once I signed the agreement, everything was out of my hands and since there was nothing I could do to expedite the long process that it takes to make animation, instead of sitting idly by, I created a series to embolden and empower girls. *Junior Outcasts From Outer Space (JOFOS)*.

The animation landscape is a challenging and daunting arena to navigate, especially since I don't come from that medium, but I'm not giving up. Whether it's *Miles Away, JOFOS, GG: Girl Genius, Ebonwood* or any of the other exciting projects we plan to produce, they will all contain elements that will be entertaining but still beneficial to the viewers and anyone exposed to them. I'm committed to our animation making a positive impact on future generations of young people, just like old cartoons made a memorable and positive impact on me.

CHAPTER TWO
STIGMA

The stigma of violence played a major factor in my life for a long time, especially during my formative years. Over time, the violence and challenges of my early years graduated to other forms of aggression or brutality while I was growing up. Many times, as is the case in most low-income neighborhoods, crime turned to violence. I mentioned that I was scared to fight when I was younger. As a result, I was fraudulent when I stood up for myself. I talked a good game but didn't know if I could back it up. Instead, I would overcompensate and be extra nice to get people to like me, especially the guys who I thought wanted to fight me. Other times, I would be extra loud and demonstrative and bluff my way out of it. I went to a therapist years ago. What I got from the sessions was that the person I feared most was my mom and due to the things I went through, I had developed major self-esteem issues, including an inferiority complex that I covered with laughter and a smile. The doc told me that trying to befriend everyone was my coping mechanism. I also learned that because I could never (and would never) hit my mom back, I could've subconsciously developed a fear of what would happen if I fought back against anyone. Where I come from, if you don't fight back you are not considered a man. Because I wouldn't fight back when I was being bullied, I grew up feeling like a coward. When I was younger, I carried myself with as much confidence as I knew how but I was secretly covering a major fear of being confronted. As a kid, my deepest desire was to protect my mom, my sister and myself. I wanted to learn how to fight to be able to defend the people I loved. Back then I didn't fight unless I felt like I had no choice (except once when I was the aggressor; I heard a guy was coming after me, so I went to him). There were also way too many other acts of violence in my life that shaped my outlook and trust/distrust of people. Those experiences helped forge my inner strength.

When I was around ten years old, there was a family with about six mean-spirited kids in the school I attended. Brothers, cousins, everything. They were like a little gang. I got picked on by at least three of the six. We were living with one of my mom's coworker's in this woman's house that she ran like a boarding house. The owner was nice enough, but she could also be mean. She had an older woman who was one of her boarders. The older woman had grayed white hair and no teeth/false teeth and normally sat around the house, smoked Pall Mall cigarettes and drank coffee all day. I liked her though. She was a quiet lady who would get really cranky sometimes, but she was usually pretty nice. There was also a guy living down the hall, mid to late 40's (he may have been younger but seemed older to me) and he was a creepy ass pervert. I couldn't stand that guy. I hated the way he looked at my mom and my sister, and the other younger woman in the house. If I remember right, she was the owner's niece. She was in her early twenties, I think. She was a nice person. I had a huge crush on her for a long time. The owner also had a foster-son in the house. I think he was 3-4 years older than me. I didn't like him much either. He always acted like he was better than me at everything. Anyway, I would routinely get chased home to the boarding house by the three kids from the family of mean-spirited kids. A few times they caught me, kicked my ass and tore up my clothes in the process. A couple guys held me while the other ones punched me. When I hit the ground they would punch and kick me until I eventually got up and ran home. I was ashamed but would tell my mother that I was being chased home. It was always even more embarrassing because it felt like the whole boarding house had an opinion about what I should do. My mom told me to fight back but I was too ashamed and embarrassed to say I didn't know how exactly. The owner's adult son showed me a couple things but I never remembered what he tried to teach me. So instead, I pretended that I knew what to do. The acting didn't stop there though. After several more times of getting chased home, one day I stopped a short distance from home and tore my own clothes and made myself dirty, as if I had been rolling around on the ground during an imaginary fight. I remember going home to the boarding house, nervously pretending that I had gotten into a fight and proudly telling my mom that I fought back. She seemed so proud of me. Genuinely proud of me. I barely ever did things to make my mom proud so I hadn't felt pride from her for who knows how long. Everyone else in the house seemed proud too. They all sounded proud that I had finally stood up for myself. No one knew that not only did I feel like a coward for still running away, but I also felt ashamed for being a liar about my cowardice. But I felt good when they said positive things about me so I kept the lie going. It got to a point where I would get chased home and instead of just running home, I would run and get away and then tear my own clothes and lie about fighting back so my mom would continue to be proud of me. It backfired though because after a while my mom got pissed that my clothes kept getting torn. I realized I had taken the lie too far. I stopped tearing my clothes after that, even though for a while I still pretended that I was fighting back. I loved hearing my mom tell me she was proud of me, even if it was based on my deception. Eventually the bullies got tired of me, moved on to their next objects of persecution and continued bullying other kids.

It wasn't just the violence of being bullied that seemed to follow me. I also faced extreme racism as a Black boy growing into a young man in Indiana. I was called nigger a lot when I was a kid. It was usually by White guys yelling at me as they were driving by. But in my hometown, Indianapolis racists were much more open with their bigotry and would say evil things even if they were just walking down the street. Everyone was not racist, but the ones who were, were very vocal about it. I don't recall if I felt racism in school when I was in elementary grades, but as I got older I could definitely feel when students in middle school and high school, and people in general, were being racist. I was forced to deal with a lot of disgusting racial encounters. After painful learning curves, to the best of my ability I learned to not give racists and their negativity any energy. Suffice it to say, the negative racial history and toxicity that belongs to my home state of Indiana affected me in emotionally destructive and psychologically detrimental ways for a number of years. It took time but I worked through my PTSD from those times. I've always detested dealing with people because of their racial biases. It has never made sense to me. I have never hated someone over the color of their skin and never understood the racist mindset. Still, whether I understand it or not, like probably every other African American, every other Black person, situations motivated by racism have happened to me so many times in my life, I've lost count. And I must navigate those situations carefully to stay safe. When I was younger, usually fights broke out, depending on where we were and what the group was doing.

Some buddies and I attended the Qualifications for the Indy 500 when I was in high school. We skipped school and went to the racetrack for the day. Granted, if I had taken my butt to school where I should've been, none of the following would've happened. Inner city life. I went to the track and it was pretty special watching people from all over the globe descend upon my hometown. The sounds of the race were deafening, the energy was electric and it was an incredible racing spectacle. More interesting to me at the time was a wild party section outside the main racing area, called the Snake Pit. I saw all kinds of stuff a teen shouldn't see—people having sex out in the open as other people cheered them on was all over the place. In other sections there were crowds of people getting so drunk they were falling all over each other, but having the best times. It was a mass of race fans partying their asses off. A crazy time with cool people, and so much fun. Unfortunately all of the people weren't cool. There are some die-hard racing fans who hated my blackness (and the other Black people) being there and ruining their tradition and celebration, and alcohol only intensified their venom and racism. Sadly, I was used to bigotry, so what I encountered there didn't affect me any worse than what I had already been dealing with throughout my life. What it did was put an ugly stain on what would have been an enjoyable time on my first exposure to the motor speedway. A lot of strangers from the crowd got into a massive brawl with the racists (not sure what sparked it). I acted like I was tough but I was scared. I had never been in the middle of a riotous group like that. We ran before the cops broke up the melee and started arresting people. Because of that mess we never even made it to see any of the cars that were qualifying. Years later, I got a chance to make it back to the Indianapolis Motor Speedway and now understand why millions of people love the Indy 500. The race is phenomenal. They told me the Snake Pit had been gone for years. I'd like to tell you that the racism was gone, but it's more likely that the people with that ugliness in their hearts didn't want to act racist around that Star Trek guy. It's funny how fame can wholly change an experience. It's sad that our world works that way.

As a kid, when life outside home got to be too much, I wanted to go home and feel safe. But I didn't always feel safe at home. My mom never randomly hit me or anything, but I got in trouble a lot and didn't know if I would get hit by her on any given day, so there was no constant feeling of safety. My step-dad usually had shitty energy and we never knew what mood we'd catch him in, so there was no feeling of safety when he was around. When I was about 9 years old, I got tired of him beating my mom and me not being able to do anything about it and I ran away. My mom told me I tried to run away from home several times (I don't remember those times), but one day that I do remember changed my young life.

We were living off of High School Road. My mom and step-dad were in their room with the door closed, arguing. I listened for a while before expecting him to start hitting mom. I got it into my head that I was going to go live with my Aunt Sharon, who was living in the family house we left on 44th street. I don't know what made me think I could decide I was moving out, but I still tried it. I snuck out of the apartment and jumped on my dirt bike heading to my aunt's house.

I didn't think about it at the time, but it was too far for a nine-year-old to be going by himself. Aunt Sharon lived about 15-20 minutes away by car from where we lived. I didn't even know her exact address but I knew how to follow the streets to get there. I knew that if I took the main road (38th Street) past the cemetery — Crown Hill Cemetery, one of the largest cemeteries in the country and to a 9-year-old, the scariest – I would see the street I was supposed to turn down to get to her house. I didn't even get a quarter-mile from home before I ran into trouble. As I was riding my bike and crossing the intersection at 38th and High School Road, I was hit by a car. I didn't get hurt but it did scare the hell out of me and I jumped up and started running, leaving my bike in the street, which was damaged from the impact and unrideable. I remember it being a woman who hit me and she tried to calm me down and get me to come back. I was disoriented and confused so I went back to her. The woman said she would have to take me home so she could explain to my parents what happened. I tried to talk her out of it, but she insisted and put me and my bike in her car and drove me back home. It wasn't very far but the ride felt like forever. The whole drive back, all I could think about was what would happen when we got there.

When the woman who hit me with her car took me home, I don't remember who answered the door. The woman explained what happened and when she left, I was sent to my room. Mom and my step-dad didn't start yelling and mom didn't start hitting me. They actually talked quietly in their room with the door closed. I didn't know what was coming next. I thought it was a set-up. I believed mom sending me to my room was just the calm before the storm that would rain down on me, so I got back to my mission of "moving to my aunt's."

Step one on my mission I knew I would need clothes, so I threw all my clothes into two large trash bags (the green Glad-type) and snuck out of my house again. The bags were too heavy for me to carry so I left them behind some bushes that were in front of an apartment that was about six units away from ours. I was going to go back and get my clothes later. Afterwards, I headed back to 38th Street, back to my aunt's. I remember feeling a weird sensation in my body as I walked past the intersection of where I had just been hit. I was almost afraid to be near the spot. I looked at it and shrugged it off and started walking. After a couple miles or so, I got hungry. I knew I needed to get some money so I could get food. I didn't know what to do so I walked up to the Speedway gas station (not the current one, the old one that was closer to the edge of the road) and asked people if I could clean their windshields for any amount of change they would give me. Some people said yes. Sometimes it was a quarter, sometimes fifty cents. The male employee who was working there came out and asked me what I was doing and I told him I was trying to make some money so that I could buy something to eat. He didn't stop me or ask where my family was. He looked like he thought it was cool that I wanted to make money and allowed me to keep "working." After making four or five dollars, I bought myself chips, orange pop (soda) and some candy and got back on the road. (When Aunt Toni found out that the man at the gas station let me "work" there, she actually went back to the gas station and cussed out the employee.)

After the gas station, I walked for several more miles. I was scared every time a big car drove by, especially the semi trucks. The wind gusts caused by semi trucks almost knocked me over a few times. It's crazy for me to think that no one stopped to find out why a child was walking alone along the side of the freeway. But it was 1980. Go figure. Anyway, I realized it was going to get dark before I made it to my aunt's house and I started to get anxious. I was scared of the dark. I was scared, terrified actually, to walk past Crownhill cemetery. I was nervous to go by it during the day in a car, I couldn't fathom walking by it at night, alone. I started imagining all the dead bodies that would come out or ghosts that would try and get me. My imagination ran wild and I really freaked myself out. I knew I couldn't go back home but I didn't know where I could go instead. I prayed to God to keep me safe. I did what I was taught, I prayed and believed God would protect me, and the only thing I could think to do was to head to our church, Puritan Baptist Church. I thought I would be safe once I got there. Because the cemetery takes up so much real estate at 38th and Dr. Martin Luther King, Jr. Blvd, with the route I had to take to get to Puritan, I still had to walk past it for at least a mile. I was terrified. I moved as fast as my little legs would carry me but dusk was quickly approaching.

When I finally made it to the church and thought I'd be safe...no one was there and the doors were locked. I didn't think about the fact that people don't stay at church when it's not Sunday, especially since we had been to the church during the week for vacation bible school. I got overwhelmed and really scared and started crying. Not knowing what to do, I sat on the steps and tried to hold in my tears but ended up crying harder. I prayed to God to help me and make me safe. After a little while, a boy who was about ten or eleven years old walked up to me and asked what was wrong. I recognized him from Sunday school and church. He lived across the street from the church and saw me sitting on the steps. I didn't know his name and was so upset I didn't ask. We weren't friends or anything but we always said hi to each other. He was a kind kid, chubby with a round face. His t-shirt and shorts were ragged and torn and he was dirty, not quite Pigpen from Charlie Brown, but not far either. I didn't care. I desperately needed a friend. I told him I ran away and everything that happened and he told me that I could stay with him at his house. I asked what we would say if his parents asked about my parents. He said his dad didn't live there and his mom didn't pay close attention to him.

At the kid's house the first thing that hit me was a really overpowering mildew smell throughout, and it had dirty dishes and clothes scattered on the floors. A mouse (or something) scurried away as we stepped in the door. To the left was some sort of living room area, large amounts of weathered clothes were strewn across a tattered couch with holes in it, one of the legs was broken which made the couch lean at a weird angle; it was fairly dark in the room, which was being lit from the hallway light, the small lamp in the corner didn't seem to put out much light. I just wanted to get to his room. I didn't think anything of the mess because our place was usually dirty at home, even though my mom always made us clean (especially the ritualistic early Saturday mornings when we cleaned the whole house). As he walked me to his room, he called out to his mother in the other room and told her his friend Anthony from church was gonna sleep over. She called back to him that it was okay and said dinner would be ready soon.

In his room, roaches ran down the walls and across the floor. I think he was a little embarrassed because he looked at me as he tried to shoo them away. I told him I didn't care because we had roaches too. I even helped him kill some of them. We laughed a little about how much we hated them. When dinner was ready, we got our plates and ate in the boy's room. I never met his mom. She made our plates and left them on the counter. We ate dinner and I didn't talk much until he fell asleep.

The next morning, I was up early. I didn't really sleep. My eyes closed and I dozed off but I kept jumping at sounds around the house, so I never actually got to rest that night. By the time I saw the sun coming up, I was ready to hit the road. The boy got up with me and gave me a washcloth to get cleaned up. Before using it to wash myself, I used the washcloth as a toothbrush because my mouth felt dirty. I wrapped the cloth around my finger, squeezed toothpaste I found on the counter top onto the cloth and used my finger to "brush" my teeth. After rinsing my mouth, I rinsed the toothpaste out of the cloth and used it to wash myself. I put my dirty clothes back on and went back to the boy's room. He got me a bowl of cereal, which I quickly ate and got back on the road to my aunt's house before anyone else in his house woke up. I thanked him and told him I'd see him in church. I don't remember his name, but he and his family were kind to me in one of my darkest moments, so I'll never forget them.

I headed back up Dr. Martin Luther King Junior Street, which at the time was still called Northwestern. I went east on 38th Street until I got to the street I recognized to get me to my aunt's house. I had to pass the cemetery to get there but I wasn't as afraid during the day. I knew that God would get me safely to where I was going.

I finally made it to Aunt Sharon's house and she swept me up in a big hug and asked me where I'd been. She said everyone was worried about me and that I shouldn't have left like I did. I told her about my journey from the day before and that I wanted to stay with her instead of staying with my mom and step-dad. Of course, my aunt said that I couldn't do that and she had to call my mom to come and get me. I was immediately afraid of what my mom would do when she got to me. I waited, wondering what would happen when she arrived. After a while my mom showed up but instead of yelling and going in on me, she just hugged me and looked really sad. I apologized for running away and asked her if we were going home. She said, "No. We can't go home." I didn't understand what she meant. We stayed there for a while longer until a police car pulled up outside. I was still confused as the police officer came up to my aunt's door. I asked my mom what was going on and she explained that because I ran away and stayed away from home overnight, she had to report me as a runaway. I started crying and told mom that I didn't want to go anywhere else and I wanted to go home with her. My mom started crying and told me that I couldn't go with her. As I screamed and pleaded with mom to not let me be taken, the officer pulled me away from her and put me in the back of his squad car. I kept crying and banging on the window as the officer drove away with me in the backseat. Helpless to do anything about it, my mother stood in front of my aunt's house crying.

The police officer took me to a juvenile detention center. I think it was the one off of Keystone Avenue. They processed me however they do for youth offenders and stuck me in a room/cell with other kids. I remember being more scared than I had ever been. I kept crying and asking to see mom. The other boys told me I wouldn't get to see my mother until I went to court and saw the judge. I didn't know how long that would take so I pestered the guards and asked them if I could see the judge so I could see my mom. The guards eventually got tired of me asking and told me to shut up and that I'd see the judge when they were ready. I don't remember how long I was there before I went in front of the judge but eventually I did. I think I was there for a couple days. I went through one day there and one of the older boys warned me to stop crying or some of the other older boys may pick on me. I nodded and made myself stop crying. That night, they put me in one of their standard cells. It was gross and smelled like pee. I felt completely alone in the world when the door locked and I was by myself with only a small window to the rest of the facility. I prayed for God to get me through it and cried myself to sleep. The next morning, I woke up and banged on the door to get out but I wasn't allowed to leave the room. I felt like I couldn't breathe, felt claustrophobic. I stood close to the door and kept asking them to open it and let me out. Eventually they opened the door.

When I went before the judge, I remember being put in a holding area with about seven or eight other boys seated on an old wooden bench. I could see my mom on the other side of the glass that went the length of the bench, but I couldn't talk to her. I felt desperate to run to her. Regardless of what life was like, that was still my mama. But I couldn't go to her. I sat restless until they finally called my name. They put me behind a podium while mom stood and talked with the judge. I didn't understand what they were talking about but when the judge was done, I asked mom if I could go home with her, and she just started crying. The bailiff came over and took me back to the room with the other boys. I cried and tried to resist but I was taken away. I kept asking questions and was eventually told that the judge had deemed something was going on in my home and that it was unfit for me to return (I don't remember the exact terminology they used). I asked when I could go home and they said that would depend on my mom and however long it would take for her to get our home together. Again, I felt completely alone and cried more. I was remanded to the custody of the state and sent to the Children's Guardian's Home. The Guardian's Home was a facility for wayward youth, abused, neglected, discarded and alone. I was made to stay there while mom was given time to make the necessary changes at home before I could go back with her.

When I was taken to the Guardian's Home, I immediately thought of running away from there and trying to find my way home. I didn't remember how to get back but I didn't care. I don't recall that there was anything specifically wrong with the facility. It was a big building and looked like it had been gutted and converted into a dormitory. It was old and worn down with an old house smell but looked clean enough. I saw a lot of other kids there. My chest got a knot in it when I saw them. I didn't want to be taken from my mom. I just didn't want my step-dad hitting mom or me, or for myself to be hit by my mom anymore. Regardless of whether I wanted to be there or not, I was there. I knew I didn't want to be in a building with a bunch of other kids I didn't know, kids who all looked more miserable than I was. As I was instructed on the rules of the Home, the Administrator looked directly at me and pointed out that there were no bars on the windows or locks on the doors. I looked over at them to confirm what he was saying. He was telling the truth. The place had regular windows and regular doors. He told me that he read my file and knew I ran away from home. He then gave me a choice. He said if I chose to run away, I could. There wouldn't be anyone to stop me. BUT…if I ran away I would have to stay in the juvenile center until my mom could get me out. And no one knew how long that would take. I didn't want to go back to Juvie, so for me it was an easy choice. I didn't run away. I decided to wait for mom to come and get me. I adapted to the environment. I was scared and hated being there, but I made the best of it. I knew God would keep me safe. My mom came to visit me every week. I don't remember which day, maybe Saturday, but she never missed a visit. She always came and let me know how much she loved me and was trying to get me home. I stayed as strong as I could for her but cried every time she left and would cry myself to sleep that night, and every other night too. I just didn't let anyone see or hear it. I didn't get picked on while in the Guardian's Home. I did see some kids get beat up from time to time, but no one bothered me. Still, I always stayed anxious, not knowing if someone would come for me. The administrators in charge enrolled me and the other kids in a new school and I hated it because I was the new kid again. Only this time I was introduced with the other kids from Guardian's Home as being from the group home, so everyone in the class stared at us as if we were to be pitied. I never forgot that feeling. It was awful. I felt like I was nothing. The other time I felt like that was some time later during the Christmas holiday. We were taken to a banquet hall that was filled with men and women in fancy suits and dresses and we were recognized as being from the Guardian's Home. I'll never forget that event because whether the organizers did it intentionally or not, I felt like we were being paraded around as the charity cases. Of course, I didn't know how to express that but I remember the room of people looking at us like we were needy. We *were* needy, but I felt like we were beneath them with all those people staring at us like that. They had pleasant smiles on their faces but in my spirit I felt like they were looking down on us. On the ride back to the Guardian's Home, I made a promise to myself to do something with my life so I would never feel like that again. The time away from my mom being alone at the Guardian's Home showed me that I could handle more in my life than I realized. Even if I bent, I wouldn't break. I knew God would get me through the worst times.

After a number of months, mom and I went back in front of the judge. The consistency of her visits and whatever changes mom made at home worked because the judge said mom had improved her living conditions and allowed me to go back home with her. When I made it back home, I promised myself I would never run away again, no matter how hard life got. And I never did.

CHAPTER THREE
FIGHT or FLIGHT

Difficulty at home, being bullied and the actions of racists weren't the only acts of violence that plagued my life when I was younger. As I got older it seemed like there were always fights going on wherever I was. It was like people didn't have anything better to do. It felt like fights were part of everyday happenings. When I was a teenager, I stayed away from home more and started going out to under-21 dance clubs. 21 Jump Street was the first dance spot I remember going to where I got inspired to learn how to dance, and learned to maneuver so I didn't get trampled when fights jumped off. I was fourteen. I couldn't dance at all before going there. Seeing people do the Eric B and Rakim dance to "Move the Crowd" got me hyped and made me want to find my voice on a dance floor. I fell in love with dancing that night. I didn't learn to dance that night, but I fell in love with the art of dance. I was determined to get better. I wanted to keep learning how music moves through you. That plan was spoiled because that same night, more drama got in the way. People were grooving on the dance floor. I tried learning the moves but I was pretty awful, my timing was off. You have to move your shoulders up and down to the beat while your legs slightly buckle in the same direction with your feet sliding at the end of the move, then repeating that process in the opposite direction. I couldn't get my body to cooperate. The harder I tried, the worse I got. I bumped into people and made them mad because I was messing up their groove. Still, as bad as I was, it was all good - until the first fight broke out. Then the same crowd that was in a vibe and gliding across the floor in unison, suddenly got caught up in the middle of a brawl that had nothing to do with us. The dope vibe and energy turned into a frenzied stampede of fear and screaming. I was focused on learning the moves so I never saw how or where the fight started. I just remember girls screaming and guys yelling "What the f*ck?!" as they struggled to get out of the way.

The guys fighting kept beating the hell out of each other as we all tried to maneuver around them. People were trampling each other to avoid getting hit or getting pulled into the fight. The night was obviously over in the club, but the fight spilled to the streets and kept going until the police started arresting people. We ran to keep from getting locked up. It was the same havoc and mayhem no matter what club we went to – Oliver's, Shenanigans, Dawson's Lake, Down Under, USA West Skating Rink – a bunch of other spots always had mess jumping off, with guys and girls getting into fights all the time. Every weekend different groups of guys were starting some shit. Fights also constantly broke out at the Circle, an area in downtown Indy that is home to a Veteran's Memorial. I witnessed guys who were in a gang beat other guys to the ground, stomp their heads into the street and then run off laughing at the pain and devastation they had just caused. Those vicious cycles continued for full summers, over many years.

I just loved to dance. And hang out with my buddies. And try to talk to girls and just have fun. I say "try" because I never knew what to say to get girls to like me, so I danced. Back then, I learned that most women love to dance and they love guys who know how to dance. I didn't have any "game" but I never needed "game" or to be able to fight when I became a dancer. I would make girls laugh and we'd get on the dance floor, and natural instincts took over from there. My group of friends weren't about all the fighting, either. They avoided fighting as much as possible, but when pushed to the limit, they didn't back down. Chuck, Wyndell (RIP), Nally, JC, J Ping, Deon, Chris (RIP), Rawley, Dewayne, Tim, Jaava – my guys. My guys became my Brothers and we were there for each other.

My best friend in high school, John, and I were inseparable. We were dance partners and worked our way up to become known dancers in our area, and we got a certain level of respect because of it. We were called the *Bad Boyz*. We won a lot of local dance competitions and made somewhat of a name for ourselves in Indianapolis. John and I practiced wherever we needed to in order to get the routines down. We choreographed our own routines where we strung together different dance moves we knew and worked out the transitions between moves. We did the Roger Rabbit, Cabbage Patch, Running Man, Snake, K-Swiss, Robocop, Tootsie Roll, Butterfly, Reebok, Wop and any other dances from the mid to late 80's that we decided to throw in. We practiced for hours and hours, day after day until we got every section right. Once we locked in a few of the moves, we would hit up one of the under 21 clubs to practice in front of a crowd. We got the routines solid and would sign up for competitions at whatever spot was holding one. As for the look of our outfits, we just went with whatever we felt like at the time. The pants were usually black oversized "MC Hammer pants" with oversized shirts. We changed the color of the shirts from contest to contest and had BAD BOYZ written in big letters on the shirts. Most of the time the prize was a small cash prize, usually about $250-$500, occasionally more. We definitely always needed the money, but I felt like the biggest win for us was knowing we gave our all, crushed the routines and had bragging rights to know that we were the best. Some of our most fun times were on weekends at the club getting in big dance circles with our large group of dance buddies (Chuck, Wyndell, JC, Deon, Chris, Rawley, Tim, Donnie, Mark and anyone else brave enough to step up). We also did line dances and other group routines that everybody joined in (like the Electric Slide), but individual battles in the circle were a staple for those of us who were the real dancers.

We never had the opportunity to be discovered like dancers do on shows like *World of Dance* or *So You Think You Can Dance?* or *America's Got Talent*. I don't think dancing had the respect back then that it does now. I would've LOVED to have been on a show like one of those. We didn't have the technical intricacies and nuanced moves and isolations of groups like Les Twins (who are phenomenal), but we were dope. I think *Star Search* was in the early years around the time I was dancing, but we didn't know anything about the process of getting on a television show and we never pursued it. I definitely wasn't thinking about Hollywood or being a part of it. John and I were happy and content to win competitions on the weekends and split the pot. We were big-ish fish in a small pond. We were friends and danced as partners and eventually grew apart. (Donnie and I became dance partners afterwards.) The last time I saw John, a different act of violence (unrelated to dance, or being at a dance club) was the backdrop.

I got into a beef with a guy who got pissed and originally wanted to fight me because I had sex with a girl he had an off-again-on-again relationship with. He and I were cool at one point until he got jealous that I slept with her. The girl and I only had sex once, and never again. He still lost his shit. I never understood why. She wasn't his girlfriend. She was a cool chick and her place was a hangout spot for a bunch of us. She was single, I was single and he had a girlfriend at the time. The girl I slept with was a "friend with benefits" for him, at least that's how she described their relationship. She wanted more but he had a girlfriend. None of that had anything to do with me, though. Why the f*ck did he get so pissed at me? He was in his feelings. He let it get back to me that he was planning to whoop my ass as soon as he saw me.

I was in a bad Gemini mood one night and when the guys told me (one guy's name was Mark, I don't remember Mark's buddy's name), I got pissed and hyped myself up to go fight him. They agreed to drive me to where he would be. I was doing too much. I put on my ninja uniform and everything. I completely disregarded the principles of the martial art. Stealth and secrecy. I didn't think about any of that. Mark and his buddy had been in a lot of fights and I was trying to make myself look tough in their eyes. I even put climbing spikes on my hands. I had seen them used in martial arts movies and had practiced with them a few times, but never to use in a fight. I had only used them to climb trees or buildings. But I knew if I did use them, they would inflict major damage of some kind, and I didn't know what I was walking into so I went ready for war. Even though I really wasn't.

We made it back over to where the girl lived. The guy was there visiting her. I didn't know it but John was there, too. The guy came outside when he heard I was there to fight him. He saw me in my uniform, yelled out something and said, "I got something for yo' ass!" and went back inside. He disappeared into the apartment and seconds later came out with a wooden bat that he banged on the side of the fence to announce his arrival to the battle. I was nervous. Scared, actually. I didn't know what I was gonna do. He swung the bat at my head and I instinctively ducked and his swing went right over my head. I didn't have time to think about the fact that his swing probably would have killed me if it had connected because everything happened lightning fast. His momentum made him spin around which gave me the opportunity to grab him in some awkward way and slam him to the ground. I didn't use any kind of technique because I wasn't sure of what to do. Of all the techniques I had learned, no combinations or sequences popped in my head. That's where I messed up. As he was falling down he grabbed my uniform and pulled me to the ground with him. We struggled around on the ground for a few moments. I didn't do any damage with the claws, even though they probably scratched him a little, but I never tried to actually use them. They were just on my hands and got in the way. I didn't have the killer instinct to do permanent damage to him. I could've blinded him or scarred his face or body for life. But somewhere inside, I knew that if I really mangled him or killed him, I was going to jail for a long time. He wasn't worth it. Deep down, I didn't even really want to fight him. We had been playing cards about a week before that.

He wriggled free first and stood up before me. I lost track of him and as I was standing up, he came down on my head with the baseball bat. Surprisingly, the blow didn't knock me out, I stood straight up. I later learned that my head was split open (had to go to the hospital and get stitches for that one), but I didn't know it due to the adrenaline of the moment. Mike Tyson once said, "Everyone has a plan until they get punched in the mouth," which is the same sentiment as the Helmuth von Moltke quote, "No plan survives contact with the enemy." Well, I didn't have a plan, and getting hit with a bat damn sure jumbled my thoughts. I remember it scared the shit out of me. I hastily tried to take the claws off and said something like, "Put the bat down, let's have a real fight." But I couldn't get them off because of how they were secured to my hand. Mark and his buddy and the other guys watching stepped in and broke it up. Mark and his buddy got me in their car to take me home. As we were driving away, the guy kept saying shit like, "I'ma f*ck you up the next time I see you! Don't think this is over motherf*cker!" The next time I saw him, he and his buddies confronted me and Donnie at the mall.

I tried to move past the incident but the guy never let it go. He approached me awhile later at Lafayette Square Mall, "the Square," a mall on the West side of Indianapolis.

I was minding my own business, standing inside a shoe store with Donnie and all of a sudden the guy I got into a fight with a month or so earlier stepped to me. He had two guys with him. He started running his mouth about the fight and how he was gonna f*ck me up. But he never swung at me. He just kept talking shit. Donnie was urging me to stand up for myself and go ahead and fight him, but I didn't. I had never been in that position before. I didn't know what to do. I had already fought him and been hit in the head with a baseball bat by him, so I wasn't necessarily scared to fight him. I just didn't want to. Donnie and I were having a good day and my energy didn't jump into fight mode. The guy and I had actually been cool at one point. I didn't hate him. But as he wolfed, a thought flashed through my mind: front thrust kick – kick him through the glass display case. I had a powerful front kick and guessed he wouldn't be able to block it. My next immediate thought was: you'll go to jail for assault. Before I could think of doing anything else, the store manager told us to get out, to take the fight outside. As we were heading outside, the other guy kept talking shit about what he was gonna do. My mind raced about what was about to go down as we walked toward the mall entrance. When Donnie saw the security guard, he waved him over and told him about the guys starting a fight with us. The guard didn't want to get involved and said to take our beef off the property. As soon as we got outside, the guy got me in between some parked cars with his buddies on each side of him. My heart was racing, fight or flight instinct engaged, but I stood my ground. I got into a slight martial arts stance with one foot slightly back and calmly said, "Come on." I was anxious but ready for whatever. I knew Donnie could handle the other two if they jumped in. The guy breathed hard, huffed and puffed and stared me down, but he never charged. He turned on Donnie, "Naw, you know what? I want yo' ass," he said. "This nigga who wanna tell every motherf*cking thing!" I was confused. It didn't make any sense to me that he would suddenly go after Donnie, who had nothing to do with our beef. The guy and his goons walked around the car and approached Donnie. By that time, Donnie was advanced in ninjutsu himself so I wasn't worried about him. He actually took over my training from George at one point. As they walked around the car, Donnie didn't back down. "Naw, ya'll don't want none of me. I'm not him." He was right. He had trained a lot longer than I had and had been in plenty of fights already. He was already combat tested.

"Naw, f*ck that, you snitch!" the guy yelled at Donnie as they kept advancing towards him. It happened quickly. They were face to face and the guy and one of his goons went after him. I just stood and watched. I don't know why I didn't rush over and grab one of them from behind like I'd seen so many times before. But I didn't. I found myself a spectator wanting to see what Donnie would do. I asked the therapist about that moment too and why she thought the guy went after Donnie and not me. She said it sounded like the guy was acting from a space of ego and may not have really wanted to fight me, but was posturing for his friends. Subconsciously, he may have been afraid of *me*, knowing that he hit me with a bat and it didn't do the damage he thought it would. If a bat didn't stop me, what would his fists do? I never thought about that. She then said I didn't move to help because, subconsciously, I may have wanted to see Donnie "in action," to see him put to use all the training I had received. I guess that's possible. But whatever the reason, I didn't react. I watched. And later, carried the weight of feeling like a coward because of it. Anyway, after a second, the guy threw a punch at Donnie who got off a few blows and flipped the guy over his shoulder, before one of the other two guys jumped in (the third guy didn't do anything). There were a few punches thrown and after another couple seconds, I see Donnie swinging his arms. Suddenly, the guy and his goons start yelling and backing up, running away from Donnie. The main guy yelled, "Aaargh! He got brass knuckles!" I looked over at Donnie and saw what the guy was talking about. They weren't brass knuckles, they were nunchucka, nunchucks. Small, red, paint chipping, metal nunchucks. I couldn't see the chipped paint at the speed they were moving, of course, but Donnie trained me and I knew what they looked like. I had practiced with them before. Donnie was wielding them like an expert. He suddenly had the upper hand and was chasing the guy and his goons. All three of them together didn't keep trying to fight him. I felt a little less like a coward. All I could think was, "Where the hell did he have those hidden?" The guy and goons fled and we got in Donnie's car and headed home. Donnie never said anything about me not jumping in. I decided that day that I would rather accept getting beat down in a fight than let a friend fight alone. I would never let Donnie or any other friend down again, no matter what happened to me. A few days later, Donnie's girlfriend at the time made a comment to me about whether or not I would "really have his back," or if I would "just let him get his ass beat like you did at the mall." I froze when she said that. She looked at me like I was a piece of shit, but because he was my friend, she had to deal with me. There was nothing I could say. We looked at each other and moved on. At that moment, I felt bad all over again. I hated that feeling. I swore I'd never feel that way again.

CHAPTER FOUR
CIVILIZATION

While I was still in high school, even though I was in school and dancing whenever I could, I still wanted to learn to fight to protect myself. When I was fourteen I met George, a normal looking guy who was actually a master (and now a grandmaster) in Koga Ryu Ninjutsu. I didn't know someone could be a master at his age. He was only a couple of years older than me. George actually went to high school with my sister Nikki but I didn't know that for a long time. George and I first made contact at one of the under-21 clubs. I heard rumors that he was a martial arts master and I started hounding him to train me. I used to watch a crazy amount of old Kung Fu movies with Shaolin Monks and day-dream about being a Kung Fu expert. *Five Deadly Venoms* is still my favorite of all time. George wasn't a Shaolin master but he was the only martial arts master I knew.

When I initially asked George to train me, Donnie intervened and told him I wasn't ready. I didn't know George had already been training Donnie and Mark in the art of ninjutsu. No matter how many times I asked, George kept saying no. I didn't understand what Donnie meant until later. When Donnie was away one summer, George allowed me to become his student. Over time I came to understand what Donnie was talking about. He wasn't just being a hater and keeping me from learning how to fight, he knew I needed to harness my energy and not be reckless with the knowledge I was given about the ninja arts. Donnie knew I could do major damage to someone else or to myself if I didn't show respect to the arts. I can't go into any details about the stuff we did (that's part of the rules of joining a ninja clan, you're not supposed to divulge the secrets of the society), other than to say we trained in fields, wooded areas and different terrains, not just in a classroom or gym or dojo. I trained in hand-to-hand combat, dealing with multiple attackers, disarming people with weapons and weapons training (ninjato/ sword, shurikens/throwing stars, bow and arrows and nunchucks). We learned real-world applications for techniques we were taught, like if someone is approaching in a threatening manner to use a front kick to keep them at a distance. I never achieved mastery in ninjutsu but I learned some stuff that I can never unlearn and that I hope to never have to use. But truth be told, I'm grateful I learned what I did. Just in case, God forbid, something apocalyptic ever jumped off. There's a lot of ugliness in the world. I learned how to rid the world of some of that ugliness if I was ever forced into that situation.

Anthony Montgomery, Black Belt
Dohyun International Hapkido Federation

After having trained in Koga Ryu Ninjutsu under Grandmaster Seika, I have also earned a Black Belt in Hapkido under the tutelage of Grandmaster Song through the Dohyun International Hapkido Federation, so I can more than protect myself and my family now. I lived with a subconscious fear for so many years. That finally changed after achieving my Black Belt. Given all the hard work I put in to earn my belt, combined with the skills I learned in ninjutsu and having the knowledge of how to apply various techniques in real-life situations, not-to-mention surviving my own battles and living to tell the tales, I finally arrived at a place of peace and self-assurance that I can defend when necessary. I finally gained the confidence to know I could protect myself and those I love, no matter where I am in the world. I was finally not afraid. With what I've been able to attain in my life, I was brought to a different awareness. I thought learning to fight and being a fighter would make me feel stronger, make me feel like a success. I've learned that my success in life is not predicated on me being a fighter. But like everyone else, I must fight through whatever stumbling blocks and learnable lessons life throws at me.

I've learned that life isn't always about fighting. Sometimes it's just about healthy competition. Indianapolis has some great sports teams, even though I didn't always root for them. The Indianapolis Colts are in my hometown but I was a San Francisco 49ers fan growing up. I loved Joe Montana, Steve Young and Jerry Rice. I was fast and always wanted to "go for the bomb" when I played football with neighborhood kids, thinking I could feel what it must be like to be Jerry Rice. I wasn't even close to being him though. When I went long, I usually dropped the ball and the kids got pissed, and then never threw to me again. I always felt like a loser when I went home. But I felt like a winner when I rooted for the Niners. Even though I'll always have love for the Niners, I became a Colts fan later in life so I've got to say to owner Jim Irsay, former head coach and Hall-of-Famer Tony Dungy, Hall-of-Famer Peyton Manning (one of the greatest to ever do it!) and the whole 2006 championship squad, "Thank you for bringing a championship to the hometown!" Colts blue, through and through!

Robert Mathis (Indianapolis Colts, OL) and Anthony Montgomery
at Food 4 Thought charity event

A full-circle-moment occurred for me after I gained success as an actor and was asked to go back to Indy and do a charity luncheon event where I would work as a waiter with Robert Mathis, all-pro Outside Linebacker for the Indianapolis Colts and other professionals in their fields. I was excited to be giving back to my city and doing something in conjunction with the Colts. We took orders, served drinks and food and had a lot of fun offering our time to benefit local organization Food 4 Thought. I was having a great time being able to help. At one point, however, it also became awkward for me when I delivered a drink to an older White man who had what I can only describe as an "I'll tolerate you" energy about him, even though he feigned a gruff smile. I brushed the thought off, working to stay in the positive spirit of what the function represented, and kept doing what I was supposed to do, making sure everyone was good and had everything they needed (much like I did when I was an actual server). But then I interacted with a different man, again, older and White, and there was a similar energy from him. The moments took me back to an energy I got from a guest who treated me like a servant at a restaurant where I worked on the Southside of Indy. At the restaurant, three mid-thirties White guys sat in my section. I said hello to greet the table (and treat them like guests in my home, which we were trained to do) and one of the guys started with, "Just take our order…" I looked at the guy, then his friends. Oh hell no. Without saying a word, I turned around and walked away from the table and had one of the other servers wait on them. I never told anyone at the charity function but I felt similarities of the restaurant experience at their event. It wasn't until a couple of weeks later when I spoke to someone connected with the event who offered an alternate mindset for the event guests. After our talk, I realized the people were probably not looking down on me at all, that they may have been actually looking at me with more admiration that I would be donating my time in that way. The realization took away the bitterness and humbled me. It gave me a different perspective and allowed me to see that everything I thought I was feeling was completely conjured up in my own mind. It made me think on a deeper level about how I have to be aware that my past negative experiences could have an impact on how I view things that aren't what they initially appear to be.

Indiana Pacers are the hometown NBA team. The Pacers are cool and I wanted to see them play when I was younger. I remember going to Market Square Arena with a couple kids I hung around trying to sneak into a game because we didn't have money for tickets. One of the guys had a scheme to get tickets we found and use them to get past security and into the game. We got close to one of the exits and found whatever discarded ticket stubs we could use that weren't ruined. After getting the dirt off the stubs, we tried to get through security. But it didn't work. The older Black security guard had seen it all before and chased us away, before he called the "real police." I just wanted to get to see Hall-of-Famer Reggie Miller in person. I loved Reggie, who was a titan when I was younger (especially in those battles against the New York Knicks with Spike Lee cheering them on). Despite being from Nap, though, I LOVE the Chicago Bulls. Michael Jordan, first and foremost, along with Scottie Pippen were the most lethal one-two punch I had ever seen, as well as all the other players who contributed to the greatness of that dynasty: Steve Kerr, Horace Grant, B.J. Armstrong, Toni Kukoc, Dennis Rodman – basically, the Bulls of the late 80s to late 90s. Like every other kid out there,

I wanted to "be like Mike." I had pictures of him up on my walls, my favorite being the "Wingspan" image. I was always trying to rock Bulls gear. I wanted Jordan's but couldn't afford them when I was a kid, so I was proud to buy my first pair as an adult. The Jordan 3s will always be my first sneaker love. I was so obsessed with them that I searched everywhere but couldn't find them and bought myself a pair when I went to Canada. I didn't pay attention to how the shoe sizing ran and I couldn't fit the pair I bought. I never tried them on in the store because I assumed they would fit. I was furious. I gave my 3s away. That hurt for a long time. I used to dress like I could play ball (oversized shirt, baggy shorts, headband, knee brace, etc.) but my game was not like Mike. I remember a game where I had a wide-open layup and I ran so fast (and didn't have control of myself or the ball), I clanked the ball off the backboard. I did that a lot. Eventually my buddies told me to just be a rebound specialist like Dennis Rodman. I did, and kept working on my shot. I'm not great but I have my flashes of greatness. I stick to living out my fantasies of being Michael Jordan every once in a while on the court and enjoy continuing watching the Bulls' games. I kept following the team after all my favorites were gone because I love the city of Chicago – one of the greatest cities in the world to me. I'm a Bulls fan for life. I'm not a bandwagon fan, either. I celebrate the victories and I get pissed and scream at my tv when they play out of sync and can't get a win. But as mad as I get, I still ride with them. I just keep the faith they'll bounce back. Chicago red, until I'm dead! Many years ago, I enjoyed being able to give back and help inspire the kids of Chicago when I worked with the Bulls' Community Relations Manager at the time (Tony Rokita) as part of an event to motivate the kids to keep being their best and doing their best in school. I love helping encourage others to live their lives to the fullest, especially since I haven't always lived my life that way.

SPORTS FLIPS

Sports played a role in my educational development, but not in the traditional sense. I did learn the lessons achieved while playing sports but didn't realize those lessons until I was older. I've always been pretty athletic so I tried a bunch of different sports, even though I wasn't great at everything. Like basketball. People LOVE basketball in Indiana. The movie Hoosiers, with Gene Hackman, was filmed in Indiana. I love basketball. But I sucked as a kid. My hand/eye coordination was garbage. I got clowned all the time. I didn't get better until I was almost grown. I'm still not great but I have my moments. Playing pick-up games got me ready for when I played in the Gus Macker, a 3-on-3 basketball tournament in Indy (we also played in Shoot-the-Bull, a 3-on-3 tourney in Chicago) with my guys: Chuck, Wyndell, and Tom Beard (and two other guys at different tourneys). Chuck was the best with the most athleticism, Wyn had handles and could drain 3's, Beard had a smooth stroke and I was scrappy and brought energy and defense when they needed a break. I started sometimes but I usually came off the bench since they were all better than me. But, I loved getting out there and the camaraderie we forged on the court.

I used to play in open fields with kids from the neighborhoods I lived in. We spent day after day doing somersaults onto old, used, dirty mattresses. People threw them out and left them near their dumpsters and we would take two or three and stack them on top of each other to cushion our landings. It wasn't sanitary at all, but we practiced hard and learned how to tumble. Our technique was non-existent, but we were determined to be like the gymnastics we saw on TV. I almost broke my neck one day trying to do a front double somersault. We had been running around doing front flips and sticking those, round-off back tucks, and sticking those. We got hyped and wanted to do more. I got cocky because I had a good front tuck. My buddy challenged me and I told him that I could do two flips. He triple-dog-dared me, so of course, I had to do it. If only I had listened to the voice in my head that said, "Anthony, that's not a swimming pool. What if you don't make it?" Nah, I wasn't listening to any logic. We took one of the three mattresses away, using the theory that I may need the extra room to get all the way around. I went for it. I was only able to make it around one and a half revolutions. I ended up going headfirst into the mattress. I thought my neck was broken. I stayed down for a long couple of minutes before getting up and shaking it off and acting like I was okay.

I wasn't okay. My neck and head hurt for weeks after that. I never told my mom so I never went to the doctor. I'm sure I should have seen a doctor, but I was more afraid of getting in trouble with my mom than finding out if my spine was okay. That near-death experience didn't stop me from being delinquent, though. We used to run around jumping off different heights, doing backflips off of whatever we could find that gave us elevation: abandoned garages, port-o-potty stalls in the park, park picnic tables, literally whatever we could find. The neighborhood kids also used to take over dilapidated fields and play football into the night (until just before the streetlights came on). I didn't know what the different positions were so I didn't know any formal plays. I was fast so they would always tell me to "go long," "go for the bomb." I was fast but only moderately good, I dropped the ball a lot. I'd make an occasional touchdown for us and that would redeem me for a little while. I persevered through vicious ridicule and insults playing with all the different kids I met while growing up. I developed a "thick skin" playing with them.

LESS THAN ORGANIZED

I got into organized sports somewhere around middle school. I tried baseball. It was fun—boring—but fun. I wasn't good in the infield (the balls kept getting past me) so they put me in the outfield and I wasn't bad. I could throw the ball far and get to them quickly once they were hit. But I was the worst when I got up to bat. I don't ever remember hitting a ball. I also never practiced the way you have to practice to be great at a sport. I gave minimal effort and never gave it my all. I learned baseball wasn't my fit and quit before wasting a lot of time with it. I developed a love for softball later in life. I enjoy playing in softball leagues when I have time.

There were many days of wandering around as a directionless preteen. One day I walked by a billiards spot and stopped and stared through dirty windows and dense cigarette smoke at the tables and all the guys moving around them with precision. I was amazed they hit shot after shot. The veteran players allowed me to come in and watch. Because they saw I had a real interest in the game (but had no money), they started teaching me the ins and outs of billiards. I learned 8-Ball and 9-Ball and found myself going day after day, for months. I eventually developed a solid game for myself. Over time, I got really good.

I tried tennis one summer and participated in a few sessions with the N.J.T.L. (National Junior Tennis League), which was holding a summer camp at a community park. I think it was Douglas Park. I wasn't the best but it was a lot of fun and I did learn my way around a tennis court. I didn't stick with it, though I do enjoy getting on the court from time to time. And I've always loved watching it.

I tried out for the football team in eighth grade. I was small but used my speed. I couldn't take a hit though. I remember being put on the line (I don't remember if it was offense or defense) and getting run over by this kid who was three times my size. I left the field and never went back. Football wasn't my thing at the time. I liked to watch games, but that was it. I wish I had stuck with it, though. I played for fun with other non-professionals when I was in college and after being in Hollywood for a while, I found a real love for the sport when I played in the Entertainment Flag Football League with Wayne, Tuesday, Desmond, Tory, Deandre, Red, Courtenay, Tony and the rest of my guys on the Terror Squad. My speed came in handy on defense against much bigger players. I finished one of the seasons with about 11 sacks. We were 5-time-EFFL Champs when I stopped playing in the league.

We made every other football team "lean back," just like Fat Joe, Remy Ma and the original Terror Squad instructed us to do.

High school brought with it track and field. I practiced with the team, trying out, but I didn't last long. I remember practicing with a relay but I don't remember which one. One day the coach let me try pole-vaulting. I liked it but never got the technique down. I couldn't figure out how to get the pole to bend to catapult me over the bar. I wasn't super strong but I had an okay

Terror Squad after our 4th championship

amount of proportionate upper-body strength, so instead of bending the pole, I just planted it in the pit and used my strength to throw me over the bar. I did that for a few practices until one day I threw myself past the landing pad and when I came down it felt like my shoulder was out of place. I couldn't raise my arm. One of the older players was close and grabbed my arm, popped it back in place and told me to run it off. I quit track-and-field soon after that.

I also tried wrestling during my freshman year. I was pretty good with the techniques. The "Fireman's Carry" was one of my favorite moves. But I didn't have any size to me and I wasn't very strong. In practice, most of my matches I would get my opponent down but before I could get the count for the win, they would flip me over, pin me, and because I wasn't strong enough to fight my way out of it, I would lose. They started teaching me escape techniques, but I hated getting pinned and started hating wrestling because of it, so I quit.

My sophomore year I was bussed to George Washington High School. It was initially a hard switch. I only went to that school because my other school shut down. I got along with most of the students pretty well but didn't want to go there so I made the transition difficult for myself. I continued getting in trouble in class and being a "class clown" like I had at all my previous schools. I never excelled as a student (I was a pretty good R.O.T.C student though), but I did find a sport I liked. I tried out for the swim team and discovered I had a knack for it. Ironically, when I was young and we lived in Texas for a brief period, I almost drowned at a community pool. When I got to high school, I found my stroke. I had fun playing around with swimming until high school and then I got serious about the sport. Unfortunately, I was forced to deal with other people's ignorance surrounding Black people and swimming. But it didn't matter. Our team was like a family. They stood by my side, and sometimes in my place, when we went to schools where students would be racist. I did my best to take my anger out in the pool and destroy the racists in our meets. My teammates were like my brothers during those years. They accepted me for who I was and I accepted them the same. We were all just students wanting to win. The fact that we came together to achieve success on a common goal despite our differences was the biggest lesson that I didn't know I was learning for life.

SACRIFICE

I loved being a swimmer. There was a focus and joy I found while swimming that was different from the other sports I tried. I loved practice. We pushed each other to be better and be faster. I hated two-a-days (having to practice early in the morning before school, even in the dead of winter) and after school. It was grueling, but swimming 3000-3500 yards per day Monday-Friday got me in excellent shape. I wasn't big on lifting weights, and I don't remember Coach making us do a full weight training regimen, although we did lift to some degree. I learned all four swim strokes but was better at breaststroke and freestyle; I was pretty good at backstroke but butterfly was the hardest for me to learn (I'm awed by Michael Phelp's domination in the sport). We had some fast freestylers so I put the most work in on my event, the 100-Breaststroke. I got good. I had some great team battles with my teammate Ryan, who I used as motivation to make myself great at breaststroke. Ryan was better until I started. I fought hard to be better than him, better than everyone. My biggest issue was stamina in the water. I would usually do well in our school meets and often had a lead after the first 50-75 yards, but I would usually have nothing left in the tank for the last 25 yards. If I was able to maintain and push through to the end, I would win, otherwise, one of the other swimmers would catch up and pass me for the victory. Those were the most painful losses. But, because I was solid in the first 50 yards and had a fast time, I earned a position swimming the breaststroke leg of the Medley Relay, which I alternated with Ryan. And I didn't just swim. I was also a diver. I started diving one day because we needed another diver for a meet and I told Coach Shaw I wanted to do it, even though I didn't know how. That day I learned to do the basics of all the dives: front, back, reverse, inward and a dive with a twist, plus one optional dive with a higher degree of difficulty (I did a front 1½ somersault in the tuck position and occasionally in pike position). I never had a diving coach in high school, I learned to dive by trial and error. I became the backup for our best diver, Scott. I fell in love with being on the board, despite the pain from learning (smacking the water over and over until I got it right) and even busting my head on the diving board once (more about that later). As a team, we were really good and went on to win the City Championship for three years straight. I was proud of my contributions to our team's success. Our theme song was *Another One Bites the Dust* by Queen. We played it after each championship and did back and front somersaults and Suzies (reverse somersaults while making crazy faces or expressions, into big splashes) off the 1-meter and 3-meter springboards, and had a blast in the pool until we got tired. Swimming and diving taught me what it means to sacrifice for your teammates.

One day during practice I was attempting a double back somersault on the 1m springboard. I threw my head back (instead of keeping it still and using my arms and legs to achieve rotation) and ended up hitting my head on the underside of the diving board. I didn't know it but the board put a gash about four inches long and pretty deep across the top of my head. I didn't black out but due to the shock of the blow, I didn't swim to the closest ladder, I grabbed the top of my head, swam across the deep end and got out. Coach was working with my teammates on the other side of the pool, but came over after hearing commotion from the other guys. Coach sat me down and held my head closed until the paramedics arrived. I was taken to the hospital and received stitches in my head.

About a week or two later we had a big swim meet and Coach told me that we needed the points from my events to help us to win. My head was still hurting but I covered the wound with gauze, put on a swim cap, swam my events and dove. It felt like somebody was hitting me in the head with a sledgehammer every time I went into the water. But I sacrificed so that my team could win. I felt like I had to make up for not performing consistently. There were too many times that I didn't execute on the diving board. I failed. Not all the time, but enough times that I was down on myself when no one was around. I don't know what it was. The lights. The pressure. The moment. Sometimes I felt I could look like a potential Olympic hopeful in practice (at least that's how I felt sometimes, and was sometimes gassed up by my teammates to feel), but when it was time for the meet, I didn't always come through. I was disappointed in myself a lot because of that but I never let anyone know how I felt. I still worked hard. And I should've worked even harder. Because of feeling like I didn't always come through for the team, when Coach told me we needed the points I knew I had to put the pain aside and give whatever I could.

The difference between swimming and every other sport I tried was that I had found a true love for swimming and diving. No matter how hard it got, no matter how many times I failed, I never quit. I finally understood how people feel when they fall in love with their sport, the sport that moves their soul. I loved being a part of the swimming environment, even if it was just walking by an aquatic center and having a sense-memory experience of all the things that bring me joy being around a pool. Because of swimming, I've learned to love and appreciate all sports and the work ethic I know it must take to be elite in them. My love of swimming led me to become a city lifeguard for Riverside Recreation Center. Because I was such an avid swimmer, the facility manager, Stan, also had me (and other lifeguards) teach swim lessons to children and adults. I loved teaching swim lessons. It made me feel good helping people learn to be more comfortable in the water. I learned a great deal of patience during those summers. I was a lifeguard and taught lessons for a couple of years (it was an indoor pool and open year-round), until one year I learned a painful lesson about the power of water. One Saturday morning, we were spread out around the pool giving swim lessons: I was in the shallow end teaching three younger kids, another lifeguard was in a different part of the shallow end teaching kids and one lifeguard was working in the deep end with a few more advanced kids, letting them practice off the diving board and whatever other techniques they worked on. Everything was going well when suddenly someone started yelling from the deep end (I think it was one of the kids) and when we looked towards them, they were yelling about one of the kids who was on the bottom of the pool.

Everyone went into action. I got my kids out of the water and made sure they were safe and then hurried to the deep end to try and assist as best I could. The scene was frantic as the child was pulled from the water and we worked to save the young boy's life. I briefly assisted in administering CPR until someone took over from me (I believe it was Stan, who kept trying to resuscitate the child until the paramedics arrived). In the end, we were not able to save him. He was nine or ten. I've always felt devastated for his parents and siblings. I know an investigation of some sort was launched but I never found out what caused that horrifying situation. I stopped being a lifeguard not long after that. I never looked at swimming the same. I wasn't afraid of the water but I gained a new understanding of its power. I maintained my love of all things aquatic but that day changed my life forever.

THE CALL OF THE SEA

When I moved to the West Coast I fell in love with the ocean after I got used to it (and of course the beach). I quickly learned the difficulties and dangers of swimming with currents and waves. I was a trained swimmer but I trained in a pool and it threw me when a wave smacked me in the face like a wall. My vision was blurred because of the salt water and I had to struggle to find which way was up to catch a breath. I spent a lot of time at the beach and found my comfort zone. Once it wasn't overwhelming anymore, I found my love for the ocean. But I hated not seeing what I was swimming in. The

Naptown kid in me knew there were sharks and everything else that would devour me in a heartbeat. So, I tackled my fear of the unknown in a different way. I got my scuba certification (NAUI -National Association of Underwater Instructors). I trained at a dive shop near Universal City and did my pool time at a local pool. I tested for my certificate at Catalina Island, and it sucked. The water was freezing through the two layers of wetsuits I wore, and visibility was 10-15 feet. But I got it done and felt accomplished for a Midwest guy.

It wasn't until I was able to scuba dive when I went to Negril, Jamaica that I fell in love with the aquatic underworld. The water was as warm as bath water and visibility was 100 feet. The vibrant colors of all the fish, flora, and fauna were unlike anything I had ever seen. It felt like I was in an aquarium painting. I also felt small, and insignificant. I thought about my life regarding the expanse of the ocean and it was humbling. It was scary, but not in a "get me the hell outta here" way. It was more, "I'm scared but I can't wait to see what other creations God has come up with under the sea." I was hooked. I dived at the Great Barrier Reef in Australia and that made me want to dive at more of the world's great dive locations. I learned to love and respect the oceans of the world.

I love learning the valuable life skills that people gain from participating in sports. I'm a huge fan and appreciate all the great analysts like Stephen A. Smith (who's also now part of our *General Hospital* family as Brick) - love him and Molly Qerim on *First Take*, and Shannon Sharpe is a fantastic addition (and killing it in his own right with with his shows *Club Shay Shay* and *NightCap*), Tony Kornheiser, Mike Wilbon (love their show *PTI*), Keith Olberman, Dan Patrick, Chris Berman, Linda Cohn, Hannah Storm, Scott Van Pelt, the late, great, Stuart Scott and so many others who break down the world of sports and help explain all the nuances. Early in life I didn't realize the education and skills people gain being involved with sports and how those skills can help improve their everyday existence. I'm grateful to have learned the importance of sports on one's growth and development. Sports will always be part of my life. I believe sports are a vital part of every civilization.

CHAPTER FIVE
DETAINED

I have always been a good guy, but I have not always made good choices. Because I didn't have an appreciation for sports or an understanding of their necessity when I was younger, instead of getting into sports, I got into trouble. Like I mentioned, no matter what was going on in our lives at home, my mom raised me to keep God first, be a good person and do what's right. But when I was younger I didn't always listen to that. I was hard-headed, as they used to say. I was what they called a "bad kid."

I could be good when I wanted but I got into stuff I shouldn't have all the time. As I got older, I didn't improve my behavior and did a lot of dumb shit and made terrible decisions. I knew better and knew I wasn't supposed to take things that didn't belong to me, but I did it anyway. I always wanted stuff and since we were impoverished, I started stealing, even when I knew it was wrong. I blamed it on us being poor. But the bottom line was that I made all those bad choices. And I lied a lot too. I got to a point where I would tell a lie as much as I would tell the truth. I had to lie even more to cover for the stealing. It was a vicious circle I kept myself in. I felt anxious all the time and kept it to myself. My stomach was always in knots trying to keep the lies straight. I'm sorry I made so many terrible choices. I know those choices made my life's journey much more challenging and difficult than it would have been otherwise, and hurt too many people who shouldn't have been pulled into my self-destructive orbit. Sometimes I got away with the negative stuff I did, but the bad energy always came back to me at some point, in some other way. Whether the repercussions came back immediately or not, when I did something bad I always felt wrong when I looked in the mirror at night. I hated who I was when I lied and stole but I still did it. I've learned as an adult that karma always catches up with you. I did so much dumb shit when I was young – and have already paid my karmic debts for those things – that I work hard to live the best life I can, and I never lie anymore. I've lied so much in my life, the easiest lie for me to remember is the truth. I know how much pain lying causes because I've caused enough pain to last a lifetime. No matter what, I would rather deal with the fallout from the truth than the loss of trust, respect and honor from telling a lie. People may not always like what I have to say, but it will be the truth. Other than for entertainment purposes and my acting career, I work to keep drama out of my life.

But I wasn't always that way. I stayed in trouble, sometimes finding myself detained or in other perils, including situations that made me feel insignificant on this rogue planet.

The stealing started at an early age. I didn't steal all the time, but I did steal a lot. I stole from wherever: stores, relatives, my mom. It got to a point where people, including family, stopped wanting me around. I felt bad but I kept doing it. I stole throughout my elementary years. One day it caught up with me. I think I was in fifth grade, about 10 years old. There was a little bodega type of convenience store around the corner from where we lived at the time. The store owner was an older short, stocky black man who looked like he had done hard labor his whole life. He was a nice enough guy. A few kids I knew from the neighborhood used to go in his store and steal penny candy from him whenever he went to the back of the store. He couldn't move very fast and had a slight limp so they would steal candy and run out. When they knew I was trying hard to be part of the group, they told me I needed to steal some candy for everybody.

They said since I was fast, the old man wouldn't be able to catch me. I knew it was wrong but I wanted to fit in so I did it. It was easy and they were right. He was way too slow to catch me. I went back and stole candy many more times after that. One day, the store owner had gotten fed-up and set a trap for us. Set a trap for me. I went into the store and didn't see the owner. I called out but he didn't answer. Thinking he was in the back of the store, I started to walk through the gate and around the counter to take some candy. As I was about to pass the gate, an actual customer came into the store and I jumped, pretending that I was just about to look and see if the owner was around. Just then the owner stood up from between two of his shelves and helped the customer, staring at me the whole time. As the customer walked out, I was about to exit also when the owner called out.

"Hold on," the owner said, anger in his eyes.

I turned and looked at him.

"I'm tired of you lil' niggas comin' in here and stealin' from me," he said. "You lucky that fella came in here when he did. I got somethin' for ya ass."

He took out an old black .38 caliber handgun from his pocket and showed it to me.

"I was gonna shoot ya little ass," he said.

My eyes were wide, mouth agape. I couldn't believe that I could've been shot, possibly killed, over stealing candy. I stood motionless for about a half second.

"I'm sorry," I blurted out to the store owner and ran out. I never went into his store again.

But I didn't stop stealing.

Once, I stole money from a gas station to buy stuff to impress another group of kids I wanted to be friends with, trying to be cool for them so they would like me. I bought candy, juices, Pittsburgh Pirates hats (the black hats with the two yellow stripes and the yellow P on the front). I was seen by one of the people who lived at the boarding house where my mom had us staying. The young woman told everyone that she saw me buying stuff and spending a lot of money that day. What I didn't know was someone had stolen money from the purse of the woman who owned the house. I had gotten a reputation for stealing so everyone assumed that I took the owner's money. I got home that night and it was like a tribunal. Everybody was staring at me with disgust. My mom started yelling and accusing me of taking the owner's money. For the first time in getting in trouble for my conduct, I told mom the truth. I didn't steal the owner's money.

Mom questioned where I got the money the other tenant saw me spending. I was scared to tell her the truth, but I did. I told her I didn't steal the owner's money, but I did steal the money. I told mom I stole it from a gas station, out of their register. She asked, "Where?? What gas station? We're going there right now!" In that instant an intense wave of fear rushed over my body. It was more than not wanting to be arrested. I was scared to be taken from my mom again. I went back to being my 9-year-old self. I didn't want to have to go to juvenile again. I didn't want to go to the Guardian's Home again. I didn't know whether or not where we were living would be considered a good environment for us to live in by the court. I was so scared of being taken from my mom again, that I lied and told mom that I did take the money from the owner's purse. My mom was furious and smacked me so hard in the side of my head that periodically I get a ringing in my left ear to this day. Everyone treated me like a pariah after that. Mom put me on punishment for a long time. I wasn't allowed in the owner's room anymore, and she had a nasty attitude with me from that day forward. The rest of the people in the house acted like I wasn't worth shit for a long time after that. It was awful. I found out later that the owner's foster son had actually stolen the money from her purse, but because I was known to steal and lie, no one believed me.

After that, I never told the truth any time I got into trouble. I didn't tell my mom the truth about that night until I was an adult. I wanted her to know that even though I lied most of the time, in that moment I did tell her the truth. Not that it mattered, but for some reason I still wanted her to know. And to know that if I could do it again, I would've taken her to the gas station so she knew I wasn't lying to her, even if it meant possibly going to the Guardian's Home again. Even though I was wrong for stealing, I didn't lie about it.

A really dumb thing I did as a kid (11 years old) was not only talk to a stranger, but I actually got into that stranger's car when he lied and offered me work. I'm pretty hard on myself by calling it dumb. I understand I was a naïve boy who was scarred that day, but I knew better than to talk to strangers. I knew better. I was disgusted with myself for years because I allowed my gullibility and desire to get money to be the root causes of me being molested by a stranger.

I was coming out of Kentucky Fried Chicken on Meridian Street, not far from downtown. I think it was at Meridian Street and Fall Creek Parkway. As I was getting on my bike, a Black man in a dirty dark blue car pulled up and asked me if I wanted to do some work to make some money. Something about him didn't seem right. I didn't trust my instincts, though. I should've gotten on my bike and rode away as fast as I could, but I didn't. I asked him what kind of work it was and how much he would pay me. The predator said it was to help him do some yard work around his home and he'd give me $50.00. That was a lot of money to me. I told him I could follow him to his house on my bike but he said it would be quicker if I just got into the car with him. Foolishly, I agreed. He got out and put my bike in his trunk and told me to get in the front seat. I remember the car was filthy inside: empty cigarette packs and cigarette butts all over it, dirty dishes, dirty clothes, empty, crumpled McDonald's French fries and Big Mac containers and bags. And it smelled like piss and shit. The predator made small talk ("I'm glad I found some help." "This won't take long." "You look pretty strong." Shit like that.) as he drove north on Meridian Street until he got to some fancy homes, around 60th Street or 70th Street, I think. He pulled over outside one of the homes on a quiet street. It was a nice upscale neighborhood with manicured lawns. Random cars lined the street but no one was around. I didn't think anything of it and wasn't alarmed by the area because I recognized it from when I was younger when we used to ride around in different neighborhoods on our bikes. I had my bike and knew how to get home from where we were so I don't remember being as scared as I would have been if it had been an unfamiliar location. The predator parked on the street instead of pulling into the driveway of one of the residences. He pointed to the nice house and told me he lived there but he needed my help with something before we did the work. It never occurred to me that a dude in a shitty car like his probably wouldn't live in a house like that. I was just focused on getting the money. I asked him what he needed help with and he told me to get on his lap. I got scared that he would try to hurt me but I didn't run. I told him I didn't want to do it and that I just wanted to do the work around the house so I could get the money and go. The predator said we would do the yard work when we finished. He told me he'd give me an extra $20 to help him. I told him that I wasn't gay and didn't like boys. He said he wasn't either, and that he just needed my help. I started thinking about the $70 and stuff I could buy. I don't remember what he said but he talked me into taking my shorts down. I sat scared with my hands covering my privates. I had never touched a girl so I didn't know what he wanted me to do. He put me on top of him between his legs facing him, my legs dangling. I didn't understand what was happening as the predator held me up close to him and humped until he had an orgasm. I remember his stinky, hot breath saying, "Are you sure you haven't done this before? You're really good." I craned my neck away from him as I shook my head and asked, "Are you done, yet?" When he finished, I got back in the other seat and pulled my shorts up. He used a dirty tee shirt from the backseat and wiped his semen off himself and threw the shirt to me so I could wipe it off me. He tossed the shirt in the backseat and pulled his pants up. I felt sick. Humiliated. Disgusting. Gross. But I kept thinking about getting the money and what I would buy my friends. I asked if we were going to get to work. The predator told me to get out of the car and wait for him while he went to the store to get some things we'd need to do the cleaning. He took my bike out of the trunk and put it on the sidewalk and told me to wait outside the house until he came back. I asked him if I could have part of the money since I had already helped him. He said he would give it to me when he got back. The predator drove away. I waited at that house for hours, until it started to get dark, just before the streetlights came on. I never saw him again. After crying to myself for being so stupid, I started processing that he wasn't coming back. I looked in the window of the home to see if anyone was there, but no one was. Part of me still didn't believe what happened. I told myself I'd come back the next day and get the money from him. But as I glanced around the front room, I noticed a lot of photos of a White family on one of the walls. I cried harder. Those images were final confirmation that I had placed myself in harm's way to have an appalling experience, only to be discarded like garbage. I felt like I was nothing. I knew better than to talk to him in the first place. He could've killed me. The weight of that truth stirred in my gut as I stood crying outside the empty home. I never trusted a stranger again. What little innocence I had left was gone after that day. I stopped trusting most people after that. I greeted individuals with a smile, but secretly waited for the person to betray my trust. I never told my mom about it until I was an adult. In my mind, I thought instead of being supported and encouraged with love and understanding, I would probably get a whipping for talking to a stranger and going with him to begin with. I don't know what mom really would've done, but I wasn't taking any chances. I felt worthless enough. I wasn't gonna get an ass-whooping on top of it. Because of everything I had been through, I already felt alone in my life so that situation became a horrible secret that I vowed to keep to myself, just between me and God. I also prayed that God would let something awful happen to that repulsive person. I knew I was supposed to forgive him but I didn't care about forgiving him. F*ck him. I wanted the predator to hurt and to be assaulted in the worst ways, so he could feel what I felt. As an adult I worked through the deep-rooted trauma of being violated and blaming myself. I also released the intense hatred I had for him.

My first real job was working at McDonald's on 38th and Lafayette Road when I was 16 years old. I developed some really great work habits, as well as some inexcusable ones. I was a fast learner and usually gave my all, no matter what task I was assigned. I started in the back-of-the-house of the restaurant and learned to run the grill. I actually enjoyed learning to make all the different menu items. I took pride in trying to make the food I cooked look like the pictures. It didn't always work because I had to move so fast. I worked really hard at every job I was given and tried to do my best at it, whether it was arranging the stockroom, mopping up overflowed toilets or cleaning up vomit and garbage in the parking lot. Even if I didn't like what I was doing, I stayed upbeat and did my job, usually with a smile on my face (except when cleaning up puke and fecal matter). I did talk shit and have fun with my co-workers, but I was usually a dependable employee and earned a reputation for being a hard worker and a team player. I carried those positive traits to every job I had after that. I was proud of myself when I earned my first paycheck. I worked really hard and was happy to see the results, even if it wasn't a lot of money (minimum wage was $4.25 an hour). I felt a true sense of accomplishment. But pride in myself was overshadowed by the guilt I felt. During that time, I'm ashamed to admit, I also learned how to cut corners (like going to the parking lot and pretending to pick up trash but in truth just walking around with the other employee and looking at things, killing time and then going back inside), skim off the company and do minimal work until payday. I watched my co-workers who had more experience and followed their bad examples of slacking and getting by until they got paid. I was a walking contradiction. I could be a model employee in one moment, and a liability the next. The restaurant didn't know I could be a liability but I could be, even though I still worked hard. I enjoyed excelling at all the different work stations (making burgers, fries, breakfast foods, desserts, etc.) until I learned it all and moved up to working the cash register on the front line. I felt great interacting with customers. It was easy for me and felt natural. I did a good job on the register and was very efficient, my drawers were never short and never off, so I was moved to run the drive-thru. When I went back to the front line from the drive-thru, I learned how to manipulate the system. I learned how to ring up sales, give customers their food (always pleasant with a good attitude), get the cash, then delete the order from the system but keep the cash for the order. I had seen one of my co-workers do it and figured out the process on my own. I would get my cash before I turned in my drawer at the end of my shift. I was nervous all the time because I had to make sure I didn't take too much or too little. I was always looking over my shoulder making sure no one was paying too much attention to what I was doing. I started making a lot of money illegally like that. I knew what I was doing was wrong, but I still did it. I wanted to get money more than listening to my own conscience. I thought I had gotten discovered several times when the company did their inventory checks, but the shortages were always explained away for other unrelated reasons. I was also questioned once about my cash register numbers. My drawers were never short money. I never stole money directly from the restaurant. But I didn't know the computer had an algorithm that tracked how many items were rung up and deleted. When my supervisor asked about the numbers during a system audit, I thought quickly and explained that I always had people who changed their minds at the last minute. My supervisors bought the story. I was a good employee so they had no reason to doubt me. I never got caught and ended up quitting before I was fired.

I eventually paid for my crimes against McDonald's and became another statistic of the judicial system when run-ins with police started after I turned eighteen. I worked for a clothing store in downtown Indianapolis and got arrested for internal theft and given a misdemeanor charge which became a part of my permanent record. I was so disappointed in myself for getting arrested but on the course I was on with my life, it was inevitable. I learned that if you work for a company and steal from them, you're treated more harshly than if you walked in off the street and stole from that company. I was a sales associate and was trained to run the cash register in a high-end men's section. I wore a shirt and tie to work and worked hard every shift. I was great with the customers and a good employee with my coworkers. But in addition to achieving high sales volumes for the company, I also used to sell the clothes in the department like they were my own. I applied the same criminal minded mentality that I developed at my first job, I just replaced food with clothes and the hustle kept going. I would look at the price of an item and knock some money off. Not a lot. Enough for guys to feel like they were saving something, but I kept it high enough to make it worth my while. Most guys were happy to get a deal and even bought more because of it. And everybody paid cash. No credit. I had a nice operation going: they picked the clothes, I removed the sensors and gave them a bag or bagged the clothes myself, they gave me cash and headed out. It was all done at the register and as far as anyone else knew, it was a regular transaction. I always kept an eye out so no one saw us. The system worked for a long time, until an old friend of mine came in to get some clothes one day. He was wearing a bandana and shorts and security started watching him. After he and I did our exchange and he left, security immediately came up to me and asked for the receipt for our transaction. My heart dropped. I knew I was busted. I pretended to look for the receipt and when I couldn't produce one, they detained me and went after him. After they arrested me, they told me they started watching him as soon as he came in because they thought he was a gang member. I believe it was racially motivated because I had done the scam with Caucasian guys in tee-shirts and shorts, with bandanas, baseball hats, dirty shirts, tank tops and everything else and security <u>never</u> approached me. But they thought my buddy was a gang banger. I believe it was because he is Black. It was bullshit because my buddy was one of the coolest people you could ever know in your life. He was a good person, him and his twin brother. And they were from a good family. Their mother was incredibly nice and always really kind to me. Though they had their flaws (like we all do), they were good guys and the furthest from being gang bangers that you could get. At first I was pissed that I got caught because he was racially profiled, but I knew I couldn't blame anyone else for my dumb decision to steal. I was more pissed at myself because I knew that what I was doing was wrong but because it got me paid I kept doing it. I hated getting caught but accepted that the arrest was me paying for other times and other crimes I had gotten away with.

I wish I had learned my lesson and stopped doing illegal shit.

I didn't, though.

I still made poor choices even after I started college at I.U.P.U.I. and was actually on the path to doing something constructive with my life. Like a dumbass, I didn't stop getting into trouble and kept trying to make quick money, instead of just staying on a positive course. One day, I overheard some guys I knew talking about a way to cash bad checks with no I.D. at a credit union in a building where one of them worked. Full disclosure: I knew both of the guys were dishonest criminals, bad human beings and overall dregs of society and I was stupid for involving myself in their scheme. I had done dirt on my own but hadn't put in any work with either of them. And the guys weren't talking to me about the criminal activity anyway. I should've stayed in my own lane. I ventured out. I stole some checks from somewhere so I could try what I had heard. By the time I got to the credit union and tried to cash my check, so many other people had done it that the company's Loss Prevention team was on to the scam and on alert. About four people came out and surrounded me and wouldn't let me leave. They questioned me about the check and who I was. I lied my way out of it. At least I tried to lie my way out of it. I had lied a lot but I had never faced pressure like that. At one point, the room started spinning and I felt like I was trying to hold myself steady. When they asked me how I heard that people could cash checks at their business with no I.D., I wasn't quick enough figuring out the next lie in my head and instead of giving a fake name, I gave the actual name of the guy who said it. I snitched. I didn't mean to, I really didn't. I knew the code of the streets. Rookie mistake. I f*cked up. I knew I f*cked up. I'm sorry I did that. Real talk. But I did it and it came back to haunt me. Not at that moment, but months later. The ensuing fight was the first time I was in a situation where all of the negative energy was directed at me. There were three of them against me. Although my buddy was there, he was an innocent bystander in everything that happened.

I didn't have my own place after moving out of my mother's house. I was homeless for almost a year and had been crashing with different friends for a while. When I started college at I.U.P.U.I, Donnie, his girlfriend and her best friend lived in a 2-bedroom townhouse they were renting on the Westside and they let me sleep on the couch. The way the living room was set up, they had one couch and one loveseat that were in the shape of an L open to the corner in the unit. A small television and an old-school square fan were in the corner. The back of the couch was towards the front door, so anyone sitting on the couch wouldn't know if someone entered the unit. Coming in the front door there was a set of stairs, heading up to the bedrooms and the other bathroom. Against another wall (the wall with the stairs) was a table that had a boombox sitting on it. On the other side of the loveseat (in what was like the dining room area) was a mini-pool table, with two mini pool cues. A couple of bar chairs sat between the pool table and loveseat. That's the setting.

On the way to class one night, a classmate of mine named Phil stopped by to pick me up because I didn't have a car. We were watching part of a basketball game on tv before heading out. Two guys I knew, we'll call them Anger and Crook, came over unexpectedly. I knew both of them because Anger was cousins with my boy John from high school. Anger and I had played cards together and kicked it several times. We were cool, or so I thought. I knew Crook from being out at the Under-21 clubs. I never had a problem with Crook, we always kept it cordial when we'd cross paths. None of us were good friends but I wasn't on alert because I thought I could trust them, at least one of them. When I questioned why they had come, they said they were waiting on another girl who was also living there. She was on her way home and they were all heading out. They came in and casually positioned themselves inside the room in strategic places – Crook sat on the loveseat and watched the game, while Anger sat on one of the bar chairs and started playing with one of the pool cues. I didn't realize it but Anger was unscrewing the mini pool cue. For those who don't know, some pool cues come in two halves: a smaller end that has the tip, and a thicker end that you hold as the base of the stick. Well, Anger was separating the thicker end so he could use it as a weapon but I didn't know it at the time. Anyway, I was sitting on the couch watching the game with my back to the front door, Phil sitting next to me on my right. Unbeknownst to me and Phil, someone else snuck into my home. Suddenly, I got struck from behind by an unknown force, struck by something or someone who hit me on the left side of my face. I was knocked into Phil, who reacted confused. Before Phil could figure out what was happening, I think Anger ran over and hit Phil in the head with the thick end of the pool cue. Phil was bloodied and could barely sit up. I didn't have time to question anything. All I kept thinking was "don't fall." I figured they would try to kill us. I was disoriented, but quickly grabbed Phil beside me and snatched up the fan in my hands. I yanked the chord out of the end of the fan and held the two pieces in both of my hands as make-shift weapons. I stood on one side of the couch with Phil lying on the floor next to me, while all three of the attackers stood on the other side. We were cut off from getting outside or to the rest of the apartment. As I readied myself for the next attack, I looked over and realized that the person who hit me was the guy I heard talking about the scam. It was the guy whose name I said when I got caught trying to cash the fraudulent check. Before anything else was said, it all made sense to me. All of it was my fault. Karma had come back around. Once I knew what I was in the middle of, I concentrated on getting us through it. In the middle of the assault, my attacker yelled that I got him fired from his job, that security had him in a room surrounded. I knew the feeling. He yelled that he almost went to jail. The truth is, he more than deserved to go to jail because he was known to be a thief, con man, liar and rapist. But in that particular instance, his life was upended because of me. He planned his revenge for a while, and even used my ex-girlfriend to get back at me so he could attack me. My ex was mad at me for breaking up with her so she hooked up with him to get back at me. That's the kind of Jerry Springer/ Maury Pauvich type of shit I used to get mixed up in when I was dating in Nap. But none of that mattered in the moment. I focused on getting Phil and myself out of there. Crook threw the boombox at me and I dodged it, leaving a hole in the wall as the radio crashed to the floor. Anger threw the thick end of the pool cue and I dodged that, too. When the cue hit the wall and then the ground, I dropped the fan and cord and picked up the cue because it was a much more formidable weapon in my hands. I had learned a few techniques of what to do using a baton against an attacker but I didn't think about any of those. I was in survival mode and I started thinking about how many of the attackers I could take out before they got me. I had personally witnessed them beat the hell out of guys at bars and stomp them into the ground in downtown Indianapolis, and they didn't stop when the guys were down. I wasn't letting them do that to me or Phil, no matter what it cost me and no matter what I had to do to them. To my surprise though, as soon as I had the pool cue, all three of the guys turned and ran out of the townhouse through the front door. When I saw them fleeing, I ran toward the door after them but didn't give a damn about any kind of technique at that moment. I was furious and was gonna make sure I got at least one of them before they got outside. With all the strength I could muster through the pain I was in, I swung the pool cue at the back of the head of the last person running out, Anger. The pool stick broke over his head. I locked the door and helped Phil upstairs to one of the bedrooms. I didn't stick around to see how he was because I immediately grabbed Donnie's samurai sword off the wall and headed downstairs. As I passed the bathroom, I saw my reflection in the mirror and realized what damage the assailant caused me. The left side of my face was swollen about 3 or 4 times its normal size. There was bruising around my eye, which was barely open with blood in it. Blood ran down my face like a small waterfall. When I saw my face, I lost it. I headed down the stairs and I was ready to kill someone. The girl they were waiting on finally came back and freaked out, yelling that she didn't know he was planning to hurt me when she hooked up with him. I wasn't trying to hear shit. She ran out of the apartment when she saw me descending the stairs with the sword and a crazed look in my eyes. Anger had come back and as I stepped out the front door, sword in hand, he dropped a brick he was carrying and ran. "Oh, shit! He got a sword!" he yelled to the other attackers as he retreated to a safe distance. I yelled for them to come back and have another go. They talked shit from a distance but never came back. But they couldn't leave because one of the guys dropped his car keys in the apartment. After a little while, I heard police sirens getting closer and saw flashing lights. Even though I was the one who was assaulted, I knew I would probably get blamed by the police for being the aggressor so I put the sword away and waited.

I didn't know it but as the attackers ran outside, one of our neighbors called the police and when the cops eventually arrived, a couple of the attackers got arrested that night. But one of the guys got away. I went to the hospital and after getting x-rays was told I would need reconstructive surgery. The attacker broke the bone around my eye. The doctor said a millimeter to the right and I would've lost my left eye. They said if I didn't have surgery, over time my eye would sink into my face. Say less. After the surgery, I was left with two small metal plates under the skin on the left side of my face, above and below my eye, but you wouldn't know it if I didn't tell you. The metal plates are a constant reminder of the pain and unnecessary chaos I brought on myself by doing something I knew was wrong while trying to make fast money. Looking at something positive from that ordeal – making it through that situation (and having already been hit with a bat from the previous fight) gave me a different confidence in myself. After years of being afraid of fighting, unsure of myself or how I would respond, I realized I don't have a glass jaw and that I could handle myself. I learned that if it came to it, I would not lay down and die. I would fight until the bitter end. I used to say that a lot, of course, but I never really knew how I'd respond since I had never faced real adversity like that. Those situations did not make me want to fight more, but I knew that if I could survive being attacked by multiple people and getting hit in the head with a baseball bat, I'd be fine if something popped off in the future. And being a Naptown guy, it deepened my "mother made you, mother f*ck you" mindset. I knew that even if I bent, I wouldn't break. "Forged by fire," as they say.

Getting attacked was f*cking horrible. I was pissed and wasn't thinking about much back then, besides running into the guy who assaulted me and having a reckoning. I wanted to whoop his ass. I have metal in my face for the rest of my life and every time I thought about it, every time I got a headache on the left side of my head near my eye, I wanted him to pay. Not long after getting jumped, I bought a gun, Beretta 92F, 9MM, sixteen in the clip and one in the chamber (with extra clips), and looked for the guy who hit me. Thank God I didn't find him. I'm grateful I don't have to ask God for forgiveness for what I would have done to him. After carrying the gun illegally for some time, I knew I was taking a chance with my life and freedom if I ever got caught with it, so I got my gun permit. I bought it legally, through a guy in the Trader (the old resale paper). It wasn't stolen and had never been used in a crime (that's what he told me but I don't know if it was true). Still, I was in the wrong for not registering it when I first got it, but I didn't care about being responsible. I didn't register it on purpose. I decided that if I was gonna get rid of that guy, and that's what I was planning to do if I saw him, I didn't want something registered getting back to me. I bought the gun with cash and the guy who sold it to me didn't make a copy of my ID. He was a White guy and I assumed he'd probably just describe me as "a Black guy with short hair," if the gun was ever found. God intervened and I never crossed paths with the assailant again. Eventually, we went to court (no, I didn't go snitch. We went to court because they got arrested the night of the fight.) and Phil and I told the judge the truth about how the fight happened. After the guy who hit me and the other attacker were caught in multiple lies about what went down and being chastised by the judge, he was ordered to pay restitution towards my medical bills. I received a couple payments before he disappeared and didn't pay anything else. I think they garnished his wages to even get those payments. I knew he'd never pay so I never expected to get the debt erased. Eventually, I released the hatred I had for the guy who hurt me. I knew it was corrupting my spirit. It wasn't his fault I made a dumb choice to commit a crime. I prayed and forgave him and wished him peace in his life. I also know that people who live negative lives, have experiences that are anything but peaceful. What goes around, always comes back around in some form or fashion. It definitely has in my life. The positive that came from that experience is that once my weapon was registered and I had my permit to lawfully carry a concealed firearm, I became a law-abiding citizen and a responsible gun owner. I frequented the gun range and got more proficient with my weapon.

Before doing the right thing and getting my gun licensed, I did wield my weapon unlawfully at times. I didn't walk around acting like I was tough because I had a gun, but if anything happened, I was ready to let off. One night we were dancing at Original Sports Bar (OSB), a local bar in downtown Indy, and my boy Chuck came in furious and worked up. He told us that some racist guys were f*cking with him and his girl (who was White) while they were walking on the Circle. The racists were yelling all kinds of hateful slurs and things. We were amped as we ran out and jumped in the car and drove around looking for them. We found them in their car and chased them down the street. I think it was Meridian, just south of downtown, heading south. I was livid. As we sped down the street, after screaming at the racists, I fired my Beretta in the direction of their car, but above it. I fired about 3 or 4 rounds. My boys were surprised but not as surprised as the racists. What no one knew was that I fired over their car on purpose. I was a hothead and I had done stupid things but I wasn't stupid. I knew if I fired directly into their car I probably would kill someone. I didn't want to kill anyone. I wanted to send a message because I really hate racists and I wanted to look hard in front of my boys. The message was received as they almost crashed their car trying to swerve and get away from us. The road forked and we let them drive off and we headed back to OSB. We reveled in the craziness that had just happened and I got a new moniker as "crazy Anthony." I didn't tell my friends but I was scared for weeks after that night. I was afraid that one of the bullets may have accidentally gone through someone's home and hurt or killed them. I monitored the news and papers for the next few weeks. Nothing ever came from that night, but I never brandished my weapon like that again.

Another brush with the law came on my 20th birthday. Literally, the day I turned 20. That time it wasn't completely my fault, though. It was Friday night going into Saturday. My buddies and I were hanging out on the Circle (Monument Circle in the heart of downtown Indy), which was a place where everyone hung out and cruised on the weekends. Cars, trucks, motorcycles, sexy girls, fly guys, people wanting to be seen like they're at the club… you get the picture. Unfortunately, egos always got out of control and fights happened down there on a regular basis. And the fights were brutal and unruly (groups of guys attacking other groups of guys, people being busted in the head with bottles, people getting stabbed), nights usually ended with a lot of bloodshed and tears. I wasn't a fighter, though, we've already established that. But I was still always down there in the mix. That night, I just wanted to party and celebrate making it 20 years in the world. Sounds simple but that's a big feat for a lot of people in the inner city. Especially aimless Black men like I was back then. Our life spans are cut short way too often, whether from our choices or things that happen to us.

But on that night, everything was calm.

It was a great atmosphere, everyone was chilling, music playing from cars, just generally having a good time. And it was my birthday. On a weekend. I was ready to turn up. I didn't want any negative energy around me on my day. I left my Beretta at home so I wouldn't have anything to carry and I wouldn't have to worry about it. I was feeling great. I was doing a few simple dance moves standing next to the driver's door of my friend's car. I had on flip-flops so I couldn't do much more than that. I was in a groove with the music when a random car pulled up with two White guys inside. The guy on the passenger side yelled, "Get the f*ck outta the street, nigger!"

My back was to them. I turned and yelled, "f*ck you!"

The driver slammed the car into park in the middle of traffic and they both jumped out. As my boys started walking around the parked cars on the side toward the antagonists and I kicked off my flip flops getting ready to fight, the racist passenger moved his shirt, flashed a badge hanging on his waist and said, "We're police officers and you're going to jail." My boys stopped and went back around the car and I put my shoes back on.

As they put the handcuffs on me, I asked why I was being arrested.

The cop said, "How old are you?"

"I'm 20," I said.

He said, "You're going to jail for curfew."

I said, "I'm 20 years old, officer, I don't have a curfew."

He said, "Then you're going to jail for pissing me off. Now get the f*ck in the car!"

And they threw me in the backseat. My boys and the other onlookers stood by and yelled what an injustice and how bullshit the arrest was, but couldn't do more than that while they watched as I was taken away. The cops were outraged as they drove. They cussed me out, asked me who the f*ck I thought I was. I remember being so scared and thinking, "What if these cops kill me?" I knew about a story of a young black teen who mysteriously shot himself (they say) while handcuffed in the backseat of a police car. I and most every other Black person I knew who knew the story had our suspicions about what really happened. I didn't want to become another victim of the same circumstance. Self-preservation kicked in again. I apologized as much as I could and tried to be cool with them. I kept trying to talk myself out of going to jail, as if that would work. They yelled at me to "shut the f*ck up!" and because I didn't know what they would do to me, I did. I shut the f*ck up. They yelled some more until we got to the police station. Then I spent the weekend in jail. I was arrested after midnight, sometime around 1:00am or so, early Saturday morning and didn't get out until Monday evening around five o'clock. When I finally went in front of the judge Monday morning, he seemed confused when I explained that I had been arrested for dancing next to a car. He threw the case out and I was ORed (released on my Own Recognizance). There was nothing I could do. I knew that what the racist cops did wasn't right but I didn't know that my civil rights were violated. I didn't know anything about hiring attorneys and filing lawsuits against law enforcement. So, I took the "L" and went home pissed. It was the worst birthday of my life.

One of the absolute dumbest decisions I've ever made was when I got mixed up with the dope game for a minute. I wasn't any good at it. At one point I was the middle man for a guy I used to be friends with. In my first year of college at BSU I lived in the dorm. Hurlbut Hall. Two guys who lived down the hall, Slick and Mick, were potheads and they were also local dealers. Those were my dudes and I stayed cool with both of them, even after we all moved out of the dorm. After I graduated from BSU, while living in Chicago, I met a guy who was a former model and owned an art gallery who became a friend/big brother/mentor to me. He gave me insight on pursuing the entertainment industry in the Chicago area. Unbeknownst to me, my new friend was also a drug smuggler. I didn't know he was running drugs when I met him, but I didn't stop my friendship with him when I found out. He was a cool guy. I didn't believe his illegal activities would affect me, so I didn't care what he did. He knew I was a struggling artist and to help me out, he asked if I knew anyone who sold weed. He told me I could be the middleman and get paid whenever they got their shipment. I remembered Slick and Mick from college and became the go-between. I got a set dollar amount off each pound they bought from him, and they usually got two or three pounds each time. I was always terrified transporting the dope, but I wanted to get money so I went against my own instincts and kept moving units. After moving back to Indianapolis and being gone from Muncie for a while, I stopped dealing with Slick and Mick because I hated making the drive (Indy to Chicago to get the product: 3 hours, Chicago to Muncie to drop off: 4 hours, back to Chicago to pay my guy: 4 hours, then back to Indy: 3 hours, unless I decided to stay and party in Chicago). Since Slick and Mick were the only guys I knew who moved real numbers, my guy in Chi asked if I wanted a small amount of coke to see if anyone I knew wanted it. He knew I wasn't a dealer and had no interest in becoming one. (No, the irony that I was doing exactly what I was opposed to doing is not lost on me.) I have zero aspirations of being a drug lord, other than portraying one in some theatrical production (like, for instance, playing Nino Brown if they remake *New Jack City* or portraying a new, enigmatic character as the lead in a reimagining of *The Godfather*, or the lead of some other fictional crime syndicate). My guy in Chi also knew I was a waiter at a restaurant on the West side of Indy and having been one himself, he knew that waiters sometimes know people who like doing drugs. Same as with the pounds of weed, he would give me some money off of whatever the buyer got. But I didn't know what to do with the dope once I got it. My close friends didn't do drugs (other than smoking weed) and I had never been around coke before. On my next shift at work, I brought it up to one of the waiters and his eyes lit up. He took me to the bartender, who was at least 10 years older than both of us and had a mullet and mustache that resembled a 70's porn star. The bartender told me he could move the dope for me with "people he knew" and for me to bring it to him. I was naïve. I didn't know the "people" he was referring to were himself and the waiter who brought me to him. I had smoked weed but had never done coke and didn't know how crazy people really get over it (other than what I had heard and seen in movies). I fronted them the coke. Rookie move, I know. But my guy in Chi fronted it to me, so I thought I was doing smart business. That's when I learned, first hand, you can't trust a coke-head, and I didn't even know they were. "Cocaine's a helluva drug." – That's a fact, Rick James. They were two blue collar White guys who seemed like regular folks. As days went on, the younger guy always had an excuse why he didn't have the money and kept avoiding me, and the other guy would tell me he was "working on it." When I confronted the bartender at work one day after their bullshit placation for more than a week, he puffed up his chest and said he didn't have the dope and he wasn't gonna pay me for it. He had snorted it. He didn't say it, but I could see in his eyes that he had. He asked what I was gonna do about it. Good question. I didn't want to fight them or have my guy that I owed hurt them. I worked with them and thought they were good guys, besides being coke-heads, I mean. I was embarrassed and pissed that the guy played me like he did, but I didn't do anything. We were at work. But I also wasn't letting him get away with it. I got stealthy with one of my boys and flattened all four tires on the guy's car. It wasn't the "street" thing to do, which would have been to bust him in the mouth in the middle of the kitchen at the restaurant and beat his ass until he understood that he had better pay me or I would f*ck him up until he did. That's a movie. And it may be real life for some people, but I wasn't getting into a fight and losing my job. I wasn't fighting somebody over something I knew I shouldn't have been doing anyway. I would've been an even bigger idiot than getting mixed up with dope to begin with. But it cost the coke-head the most in the end. Replacing all four tires, plus getting his car towed and all the headaches I'm sure he dealt with, cost him more than the amount he owed me. But I did learn my lesson. I paid my guy in Chi the money for the coke, never dealt with my former co-workers again and ended my short stint making illegal money that way. I knew I wasn't supposed to be in the drug business.

But that knowledge didn't stop me from making another dumb choice that got me arrested again, and could've gotten me killed.

I matured and stopped stealing decades ago. Taking things that didn't belong to me only brought drama into my life, even if doing it did solve some temporary stressful situation I was in. Not to mention the fact that I always felt like shit when I was alone. In my soul I never felt good or accomplished after stealing anything. I knew I was a better person than I was being. I have repaid my karmic debts for the negative actions I've taken. I completely stopped doing bad things. The last criminally self-destructive decision I have ever made, the last time I got into any kind of trouble happened over a quarter-century ago. My guy in Chi offered me $10,000 to drive a car from Tucson, Arizona to Chicago, Illinois. He told me he had had a mild heart-attack and couldn't make the run, but it was big for him. He said I'd be flown First Class to Tucson, put up in a motel for the night and someone would show up the next morning and take me to the car. He said he'd give me ten grand in cash when I got to him in Chicago. Something deep inside me screamed, "NO!" But I didn't listen. I needed money, more than ever. I had already learned the drug world wasn't for me and made sure he knew that, but I was upset with my daughter's mother and wanted to use the money to pay for an attorney to fight for my rights as a dad. I knew better, but my emotions were on overload so I said yes. I justified the decision by saying it wouldn't be any harder than driving from Indy to Chicago to Muncie; Tucson to Chicago would just be a longer stretch in the car. It was the dumbest decision I have ever made in my life. At the time, I had the best job I could've asked for on an adventure show with young people ages 12-17 years old, traveling and adventuring around the world. I wasn't filming all the time and still had three regular jobs while auditioning, but I had been on an incline doing something positive with my life. I allowed myself to get derailed because I was upset. As they say, the road to hell is paved with good intentions. I was angry and hurting, so I didn't care. Like so many times in my past, I made a damaging life choice instead of doing what I knew to be right. But when the time came, I felt wrong every step of the way. I continuously felt like "I can't believe I'm doing this. I'm not supposed to be here." I ignored my better judgment. I ignored my inner voice. I lied to myself and acted like what I was about to do wasn't so bad. I tried to treat the situation like a quick trip and took a backpack and snacks so I wouldn't have to stop for food. But it didn't matter. As much as I tried to normalize what I was doing, something inside me still felt off. I kept getting signals to turn back but I disregarded the signs. My stomach was queasy when I was heading to the airport to go to Tucson. I had a headache on the flight. I didn't get any rest because I slept anxiously, worrying throughout the night. I tried to be cool but I was beyond nervous the next morning when a 30-something-years-old Hispanic male showed up at the motel door to take me to the car. He wore jeans, a black leather jacket over a red flannel shirt and a black cowboy hat. The guy didn't say much, other than telling me the keys were in the car and the gas tank was full. I said, "Okay," and didn't talk anymore. He dropped me off at the car, a black town car, and drove away. I looked around to see if anyone was watching. No one was. It was a normal day in the neighborhood. Normal for everyone else, not for me. I was scared. But I was in it. I had to see it through.

I got really light-headed when I was about to get into the car, I had to steady myself before opening the door. Looking back, I believe that was God's final reminder that I was going the wrong direction. But I paid no attention to the message. I stuck with my bad choice. I didn't check the car out, I just got behind the wheel, got the keys from the visor where I was told they'd be, started the engine, looked at my map directions and drove. My heart raced the whole time I was in the car. Several minutes into the drive, police sirens sounded and I saw a highway patrol car approaching in the rearview mirror. I couldn't breathe. I didn't know why they would be coming for me. I wasn't speeding, I wasn't swerving, I wasn't doing anything wrong. I started thinking the worst. Did my guy in Chi set me up? Why would he do that? What would his end game be? Nah, not my guy. My mind raced. I maintained my speed, slowing slightly while checking the mirror. After a few moments, the police car, lights flashing, changed lanes and sped past me towards its destination. I thought I was gonna be sick. I paid close attention to the road and made sure I didn't give the police any reason to stop me. I was antsy the entire ride. My nerves never fully settled but after driving for hours, I finally started to calm down. When I stopped to get gas in Albuquerque, New Mexico, I checked in with my guy in Chicago. I called to tell him everything was going okay. I wasn't doing anything to draw attention, I wasn't making a scene, I was just making a call. While I was on the phone, I was approached by two undercover New Mexico police officers. They presented their identification and asked for my license and registration. In that instant, my whole world stopped. My fear was realized. I felt immediate loss thinking of my daughter. I felt like a pathetic loser for letting her down. I remember a numbness coming over my body at the crushing realization that I had failed her, I failed myself. But I didn't have time to be numb. I had to focus. I had to concentrate so I could try and minimize the collateral damage to my life. I wasn't gonna snitch on my guy, but I didn't want to do time for whatever they found in the car. My guy in Chi heard the cops announce themselves and hung up. They questioned me about the car and I explained that it wasn't mine, that I was driving it to a friend who had a heart attack. I stuck with the story. They checked my license and had me check for the registration. We learned together that the car was a rental. I took out the rental agreement and gave it to the cops. One cop stayed with me near the driver's door while the other one went behind the car and called the rental company. The time I waited for him to get off the phone was probably only a couple minutes, but it felt like an eternity. The rental company gave them permission to search the car. The cop behind the car repeated his earlier question before he opened the trunk.

"You're sure nothing in this car belongs to you?" he asked.

"No, just my backpack," I answered.

The cop opened the trunk, closed it immediately and told his partner to place me under arrest.

"I don't know what's in the car!" I protested as the other officer placed the handcuffs on me.

Which was true. I didn't know what was in the car. I knew *something* was in the car, but I didn't know what. But, I didn't tell them that. They walked me to the back of the vehicle where I saw a huge bushel of raw, unprocessed marijuana sitting in the middle of the trunk. It was in a round shape, about three feet tall by about two and a half feet wide. It had cellophane plastic surrounding it, holding it together. The cellophane had a four inch wide red color around the center and the plastic had black writing on it, maybe some sort of insignia. I couldn't tell for sure. I was arrested.

When we got to the police station, I overheard the weight of the contraband was 100 pounds with a street value of a half million dollars. The police interrogated me and told me they'd been monitoring my guy from Chi for months. They said I was being used as a mule. I didn't believe them but I didn't care if they were lying. I didn't care if they were telling the truth. I just wanted my part in the nightmare to be over. The police tried to get me to flip on him, but they quickly realized I didn't have anything to offer. I explained to them that I'm an actor who lives in California and I didn't know anything about, or have anything to do with his drug dealings. I explained that I made a bad choice to get money to take care of a situation in my own life and that I had never done it before. The police used my confiscated phone to call his number but he didn't answer. They had me leave a message. I didn't hear from my guy in Chi again for six months. I sat in jail in Albuquerque until my personal manager at the time found a bail bondsman and got me out a day or so later. I was visiting home when I got the call to go to Tucson so when I was released, I went back to Indianapolis, got all of my things and got on a plane back to California. I was in a hurry to get back to my business of building a better life. I had several episodes of my adventure show to film, so I went back to work. My manager told me to keep quiet, so I never said anything to production and I prayed that the show would never find out because I knew I'd be fired. Not long after being back in California, I got a call from a random attorney saying he was going to represent me and my guy in Chicago during the case. I had enough street knowledge to know that if I was represented by the same attorney, and if the police were telling the truth and I really was used as a mule, then I would be sacrificed as a pawn. There was no way I was letting that happen. I told the attorney I didn't need his help and that I would get my own attorney and hung up. I didn't know how I would find a good lawyer in a different state but I knew I had to find one. I found an attorney in the Albuquerque area using the internet. I actually never met my lawyer face to face. I told them the situation and said all I wanted out of it was "to get my life back." They told me what I was really facing: twenty years in prison if the case went Federal and three years if it went State. As terrifying as those scenarios were, I was glad it was only weed in the car. If there had been any other harsher substance, I could have been looking at going to prison for the rest of my life. My attorney said for me to just focus on my career and that they would take care of it. So, I did. But every day for months, right before I got into my car, or started my car, I would always say a prayer because I was worried that someone would blow up my car. Where I'm from, people can get killed over a pair of sneakers, so I knew I could definitely be killed over people missing out on $500,000 worth of product. That's not a movie. That's real life. I didn't tell anyone and I didn't show it to folks but I was always looking over my shoulder. I was in a constant state of fear. One day after many months had gone by, I got a call from my attorney in Albuquerque saying very simply, "You got your life back." I didn't ask or care about the details of how or why I was out of it, I was just grateful to be out of it.

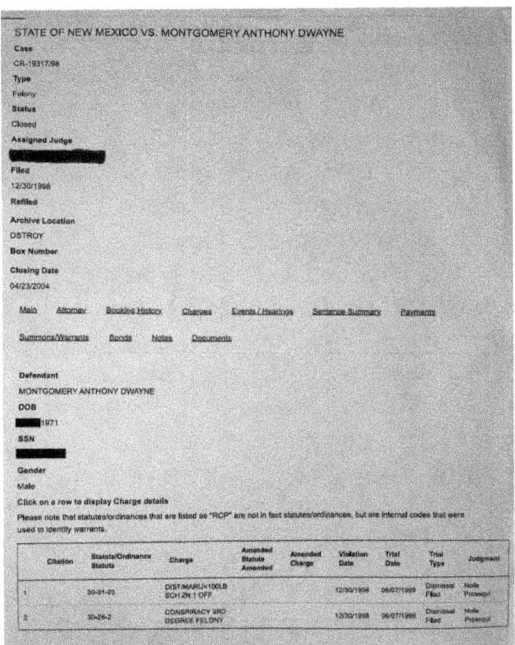

Redacted New Mexico arrest record

I got off the phone and silently sat. I thanked God that the legal part of the situation was finished. But I knew the ordeal wasn't over. I still had to deal with the street element before the drama would truly be done. Roughly six months after my initial arrest, close to my birthday, I got a call from my guy in Chicago telling me he was in California and asking me to meet him. I knew that day would come, I just didn't know how it would go down. He asked me to meet him in the hotel lobby of the Sheraton Universal Hotel. Because I didn't know what was going to happen, I went to my boy

(Sekou-who was one of my best friends) and told him if he and Elimu didn't hear from me by the end of the night, they should look for my body at the Sheraton. Sekou questioned what I was talking about. I explained and he asked if I should go to the police or something. That's not where my mind was. I went home and got my Beretta and went to the Sheraton. When I got to the hotel, I scoped out the place to see if anything looked off or suspicious in any way. My guy from Chi was sitting by himself having a drink, non-threatening. We met and gave an awkward "what's up" embrace. He slyly tried to feel if I was wearing a wire. I wasn't. But he did feel my gun. I told him if he was on some bullshit and if anything was gonna happen to me, that we were *both* gonna die that night. He knew I meant it. But because he also had been like a brother to me before everything went down, I didn't want to kill him or be killed myself. To my surprise, there was no animosity from him at all. He said he knew that I would be guarded meeting with him and that's why he wanted to meet in a public, open place. He was right. I didn't know if I could trust him anymore. I hadn't heard from him for six months and I didn't know if he really had used me as a mule and set me up, or if I was just a guy who got caught up in a drug sting. He told me he did not set me up and that the cops coming up to me was a random coincidence. He said he had to stay away so long to let everything die down. Because of our history, I chose to believe him, that he wouldn't do me like that. I let my guard down a little, but never completely. He said he took care of whatever the debt was with his connects on the other end and that I didn't have to worry about it, or anyone coming after me. He said I could continue living my life without any worry. I wasn't sure if I should be relieved because he said he got me out of it, or pissed that I was in it in the first place. It was my decision to say yes to his request for me to drive the car, so accepting that it was my fault, I was just extremely grateful for whatever he had to do to make sure no one would bother me or my family. I nodded my appreciation of his statement. We talked for a bit longer, wished each other well and I left. After that interaction, I knew that chapter of my life was finally over. I never saw my guy from Chicago after that day.

I promised God that if He fixed it, I would turn my life around. I knew I wouldn't be perfect but I promised to be better. As only God can, He got me through that situation, just like all the other dumb choices I've made in my life that He carried me through. After that major intervention, I have kept my promise and have never gotten into trouble since. I will never consciously allow myself to get in trouble again. I finally acknowledged that my life is valuable. I owe myself the best life I can provide. I have more to offer the world than to be on the wrong side of the law. There are no accidents and I believe God allowed me to get caught. If I had gotten away with it, I probably would have made another bad choice if I ever found myself in a situation where I needed a lot of fast money. And because my guy in Chicago was like a brother, and a good dude in general, if I didn't get caught, I would not have gotten him out of my life, nor any of the other people I was hanging around who were good people but doing illegal things. But with the lives they chose for themselves, I wasn't supposed to be part of their journeys and I could not have them be part of mine. With the blessings God has in store for me, my family and my life, I have to surround myself with positive energy and great people. Eventually, I made it through nearly two years of psychological and emotional hell during those trying times, and I decisively cleared my circle and the team around me of any wrong-doers. I received confirmation that I made the right choice of living a positive life and focusing on my career and being my best as a man and an actor when I was blessed to join the Star Trek Universe. My life has never been the same.

I've done a lot of things I'm not proud of, but I am proud of the fact that I haven't stood still in my life. I have moved towards evolving into a mature, responsible and honest human being.

Along the way, I stopped doing all that dumb shit and I stepped into being my better self. Because I know the difference between right and wrong, I do what's right. It's that simple. Doing what's right brings peace. Doing dirt brings chaos. I choose peace.

CHAPTER SIX
THE COMMUNICATOR

When I was a kid, mom and I didn't have conversations about sex so most of the questions I had were left unanswered. The closest I got to her talking with me about things like that was one day when I asked her what a "wet dream" was. I heard some boys at school talking and I was curious but embarrassed to ask them what they were talking about. Not thinking anything of it being inappropriate to ask when guests were over, I posed that question to mom in front of her friend instead of when it was just the two of us.

Talk about bad timing. Mom gave me some off-handed answer that I didn't quite understand. She and her friend laughed it off, but I was embarrassed by the response and them laughing. I never asked her another question about sex after that.

After the sexual-related trauma I suffered as a kid, I didn't have an interest in sex for a long time. But an overwhelming attraction to and fascination with girls gave me the strength to not let the horrible experience of that day stop me.

The main person I remember guiding me in the right direction regarding girls (and different aspects of life for the short amount of time he was part of my life) was Billy. He was around when I started having a real interest in girls.

Billy taught me to treat girls kindly and with respect, to be a gentleman, to open doors and pull out chairs for them to sit. He told me to be calm around girls and to just be myself to get them to like me. But I didn't know what "be myself" really meant because I was never truly comfortable in my skin. As a result, I was never truly comfortable around girls. I was embarrassed to talk about them, so Billy and I talked a little, but I never told him how I felt so he could help me work through those feelings. I just kept it to myself and acted like I understood what I was supposed to do. As a result, I was awkward around girls for a long time.

Growing up, plenty of girls 'liked me', just not in that way. I was in the friend zone because I was the so-called 'good guy', and so wasn't exciting to them. I hated it. I didn't hate being a good guy, I hated the perception that being a good guy was soft and weak. I hated the fact that the cool guy or the asshole guy always got the girl and the good guy stayed in the friend zone. I wasn't the cool guy. I didn't want to be the asshole guy—even though it felt like many girls liked the asshole guys way more than the good guys. So, instead of just being the good guy, I had a plan— I would be the funny guy.

Problem number one (and the biggest one)—most girls don't get hot over the goofy guy. At least, girls didn't when I was coming up. Problem number two — I didn't know what to do or even what to say to girls. When the funny guy plan did finally break through the wall of being scared to talk to girls and girls seemed to be responding, because I didn't have any "game" it was just back to being silly. After I became a dancer, that changed.

Another major hurdle for me when I first discovered girls was for some reason, most of the Black girls didn't romantically like me because I wasn't "hard" enough. I guess I wasn't tough in their eyes. Worse than that, a lot of the Black girls told me I wasn't black enough. I heard that one a lot. It made me question my self-worth. I always wondered what that even meant. I was raised by a Black mother, Black grandmother, with Black siblings, my grandfather was a Black man, I have a Black father, Black aunts, Black uncles, and Black cousins. I've been racially profiled, accused, judged, and condemned because of the color of my skin, just like almost every other Black person in America has in some way or another. How the hell can another Black person (female or male, because some Black guys have said that same nonsense to me) look at me and declare that I'm not black enough? Ultimately, I realized that I didn't live up to those girls' standards of what a Black man was. Believing I didn't meet some unknown set of qualifications I was being judged for, for acceptance among some Black people gave me a complex for a long time.

While I was still attracted to Black girls, since the ones I liked didn't like me, I started dating White girls. I quickly learned that it didn't matter what ethnicity the girl was if we had a real connection. People are people. But dating White girls came with its own set of issues. I got nasty comments from some Black girls calling me "sellout" and some Black guys calling me "Uncle Tom." I couldn't win for losing. I was attracted to who I was attracted to, regardless of their background. But it was Indiana and the racism I dealt with made interracial dating a nightmare. I received hateful energy and racist, bigoted taunts from some White people, mainly guys, who hated the sight of an interracial couple. But to me, again, people are people, beauty is beauty. Whether Black, White, Hispanic, Asian or whatever the ancestry, I have dated whoever I wanted, who wanted to date me. F*ck racists. F*ck racism. Love isn't color. Love. Is. Love.

After getting past the initial hurdle of the introduction and banter, although I never had game, I've always been a talker. I could make girls laugh and make them think. We would have goofy talks about random, nonsensical subjects, as well as deep philosophical discussions about life, death, and everything in between. I was always earnest and sincere, straightforward and direct so our conversations could be thought–provoking and engaging, or silly and fun. Because of that, once I got over being awkward and got comfortable around them, I've never had a problem talking with the girls in my life. My being that way became more cemented over the years. Granted, I have had to learn better ways to communicate more effectively but I didn't have to learn to open up. Admittedly, I have kept my feelings to myself when I should have shared them. Still, I had a lot of other lessons to learn about being in a relationship, but being a communicator wasn't one of them. To my developmental detriment, after suffering a devastating heartbreak as a junior in high school when my first real girlfriend cheated on me, the first girl I ever thought I loved, I became emotionally damaged, immature and irresponsible. I didn't address my true feelings about the hurt and kept all the pain inside. I became a jerk. I started hanging around guys who had terrible ethical standards when it came to girls. I knew they were wrong but I didn't have enough self-worth to steer clear of them, so I hung around and stayed cool because everyone else did. Instead of being a leader and doing what I knew to be right, I was a follower and from that low vibrational place, I adopted many of their toxic behaviors. From a wounded space, I made a lot of mistakes in my dating life, including becoming a cheater myself. I maintained the destructive dichotomy of being a good guy but a cheater through my college years, where I learned valuable lessons from two amazing women. One, who we'll call Red, had my heart more than any woman I had ever known. I never cheated on Red. She graduated before I did and was given an opportunity for a job that took her out of the country but she wanted to stay and wait for me to graduate. Selfishly, I wanted her to stay, but because I loved her so much I wanted her to be her best self. Her degree was in dance and it was a smart move to take the job as a dancer on a cruise ship, even though it meant we wouldn't stay together. Through a painful goodbye, we released each other for her to go be great. That was the moment I understood the Richard Bach quote—*If you love someone, set them free. If they come back to you, they're yours. If they don't, they never were.* Red never came back. She got married, has a beautiful family and we're wonderful friends to this day. After Red had been gone for a couple months, I got lonely and ended up getting into a relationship with an incredible woman, call her Kate. I loved Kate - as much as I understood love back then - but I was still pining over Red leaving so I never fully committed to Kate. I didn't lie to Kate about my feelings, but I selfishly took advantage of her and her love. I was thoughtless and reckless with her feelings and emotions, took advantage of her kindness, and ruined our relationship. I learned the painful lesson of not playing with a woman's heart if she honors you by giving it to you. Thankfully, Kate moved past the pain I brought into our relationship and went on to have a wonderful life with the husband she deserves.

Companied with other failed relationships (before and after college), I learned and grew from my mistakes. When I moved to California, I gave my life a fresh start and left all the bullshit and immature toxicity in the Midwest. I left my sketchy past behind. I also left all the negative energy in Indianapolis too. I knew how my deception and dishonesty destroyed my relationships, so I vowed to myself and God to not lie or cheat like I did in Indy. I planned to base every connection on a foundation of truth and honesty. I knew I would rather have a woman dislike me and what I say from telling the truth than to lose her trust and hate me for lying. Once the trust is gone, it never comes back. I hated how I made women feel, and how I felt in those situations back home. I swore to never put any more women or myself in any compromised positions. No more cheating, no more lying. Ever.

After years of dating on the West Coast and having some fun encounters, including a brief period dating an adult film star, I was single but subconsciously longing for my person when I met my future ex-wife, call her Allison. She was a beautiful, kind, incredible, strong and intelligent Black woman (earned her undergraduate degree and a Master's Degree in Business) with beautiful eyes, a beautiful smile and a cool eclectic style. I had never met anyone like her. Something in me sparked and I suspected she was the one. After getting to know her, although when we met I was looking for company, not companionship, I made the connection that my soul secretly sought. From the way we met, it felt destined.

Allison was walking with a friend down a side street that fed into Fairfax Avenue in Hollywood. I was driving past on my way to Samy's Camera. I noticed her immediately. She was wearing a weathered cowgirl hat, white shirt with a skirt, she had nice legs and was wearing flip flops/sandals with flowers on them. She had cute feet but I wasn't thinking about her feet, I was too busy looking at her beautiful eyes. As I was driving past, we locked eyes. We both smiled. I kept driving. I was in a particular headspace because I had recently watched *Serendipity* with John Cusack and Kate Backinsale. If you don't know the film, in short, it's about two people who meet one night and leave it up to fate to answer the question of whether they belong together or not. After ten years apart they finally reconnect, confirming their initial meeting was not by chance. It was meant to be. It was serendipity. Because at my core I still wanted to meet my person, I had that film on my mind when I saw Allison for the first time. I thought, "What if she's who I've been waiting on?" I drove past and said to myself "If I look in the mirror and she's looking back at me, I'll go back and say something." I looked in the mirror. Allison and her friend were standing still, watching me drive away. I chuckled to myself and put my car in reverse. I backed down the street forty or fifty feet and stopped across from them. I got out of my car and approached Allison, hands up in surrender, letting her know I meant them no harm. I introduced myself and complemented Allison, telling her I thought she was beautiful and wanted to say hi. She blushed, smiled and introduced herself and then her friend. She had the nicest spirit. We chatted for a few minutes and I asked her for her phone number. She said yes and gave me one of her cards. Her friend was a wonderful jewelry maker and I got her friend's card to see if we could possibly do some charitable work together. I was leaving town the next day and told Allison I would call her when I got back to town in a few weeks. I said goodbye and let them get on their way. I got back in my car on cloud nine. I couldn't wait to go on my trip so I could come back and ask her out. That was the plan. The problem was, after I got back from my trip, I realized I misplaced her card and couldn't find it. I retraced my steps, but it was nowhere to be found.

Several more weeks went by and I couldn't stop thinking about the incredible woman in the hat who I briefly met. She stayed on my mind as I went about my day-to-day routine of building a life in Hollywood. After a visit to see my agent at the time at their office on Sunset Boulevard, I went across the street to a restaurant called Blowfish Sushi to grab some lunch. It was a cool spot with animation cell artwork adorning the walls and anime videos playing from monitors embedded in the walls. The scene was a fun trendy vibe. After sitting at my table for awhile, an attractive woman walked past me as she went to the bathroom (I assumed). She gave me a pleasant look and smiled as she passed. I smiled back. I paid my check and was heading to the bathroom myself when the woman returned to her seat. She stopped me with a smile and a curious look on her face.

"I know you," she said, trying to place where we had met.

"No, I don't think we have," I responded, assuming she had me mistaken for someone else.

But she wouldn't let it go. "I think I met you with my friend," she said, then reminding me of her name. "I make jewelry."

My heart skipped and my eyes widened. "Wait, you're..." and I reached into my wallet and pulled out a business card, her jewelry design business card. "This is your card?" I asked.

"Yes, that's me!" she beamed.

We hugged and I told her that I had been thinking about her friend and looking for her card for weeks and couldn't find it. I didn't even remember her friend's name, just her beautiful eyes, her smile and her hat.

She reminded me of Allison's name. I asked her if she thought it would be a problem if she gave me Allison's number. She said it would be fine and gave me the number. And then she said something that made me realize I was supposed to meet Allison. She said Allison worked in the building across the street as a real estate agent at Sotheby's. Allison worked in the same building as my agent, just a few floors beneath them. I had been going past her on the elevator to visit my reps for at least a couple of years. When I thought back to first meeting Allison, and then running into her friend the way I did, I knew meeting Allison was supposed to happen. Serendipity. I thanked the friend and we went our separate ways.

I called Allison and we scheduled to go on a date. I didn't put any pressure on our situation because my life was a little complicated. But the more time I spent with Allison, the more I felt something deep in my spirit pulling me towards her. I believed she was going to be my partner for life. I believed it so strongly that I talked to Christine, my spiritual sister and dear friend about her. After a near-fatal illness that left her legally dead for about a minute and a half, Christine was blessed with the unique gift of communicating with spirits. When she talked to my spirit guides, they confirmed that Allison was the woman I incarnated to marry. We made a spiritual agreement before coming into this life and needed to fulfill the agreement.

The day I realized I was going to marry Allison, I adjusted my behavior and got all other women out of my romantic life. I privately made a vow to Allison and God. And I never told her. I just changed my behavior and stopped seeing other women. And that was long before we got married (for any guys out there who think you start being a husband after you say "I do"). I changed how I moved long before I ever proposed. The day I knew it was her, I made a shift. After we wed, I planned to be married until I died. I wanted what my grandmother had. Through the ups and downs, I wanted a love to last the tests of time. I was also focused on continuing my career. I had already achieved a level of professional success and I believed that having a successful career would provide the kind of life Allison wanted and I wanted for her. In the end, I didn't know how to lead us and we didn't work together to make the marriage work. When I did step up to lead, she didn't trust my decisions. We wound up being two single people operating under the banner of marriage. Nothing nefarious happened, though, no abuse, nothing scandalous. Even though we were grown when we got married, we both had a lot of growing to do. As a result, we both contributed to the dissolution of our union. I take full responsibility for my shortcomings. In some ways marriage was a major challenge for me. It was challenging because I simply didn't know what it was supposed to look like being in a marriage. At times, I was inflexible and didn't seek the tools to help me learn. I never cheated on Allison, though. There was no infidelity. On the contrary. I learned about myself that I can be monogamous. I'm proud of that fact because with my past and all the cheating I did, I wasn't sure I was even capable of being in a one-on-one relationship.

Even though my marriage to Allison didn't last, I learned I can be faithful to one woman. I'm a living contradiction to the notion that "once a cheater, always a cheater." That statement is bullshit. Men (and women) cheat until they are spiritually and emotionally mature enough not to. Speaking from experience. I have too many painful memories of letting down the girls I used to date. I was never going to let Allison down in that way. I was never going to elevate another woman over Allison in any way. I had my flaws but I made sure I stayed a good guy. I even cooked and cleaned and did all the other things a lot of guys don't like to do because they may feel like those things aren't manly. Because of the marital examples I did witness, I knew to be the opposite of what I had seen. I knew to not be abusive or demeaning in any way. I knew to show my love and to be there with my partner and stay in it with my family, no matter what, no matter how hard it got. Knowing that on the other side of the struggle is growth. Knowing that life is about the journey, not the destination. I figured I would learn as we went. I'm a good man so I knew that no matter how I guided our family, even though I may not have the "traditional" attributes of a family patriarch, I would lead us with God first and everything else would work itself out. I had faith that with God's grace, we would be more than okay. I trusted we would have a wonderful family and build generational blessings and successes. I had faith that we would have a blessed life even if we didn't "see it coming" because we had God leading the way. I didn't feel I needed a plan for what our life and love would look like because… God. I learned first-hand what many people have discovered and stated thousands of times over in many different ways: marriage is not a game. But marriage is a business. If you don't have the right business partner, your business can't thrive. If you don't know how to be a good business partner, your business can't thrive. I didn't know the business of marriage. I knew how to work hard in my life and as an actor to make a life for myself, and planned to use that same path of perseverance to provide for my family. I made a lot of promises based on what I believed was going to manifest in our lives concerning my career and my ability to support the kind of life Allison said she wanted and I wanted for us. I was a dreamer. I am a dreamer. But we never worked together to achieve family goals. (Lesson inside the lesson: You can't build a life with someone if you're not working together.)

Unfortunately, the promises I made were upended by something I had no control over. The year Allison and I got married the Writer's Guild of America writers, writers who supply material to Hollywood, went on strike and work stopped across the Hollywood industry. Any work that did go on would've required me to cross the picket lines. I'm a union guy too (SAG/AFTRA) and I stood in solidarity with my writing Brothers and Sisters and wanted them to get all the compensation, benefits, rights, and everything they were entitled to receive, so I never crossed the picket lines. I didn't work. And when work did finally start back up, it was different. As we all know, anytime there's a call to action and people go on strike, it strains the psyche of the masses. After the writer's strike in 2007, productions seemed more anxious than they had been. And there was a trickle-down effect that emerged. Movie stars, A-list actors who were typically known to do big movies that went to theaters, were suddenly doing television, which gave actors who worked consistently in television less work, so there was even less work for actors who worked periodically in television, like me. With so few jobs and so much competition, it became more of a rat race to even get the *opportunities* to be seen for consideration. The negative financial impact of the strike lasted for years. I contributed to our household using my residuals and periodic acting work before the strike hit (even though Allison had a full-time job making good money). I kept a roof over our heads and food in the fridge, but not securely. It was still the same stressful way I lived my own life. My lack of producing the results and resources I anticipated in a timely fashion caused a lot of tension between us. When I didn't bring in enough money it stressed our relationship. Plain and simple. I had so many non-industry jobs before breaking through in Hollywood (at least 20 jobs - fast food, clothing retail, restaurants/busboy/waiter/bartender, pizza dispatch, gas station attendant, Learning Center student aid (BSU), UPS loader, bouncer, emcee/DJ, hotel security guard, market research recruiter), admittedly, I was selfish and not open to having 3 or 4 jobs to support us and keep pursuing my acting career. I have worked at a lot of places, but I couldn't go back to any of them to make good money to support a family. And starting a new career wasn't on the radar. In order to bring in some sort of income, I swallowed my pride and went back to waiting tables at Chili's Grill and Bar after I had already worked on *Star Trek: Enterprise*. It was beyond humbling to say the least, especially when guests who were fans immediately recognized me from the show and I had to take their drink orders. I played it off but I felt like they were looking down on me, judging me. They probably weren't (especially given the love and reverence I have always felt from all Trekkies regarding the Star Trek Universe), but I was embarrassed about having to be there so I internalized everything. I would avoid those guests as much as I could, sometimes having my coworkers take over their tables. Or if they started asking questions, I would say I was doing research for a role I was about to play. Eventually, I stopped caring what anyone thought, stopped lying to guests, and just went to work. I sat on my feelings and did what I had to do. I didn't care how worthless I felt as long as Allison knew that I was doing it for my family. At one point, I talked to my General Manager about joining the management team. I admired the employment model they have at Brinker International and if I had to have a "regular job," it was the only direction I really considered. I figured it would be a normal transition for me to go from server/bartender to management. But I wouldn't stop there. I would set my goals on becoming a Regional Director (to gain the experience of covering multiple territories) and eventually owning my own Chili's. Because I was a hard worker and a good employee, he said he would love to have me as a manager and move me up the corporate ranks for the company, but it would mean I'd have to give up acting. The GM said the only reason I was able to work there as a waiter and still be an actor was that I could get someone to cover my shifts if I needed to go do an acting job or auditions (which is the case for all actors who are waiters or bartenders). He said that when you're a manager, you have to be there when you have to be there, and you can't just call another manager to cover your shifts. You don't get to leave in the middle of the day so you can go do three auditions, or take 6 weeks off so you can do a play. I appreciated his candor and thought hard about it. That was the first time I really considered not being an actor as a possibility. I would have to give up the constant in my life. My craft, my art. I knew I wouldn't make a lot of money as a manager but it would be consistent money, versus the monetary fluctuations of the acting life. I talked to Allison about it and she said it was up to me. I mulled over the decision for a long time. In the end, I would have been going to a job I didn't love, still not making enough money to cover my overhead so I could provide for my family (which would've definitely caused more division at home), and then stressing to figure out how to make more money with no more time. All while being miserable that I wasn't being creative and performing. Because I'm an artist first, I knew I would have regretted giving up my craft, so I passed on the opportunity. I kept the faith.

When money got too tight, I even considered becoming an acting teacher after I coached a few people. But because they were actors themselves, they didn't always have consistent money to get coaching so I couldn't count on coaching as a reliable income stream. But I did enjoy helping other actors find the truth and depth of their characters, so I sat down and thought of how I could realistically make it work. I considered that I would be able to take the acting credits I had amassed in Hollywood and relocate to a city that doesn't have as high of an overhead as LA but would still provide a nice quality of life for my family, and start a class to help other people who have aspirations of pursuing a career in acting. I also knew that being a teacher meant a complete career shift. I understood it would take time to build the curriculum, build the trust in me from the community, and build the class roster. I was willing to make the sacrifice for my family but I am an artist. I spoke to an actor I admire and respect who has a solid career in Hollywood and mentioned what I was thinking of doing. He said if I made the transition to teacher, productions might think that I wasn't as invested in being an actor and that they could get hesitant to hire me. The artist in me felt like I'd only scratched the surface of the work I still have to do in front of the camera, and I also plan to get into directing at some point. Since I wasn't ready to dedicate my life to teaching in that way, I continued on my acting path. Too many years passed and Allison lost respect for me. She didn't say it, but I knew it. I felt it in my soul. It crushed my spirit. Once her respect for me was gone, I felt like it never came back. As a man, I believe there's no worse feeling than knowing you've let your woman down. I felt psychologically and emotionally castrated when Allison deemed me unworthy of her respect. With my hard upbringing, I had more than overcome my past, so by the time I met Allison I knew I could handle anything life threw at us. I believed that if she was my rider - my ride-or-die chick - she would ride with me, I'd ride with her, and we'd be good. Because I keep God first, I know that as bad as any situation may be, it won't always be that bad. Just like I know that no matter how great a situation is, it won't always be that great. I had already established a career in Hollywood before getting married, so I had faith that I would be able to build on my past work and book more projects to cover my financial responsibilities and create a quality life for my family. But the Hollywood industry is not something you can control or count on. I was optimistically naïve. I never got another series during the marriage, or any consistent acting work, for that matter. Personally, I wasn't worried because I planned for my acting career to span a lifetime, not just a season. But I realized that the uncertainty of the industry wasn't what Allison was prepared for, even if she thought she was. Even though I was hurt, I understood where Allison was coming from. Women need security. An actor's life is anything but. There were plenty of days where I wanted to leave the marriage and go back to being single. Not because I wanted to be single, because I didn't. I loved her with my heart and soul and wanted our marriage to work. But if I had to struggle as an actor, it would've been easier to struggle alone than having someone struggling with me. I never wanted whoever my lady was to have to go through the roller-coaster ride that comes with the life I chose as an actor. I wanted to get my career set, or at least stable enough that I had security, before meeting my person. I never got to that point before meeting Allison. I did have tens of thousands in the bank and a healthy 6-figures savings before meeting her, but I also had debt because of how I was living and ran through all my money when there was no work and the acting drought continued for years. Although there were times when I wanted to leave the marriage, I never left. I made a promise to Allison, God, and myself. I made a vow and stood by it. Until Allison filed for divorce. We had fulfilled our spiritual agreement and once she voided the contract of our marriage, I strived to continue being a great dad and went to the only thing I knew I could count on, as unstable as it was and will always be. I focused on my craft, focused on work. I was used to being by myself, head down and working hard to achieve it, whatever the "it" was concerning my acting career (acting gigs mainly - feature films and scripted series, but also voice-over or emcee work, hosting opportunities – whatever performance-related jobs I could find). I got back to my Hollywood grind.

My relationship with Allison taught me a lot about myself and the compromise it takes to make a marriage work. I was resistant to change so the lessons I learned during that time were only able to slowly move me towards a better version of myself. Ultimately, there were challenges in my marriage with Allison but we loved each other and came together for a purpose that was greater than both of us. Our union was about love and we received the greatest gift we could've ever imagined from that love – our son, our little prince. My son is my heart and soul. He is a phenomenal boy and a blessing, not only to his mom and me but to his cousins, family and friends and everyone he interacts with. My son is a blessing to this world and when he decides what he wants to do with his life, whatever that may be, I know he will have a wonderful life of purpose and his contributions will help make this world a better place. Our little man is a leader, he's incredibly smart, very funny, and wonderfully talented. He's an exceptional teen who continues growing into a terrific person. My son is a really nice kid, handsome, extremely kind and a curious soul. He's polite and well-mannered, helpful and selfless. Yes, he does have another side too. He's a Taurus and can be more than a handful when he gets in one of his moods and becomes defiantly stubborn. I give him grace since I know it's typical teen behavior. Above all else, I'm incredibly proud of my son because he's a really good human being. I wish I was the kind of kid my son is when I was his age. I've felt that way my son's whole life because he's been an awesome kid his whole life. I'm honored that he chose me to be his dad. He's the best version of me that I never saw of myself. The hardest part of the divorce, the part that hurts me the deepest, is not being with my prince every day. It saddens me every moment I don't get to witness him growing into the outstanding man he's becoming. So, I shower him with love even harder during the time I do get to spend with him (even when it gets on his nerves). I'm also strict and in an effort to make up for the time that I'm not with him, I'm constantly trying to teach him everything I feel he needs to know about the real world and how to deal with situations in life. It often backfires and he gets angry because he says I act like I know everything. That's ironic because every day I walk in being his dad, I realize how much I still have to learn. But we're learning together, and my son is doing great.

After my marriage ended, I was in a painfully low place. I felt miserable that I didn't keep my family together. I felt like a failure as a man, a Black man, a husband and a father. The crushing feeling of letting my prince down weighed heavy on my spirit. I had also lost my soulmate. The person I wanted to do life with. When that notion was over and she divorced me, despite what I showed people, despite what I posted on social media, I was broken inside. I felt like I had to keep up appearances because I was in the public eye, but I wallowed in the defeated mindset of the unsuccessful marriage for a long time. I didn't go to therapy during that period because I couldn't afford it. It took more than a year and a half of tears, sleepless nights, and broken-down conversations with God (asking Him to take the pain away), continued growth on my own, and dozens of conversations with friends about perspective before I finally released the anxiety of my perceived failures and arrived at a place of peace with it all. I forgave myself. I am forever grateful for the love Allison and I shared, beyond grateful for my prince, and thankful for having had the experience of being married. I promised myself to grow from the lessons so I could be better in my next relationship.

After months of personal suffering and dealing with the loss of my marriage, I was finally ready to move on with my life, ready to re-engage with the dating world. And I didn't want to become one of those bitter people who hate their ex-spouse and the idea of marriage because of a painful divorce. I wanted to be better than that. I was determined for us not to be enemies when we divorced. I knew that many divorces end ugly, but if we loved each other when we came together, why couldn't we remember that love when we grew apart? I don't hate my ex-wife, we just didn't work. That doesn't make us enemies. She's a good woman and I want her to find her person who will add to her happiness. Also, as the mother of my prince, I would never want us feuding. In that scenario, the one who loses is our son. (Lesson for any of you out there going back and forth, putting your kids through turmoil dealing with your hellish breakup. It's hurting your little ones.) Whether I ever get married again or not, I love the union of marriage and still believe in it.

When I got to a better emotional place, I was receptive to the possibility of love again. Secretly, that's what my heart wanted. I was reluctant because of the thought of possibly having to go through heartbreak again if whoever I met didn't work out. But that's the game of love, right? You can't play the game, if you're not in the game. However, having learned from past mistakes and all the past games I played or found myself in, I didn't rush out and start sleeping with a lot of women. I didn't run around having tons of divorce sex (like so many people suggested I do). I did have sex with one woman after the divorce, and she was cool but I just wanted sex, wasn't into her, and never saw or talked to her after that night. Some of my guys thought I was crazy for keeping myself unavailable, but I had no interest in dealing with the drama that can come with random sex. I didn't rush into dating, either. I wasn't going to share my energy with just anyone. Being married changed how I approached being single. My spirit was in a better space and I was slowly opening up my guarded heart to the prospect of meeting someone, but I wanted someone with long-term potential. I privately prayed that the next woman God revealed to me would not only love me completely but that she would understand and honor my artistic love and life. I prayed that our souls would connect and intertwine. I wanted someone to love and grow old with. I wanted her to love me as I would her: unconditionally, embracing my strengths and counterbalancing my weaknesses. After declaring to God what I wanted in my person, I went about my life. When God knew I was ready, He brought me to a wonderful woman, Victoria.

Victoria was my everything, smart, creative, beautiful, sexy, kind, funny, silly, loving, supportive, a wonderful mother to her children and so many other qualities I loved about her - essentially exactly who I prayed about without knowing all the specifics of the woman God was sending me. And she's also an extremely talented artist so she understood my core and encouraged my dreams, especially my drive to build a successful acting career. I had never met anyone more perfect for me. She was exquisitely made and humanly flawed. She was who I needed in my life, for my life. We had a rocky beginning to our relationship because she was in a situation, but we shared a love I had never experienced, a love that I didn't know was possible. A love that I didn't want to share with the world, even though we're both in the public eye. Not because I didn't want to shout from the rafters how much I loved her, because I did that often, but because I didn't want the ugliness of the world trying to spoil what we had (as many people in the world love to do when they see other people happy). It was only after meeting Victoria that I realized a person can have more than one soulmate. I've often heard a lot of people talk about finding a soulmate and I've had a lot of in-depth conversations about the subject. It feels like too many people are so busy hiding behind the masks of what they want people to see that it doesn't allow them to authentically connect with other souls. I stripped away my masks with Victoria, and she stripped away hers with me. Our souls connected and I couldn't imagine my life without her. It took me some time to get there because of the barrier I had around my heart. I didn't say I love you for a long while (even when I felt deep in my heart like I already loved her), because I wanted her to be the last woman I said those words to. I had used that phrase a lot in my past, too much, but once I emotionally matured and realized what I was saying, I told myself I would not throw it around flippantly anymore. But whether I said I love you or not, I only wanted her. Once it was Victoria and me, I was all in for the rest of our lives, excited for us to discover our forever together. The problem arose because I wasn't stabilized in some areas of my life, which caused a major blockade in our relationship. After my divorce, I didn't establish healthy boundaries for myself with my son's mother regarding our son. Victoria was a supportive partner and respected and honored my involvement in my son's life. She adored my son and encouraged me to be there for him, just as I adored her sons and supported being there for them. But when my son's mother gave negative energy towards my relationship with Victoria, Victoria got tired of putting up with it. I was tired of it too, but I had to deal with it. Victoria didn't. I was caught in the middle trying to be the peacemaker. I unintentionally sabotaged Victoria and me by trying too hard to stay in my son's mother's good graces because she has my son. By the time I shifted that space within myself, Victoria was on a journey of self-discovery and ended our relationship. When she broke up with me, I felt like I lost a piece of my soul. I was broken hearted but understood. I encouraged and supported Victoria's personal growth. I always want her to be her best. "When you love something, let it go." I didn't have a choice. She needed to grow without me. When Victoria told me she found someone else, I was devastated. I tried to be a bigger person. I was happy for her, of course, because I wanted her happy, but my spirit wept. I fell into my own tortured version of the Sunken Place (Thank you Jordan Peele for that perfect visual representation of the dark void of nothingness where I felt like my spirit dwelled). I didn't tell anyone and kept up the façade on social media. "The show must go on," they say. I privately worked to heal so I could move on with my life. I gained a couple of takeaways that I can pass on:

Men – If you divorce or walk away from a relationship, if you have done right by a former spouse or partner, including after your relationship ended—meaning you weren't an asshole to them, you didn't make their life difficult, etc. – if you move on and begin a new situation, handle your business and make sure you set strict boundaries if you must continue interacting. Do not allow any negative energy to affect you and potentially ruin your future relationships. And guys, you only get to exercise this stance if you don't put your ex through any bullshit. If you do, you deserve all the smoke she brings you. Period.

Women – Respectfully, if you decide to end a marriage (or relationship) and your ex-spouse (or partner) never wronged you – meaning they never cheated on you, they were never abusive, they never did you dirty, etc. – and you have a child (or children), as long as they are a *good* father when they move on, and they and their new love interest don't bring any drama to you, it is not right to bring any drama to his new woman, his new relationship or him in any way, for any reason. Period.

To try and find a place of peace for myself, I looked for a silver lining inside the pain I felt. I looked for the blessing so I could know some good came from my misery. The truth is since Victoria has moved back to her home country she has been thriving. She was leading a terrific television series, continues doing excellent work on different shows, has been nominated for some prestigious awards (including her country's equivalent to the Emmys or Oscars in the U.S.), and has already won awards for her outstanding performances in her work. I'm not surprised. She's a fantastic actor and deserves all the accolades coming her way. When I think of all the wonderful things that Victoria has going on in her life, I realize, as much as it hurt, we had to break up for her to soar into her greatness. Her life is there and with a young son, my life is here in the U.S.. I finally found peace and solace in the knowledge that there are no accidents and that everything happens for a reason. I will always love Victoria and will always be grateful for our time together and the love we shared.

I didn't know anything about Love Languages as I went on sex quests and explored the emotional depths of my heart and soul. But I have learned as I've gone along (mine are Quality Time and Physical Touch). Another big lesson I learned about love is to not withhold my love (or the expression of that love) when I find the right woman to share my heart with. Which is not the same as not knowing *how* to open up. I knew how. I just didn't, for what I thought were good reasons. But to give us a chance to be in a complete relationship from the beginning, I can't hold back my feelings and intentions worrying that I may not be enough in some way. By being too overly cautious and guarded in my approach to love after Victoria, I lost my connection with an amazing woman, we'll call her Yolanda. I sat in a state of pain for a long time after realizing the foolish error of my ways. Yolanda was gorgeous, kind, funny, intelligent (with a passion for medicine, studying to be a doctor in research pathology), and she was also a young hottie (half my age) but with a strength that belied her years due to her rough upbringing in the Bronx, NY. I didn't know any of that when we met.

It was New Year's Eve and I had flown to New York to go out with my guy Jamal, an attorney in Connecticut who's from Harlem. I told him I needed to get out of California because I wanted to start the new year with a new energy. I had never spent a New Year's in NY and I was excited to see what it was like. The trip was last minute and I didn't have much money. I didn't care, I made the most of it. I found a cheap round trip flight and we stayed in a place that belonged to a friend of a friend, somewhere near 135th and 8th Ave. It was pretty awful, but it was cheap and in a good location and gave us somewhere to sleep. I initially wanted to experience the Times Square Ball Drop because I've seen it on television for so many years, but the crowd was massive and it was freezing. I was told we'd have to be there all day and night. I was told about the logistical nightmares of not being able to go to the bathroom or go get food. I passed. Instead we looked into a couple of different bars that were celebrating. The first one we went to was for an older crowd and pretty boring. *More Than A Woman* by the Bee Gees was playing when we walked in. Coupled with the fact that the bar looked like a setting from a *Happy Days* episode, I knew I wasn't staying there. Don't get me wrong, there's nothing wrong with that music. I love the Bee Gees (great song), and I loved *Happy Days* (The Fonz was the man) but that's not what I was looking for that night. We left there and went to a bar with a younger vibe. It was getting close to midnight so even if it wasn't good, we decided we'd stay and celebrate with the rest of the bar and then go to another spot. That was the plan. It was a bar called Stitch. Things were looking up from the start. The music was live (*Happy* by Pharrell Williams was playing) and everyone in line had great energy, excited for the night. When we got inside, like I always do when I go to a new club, I walked around and got a lay of the land. It was a cool two-story bar set-up, long bar across one of the walls, tables and chairs moved to give more room. They had a photo booth in back so people could get their photo keepsake. About four hundred New Yorkers were celebrating that night and the space wasn't very big so it was a packed house. After making a full lap around and discovering there was no one there I wanted to hang out with, we went back toward the front and stood near the bar. Jamal left me at one point to go check out a woman he saw so I posted up next to the bar near one of the computer terminals. There were a couple of female bartenders but there was only one I paid attention to. Aesthetic features, beautiful eyes and she was efficient and about her business. She had a radiant smile as she engaged with all the partygoers. She moved behind the bar with precision and skill, clearly in her element. I was incredibly impressed because although she was being hit on by nearly every guy who wanted to order a drink, she politely and professionally let them down without angering them or causing a scene. She moved with the confidence of someone who's had to develop the skill to navigate unwanted advances, while keeping herself safe. I've talked with women who are sometimes afraid to reject a guy who's interested in them because they don't know if the guy will become violent. That lunacy baffles me. I get that a guy may be embarrassed if a woman shoots him down (Lord knows it's happened to me a bunch) and yes, it is embarrassing, but you just walk away. You go meet another woman. Any man who will attack a woman in any way because she turned him down is not a man, he's an immature man-boy who should seek help to address the childhood trauma that he wallows in. But those men do exist and she clearly knew how to maneuver. I've never lived there, but I was told living in New York will give you that self-preservation mindset. Whatever it was that caused her to move so effortlessly on an extremely busy New Year's Eve, it was fun to watch. Because I was a bartender for so many years and love it so much, I'll always have an affinity to the craft. And in case you didn't know, yes, it is a craft. Have you ever had a shitty bartender? Me too. That's why I can appreciate a good one. And she was also fine. I didn't want to disturb her groove so I just watched her do her thing for a minute. I bought a drink from the other bartender and asked her name. The other bartender gave it to me. She walked back toward where I was standing and stopped at the computer so she could enter in the drinks and do her other work.

"Hi, Yolanda," I said.

She turned to me with a confused look, wondering if we had already met. I smiled.

"I asked the other bartender," I offered.

She smiled, said hi, and got back to business. I offered my name and since it was almost midnight, I asked her if I could buy her a shot for her to toast with me/us when the clock struck 12. She agreed. I took my drink and left the area to give her space while she worked. Jamal and I walked around the bar and laughed with revelers until we made our way back to Yolanda and the other celebrants standing nearby. We grabbed our shots and when the clock struck midnight, the bar erupted. Yolanda and I locked eyes and toasted. It was in a look, with a toast, we both felt something. We all jumped around and wished each other salutations. Yolanda was called away to go work in another area of the bar for awhile. She was gone so long that Jamal thought she blew me off. I didn't agree. It was in the look we shared. I knew she wasn't blowing me off. It was New Year's and she was working. I didn't worry. We connected again when she came back some time later. Jamal left and I stayed at the bar to wait for Yolanda and we partied until it closed, and then after. It was my first NY bar staying until 7:00am. I had a blast hanging with Yolanda, the staff, security and some other patrons who partied with us. Yolanda and I spent that morning together and then the next two days after that, until I had to leave and go back to California. I found a nice AirBnB that was close to the airport and we went out a couple times and got to know more about each other. After a memorable NY trip I headed back home. Yolanda and I talked when I got back and planned for her to come visit LA. She flew out a couple weeks later and stayed for a few days. We had a great time, still feeling each other out but everything felt natural and most importantly, she was comfortable. We planned for her to come back out if I wasn't able to get to NY first. Yolanda came back in February and stayed for a week. When she was about to go back to NY the pandemic hit. Full stop. Like everyone else, we weren't sure how severe the situation was, or would be, so we had to decide if she would go back to NY and ride out whatever was to come, or if we would ride it out together (also with my prince, who was spending every other week with me). We were having a lot of fun before the shutdown so it wasn't a thing for us. Since we had already spent time together, we didn't think there would be an issue if we had to stay together for another week or two. I was enjoying getting to know her and she said she felt the same. We didn't know the world was gonna shut down. When that happened, over the next year and a half we developed our own routines and kept moving with the flow. And we didn't have any drama. While we watched the news or social media and saw people losing it and couple after couple breaking up and all the different domestic violence issues that were happening during that time, Yolanda and I found a peaceful co-existence surviving together. And not just surviving, growing. That's one great thing about living in California, there's no shortage of things to do outside. We hiked a mountain, went to the beach, found spacious outdoor parks to take walks or exercise. Given the circumstances, it was great. And life was seamless when we were at home. She also got along great with my son, which would've been a deal breaker. We didn't plan it, but we grew together until the world opened up. She was my friend and my love. But she didn't know how I felt. I did what I could to show her how special she was to me during that time, but I never told her because I wanted to get my life stable before sharing my true feelings and having talks about moving her from NY to CA. I was also hesitant because she's younger than my daughter. But she was more mature than women I had dated who were nearly twice her age. Age is a number. After everything opened up, Yolanda went back to NY to check on life back there and I kept working to get stable and financially set so I could move her back to CA. She never pressured me to do that and she never knew my reluctance to share how I felt. I put that pressure on my own shoulders because I didn't want money to be a root cause if our relationship didn't work. I would never move her three thousand miles from her home to have her struggle with me. Yes, in struggle there is growth, but she didn't ask for that so I tried to limit her exposure to my financial constraints. Before I was able to stabilize myself, tragically, a terrible accident struck while we were apart (the Bronx fire) and another guy swooped into the picture. Our relationship didn't survive. I sat in the pain until it dissipated. Because I intimately know heartache, I knew I would eventually heal and move on over time, but heartache sucks, especially when self-induced. Still, at my core I believe the wonders of love are worth the possible heartache. What an unexpected journey Yolanda and I had. Our chance meeting, maybe even kismet, set us on a path we could've never imagined. When we didn't know how life would go on or what the world would be like, it was just us. She was the "last woman on Earth" with me, I was the last man with her. And we were happy. I'll always love Yolanda and wish her peace, love and happiness in her life.

After a lot of dating adventures, I've learned that a man should have his own life in order before dating a woman. I vowed to break my old habits. I decided to work on myself and make sure my life elevates. I was once told that the best way to get over heartache of any kind is to improve your own life. If it's that simple, watch me shine.

CHAPTER SEVEN
BOUND

1st Grade   *4th Grade*   *8th Grade*

Back to my youth.

I knew some kids who loved school and loved everything about it. That wasn't me. I liked learning new things but was never interested in any subject long enough to calm myself and focus on the material during my elementary school years. My mom told me that I was a smart student and would finish my work but I got bored and then got into trouble. I don't know about that. What I do know is I was the class clown.

I know I talked all the time in class and was labeled a troublemaker. I was disruptive at every school I attended. I wasn't violent or anything, I was a joker. Instead of shutting up and listening to my teachers, I tried to make the other kids laugh. That often resulted in me getting kicked out of class and sent to the principal's office, and it was usually worse when I said something funny that made my classmates laugh at the teacher. I did it even though I knew I would get my butt whooped when I got home. I still acted out (actually, multiple times I got paddled in the principal's office—and then another whooping when I got home). Mom always told me to show them I was smart and to be the opposite of what they expected me to be.

I didn't listen though.

I did what I wanted and usually paid the price. My mom once reminded me I got kicked out of every school I went to until I got older - not sure how old but I don't remember getting kicked out of middle school and I didn't get kicked out of high school, so I had calmed down to some degree by those grade levels. But I was such an interference in my early years they didn't want me back at their schools. As one counselor put it, I was bright, but I was also mischievous. When I applied myself, I typically met or exceeded expectations. But more often than not, I didn't even bother. I did just enough to get by. I never pushed myself to be my best. I didn't have any discipline. No matter how much my mom beat my ass, I still didn't straighten up. I know I didn't live up to my full potential. My mom always stressed the importance of getting an education but the emphasis wasn't placed on figuring out what I wanted to do with my life. Mom told me I could be whatever I wanted, she just required that I "get through school and get her "her" diploma," meaning my high school diploma. So, that's the bar I set my life standard by—get through school to get mom my diploma. That's it. All decisions and actions were centered around that outcome. I never cared about getting a quality education, I just wanted to finish school. That limited thinking held me back many times, no matter who tried to help steer me in the right direction.

STUCK ON STUPID

One day in fourth grade, I got into trouble and was sent to the principal's office. On my way there, I looked in the window of a closed door of one of the classrooms down the hall and saw the lights were off. The kids in there were watching some educational videos. I watched all the students paying close attention. I was fascinated at how still everyone was and how fixated they were on the screen. It wasn't like that in any class I had ever been in. Even when we watched things on video, there was always whispering and chatting, kids cutting up. This class was different. All the students were paying attention to the program. I started watching the program with them through the door. I couldn't hear it but I was taken in by whatever the subject was. I stayed there for a little while until the teacher caught me looking and came to the door. I got scared and started walking away fast towards the principal's office, but the teacher stopped me and asked if I was interested in joining them. I didn't think he was serious, but he seemed like a nice teacher. I told him that I had gotten in trouble in my class—I was on my way to the principal's office and I didn't want to get into any more trouble. The teacher told me not to worry about it and that he would talk to my teacher. I was curious so I said okay and went in. The teacher sat me at one of the desks in the back of the room, while the show was being projected in the front.

Some of the kids nodded to me, saying hello. Others looked on, wondering what I was doing there, not welcoming, but not rejecting me either. The teacher never said anything to the class. He told me to have a seat and enjoy the program. After I got over the initial nerves, I did enjoy the program and stayed around during their brief class discussion afterward. After a little while, the teacher took me to the principal's office. The teacher and principal talked while I waited. I was eventually sent back to my class. I didn't realize the teacher's class was an accelerated learning class for gifted kids.

Within a couple of days, I was placed in the gifted class to see if it would challenge me more. When I got in the class though, I didn't do the work. The material was much more engaging and sometimes I didn't understand but was embarrassed to speak up. I would look around and see the other kids who were confidently doing their work and I would feel like they were smarter than me and I would keep it to myself. Other times, I did understand it and was learning, but I did not dedicate myself to the process and ended up blowing that opportunity. I didn't respect the chance that I was given. I didn't even understand the magnitude of the opportunity.

I was stuck on stupid.

Because I was so used to cutting up in class, during the times that I didn't know what to do on an assignment, instead of working it out or asking for help, I tried to make the other students laugh and did the same silliness that I had pulled in all my other classes. However, the gifted kids looked at me like I was an annoyance. Instead of handling my business and focusing, I was too much of a distraction and ended up being placed back in my regular class.

SCARED STRAIGHT A's

I had one grading period where I shined. I was in fifth or sixth grade, I don't remember, but I was getting bad grades as usual. And my mother was fed up. She was done. She had screamed all she could scream and beat me all she could beat me. I still wouldn't do right and stop getting into trouble. Mom didn't know what else to do so she stopped talking to me. Completely. She never said, hi, or goodbye, no I love you—nothing. She didn't communicate with me for a full grading period. She still took care of me, fed and clothed me, and made sure I had everything I needed physically. But nothing emotionally.

This went on for six weeks. I remember feeling scared and alone. I felt terrible that I made my mom feel like she didn't want to have anything to do with me. I cried a lot but I went to school and focused. I worked hard in that grading period and didn't get into any more trouble or cause any problems. I was rewarded by getting A's and one or two B's on my report card. My mom was so incredibly proud of me. She smiled and hugged me harder than she ever had. She knew I was capable of greatness and was proud of me for finally doing my best. I felt great and was proud of myself, too. I basked in the feeling of that great moment for a long time.

That didn't mean I learned anything, though. I didn't maintain the work ethic that got me there. I excelled at times, but more often than not, I went back to allowing myself to be average. I stayed in that tier of educational development for the rest of my school years.

AN ACTOR IS BORN

Indiana Avenue, a street I walked down to go to Crispus Attucks High School in 9th grade, was at one time a top destination for jazz musicians from all over the globe. The same street where I acted goofy with my friends was where my late grandfather, jazz guitarist Wes Montgomery was heard by Cannonball Adderley, which started a chain of events that led to Grandpa Wes getting his first record deal. My family never went into details about how Grandpa Wes became the success he did. I learned about him as I got older. I discovered the genius he was on a guitar. He was the performer in the family.

And then there was me.

Given all the school drama I put my mother through over the years, it was a real celebration when I finished high school. I was proud. I did it. I reached my goal. But by the time I graduated and got mom her diploma, I still didn't have any direction for my life. I was an eighteen-year-old high school graduate on a road to nowhere. I moved out of my mom's house and as previously mentioned, didn't have a car or my own place and was homeless. I didn't act like it though and I didn't tell anyone, so no one knew. I floated around, partying, sleeping on different friend's couches (or pallets of blankets on the floor), or staying with girls I had sex with. I did that for over a year. During that turbulent period, I became a dad. I started college at Indiana University Purdue University at Indianapolis (I.U.P.U.I.) because my life had spiraled out of control and I didn't know what to do. I was motivated to make something of myself. I knew I had to do something with my life or I would end up in jail or dead like a lot of the guys from the different areas where I grew up. I went to college to figure out what career path I would take. Initially, I scheduled my general requirements. I figured I would decide on a profession when something felt right and until then I would take all the classes that everyone was required to take. I was beyond broke so to pay for my education I got grants, as many student loans as I could, and after I found some jobs, worked all the time to pay for the rest. I took a full course load my first semester because I wanted to hurry and get through school. That was a mistake. I should've taken fewer hours to work myself back into the routine of school. I overwhelmed myself but didn't understand that at the time.

My life changed the day I was introduced to what my major would be.

I was on my way to one of my classes when a guy was approaching me from the opposite direction down the hall. We were in the Mary Cable Building. He stopped and gave me a compliment which began the conversation. He told me I had a "great look" and asked if I was an actor. I had never considered acting before. He said he had written an original theater piece, a children's play that he would also be directing, and he wanted to know if I wanted to audition. I didn't know what auditioning was. I had only heard weird stories about it (casting couch horrors) so when he first asked, I was very hesitant because I thought he was being creepy. He assured me that everything he was asking me to do was legitimate and he only wanted me to come and read for a part in his play. I asked him what auditioning was and he told me that I would get the dialogue (the lines to say) and however it made me feel, I should say it like that. (There's SO much more that goes into the craft of acting but that was an easy direction for him to give me to see what I could do.) I confirmed that's all that would happen and he said yes. I asked if there would be other people there and he said yes, that other actors would be auditioning as well. I agreed and went to the audition. I don't remember being overly nervous, I don't remember being nervous at all. I was just curious what the process would be like, so I was open to whatever happened. I had fun, did what they asked, and gave my rendition of the character. I ended up booking the role. The play was called *East of the Sun, West of the Moon*, about an enchanted bear on a perilous quest with an eclectic cast of creatures who help along the way. I played the North Wind, a high-energy gust of wind that was used for transportation. My wardrobe was a bedazzled mask (with fake blue gemstones like aquamarine, blue topaz and tanzanite) that looked like I was going to a masquerade ball, a shawl-looking top that was multiple layers of sky-blue (and other hues of blue) fabric cut into thin strips that went almost to the floor so it had weight but moved as I ran, sky-blue tights and a pair of matching sky-blue Chuck Taylors. As the North Wind, I carried everyone to their destinations. I ran on stage and kept running in place the whole time, through the entire scene (through dialogue). When it was time for us to travel, the cast would start running in place and follow me around the stage, "riding my tailwinds," off the stage and through the audience until we reached the destination, which was back on stage. The set was changed while we were off-stage and the audience was distracted. It was a lot of work (putting the show together, tearing down the sets, doing multiple shows per day) but I had a blast. I was in my element. I was new to the world of acting as a performer but I fell in love with it. My interest was built on the fascination I developed watching church productions when I was a kid. In college, I took it all in and tried to learn a little bit about every aspect of the show when we did our play. Because I wanted to see how other actors worked, I tried to watch my castmates and how they approached rehearsals and performances. I liked watching their processes (what I saw of them) and soaked up as much as I could. One time, I got called to step into the lead role for a matinee show when my castmate got sick. I don't remember if I was her understudy (I may have been), but I led the show that day. It was my first and only time, and I remember being anxiously excited at getting the chance. Because I didn't have many lines of my own, I watched every performance and memorized the whole play. I knew all the roles. (I didn't know I could do that.) The cast helped support me when I forgot something or missed a cue, and I made it through the performance. The White Bear costume was a little short because the girl who played the role was shorter than me, but we made it work and the kids didn't care. I wasn't a student of the craft yet, but I loved being immersed in the world of the production as the main character. After that day, I knew I wanted to lead my own shows. Until then, I planned to appreciate every role that came my way, starting with the North Wind. My part wasn't very big, but I felt like it mattered in the show. I felt like I mattered *to* the show. I felt really good about myself doing it. I had never felt that kind of pride in myself – for doing something good and positive that felt so regular to me, that was as normal to me as breathing. I felt like I was supposed to be performing. I loved the feedback and loved making people feel good through my performances. The kids'/audiences' reactions were real and honest: If they loved what they saw, you knew it; if they hated what they saw, you knew it. I loved that genuineness. I loved going on that ride with the spectators, children and adults alike, and feeling their energy as they watched us perform. I felt more alive when I was on stage, even though it was just for a short time. We had a run for about three months and I learned many of the ins and outs of theater production. I dropped one of my classes and signed up for Introduction to Acting so I could learn something about acting. But, I approached my craft from a surface level. I didn't take that class (or subsequent ones) to learn about the history of acting or to be well-versed in the field, I was there to learn how to "act better." I never put it together that the culmination of all the knowledge I was going to gain, in addition to experiences over time and actual performances, would help me do just that. I pursued my college degree like I did getting my mom her high school diploma, and my future was on the line so failure was not an option.

The class was a good beginning and provided somewhat of an understanding of the background of the Performing Arts (I'm sure I would have gotten more out of it if I had focused on the material, rather than just going through the motions), but it did not imbue me with the kind of foundation I was looking for as an actor – one that gave me confidence in my acting abilities. Honestly, I felt like I didn't know what I was doing (other than what the director and script told me), and I still didn't after the class. What I was doing when I performed felt good to me and got positive responses so I continued doing it. People told me I was "a natural." I didn't know exactly what that meant but it felt like encouragement when they said it, so I never asked. I just kept doing my best. In one of my earlier acting classes (it may have been Intro to Acting), I learned about Konstantin Stanislavski and how he was a champion for realism on stage. Stanislavski's teachings resonated with me and because of the feedback I was getting, I concentrated on making sure what I did on stage and in performances felt genuine, albeit, heightened for the theater, but still grounded to feel real. I used that methodology as the bedrock in doing my work. I wasn't sure if what I was doing was right or wrong but it felt right, so I went with it. I also learned about wardrobe for performances (but went more in-depth when I took Costuming at Ball State; during that class, I channeled my mom to guide my inner seamster). I learned about hair and make-up, set design, lighting, and other departments associated with the theater. During our performance run, an actor was born. I realized I was supposed to be an actor, and that my career would be as an artist. I declared my major as a theater performance artist and kept moving from there. Every decision I made concerning my schooling after my declaration became about putting myself in a position to have a career as an actor. I didn't have a minor, although counselors, family, and others suggested that I take courses to have something to "fall back on." I was resolute. I didn't care about having anything to fall back on. I promised myself I would make a positive career as an actor, no matter how hard it was, no matter how long it took or what I had to sacrifice. And I would not sacrifice my soul to do it. Once I knew acting was going to be my life, I was bound and determined to succeed at it, no matter what.

I had a goal but was still too preoccupied with personal issues and wasn't completely focused on school my first semester. A creature of habit, I tried to keep partying but quickly went MIA from the party scene. When school first started, I hung out at the food court and had fun with my guys from school – Dohn Anthony and the rest of the fellas – we played cards most of the time or threw a football in the yard, but as I started moving towards acting, I stopped hanging out. Work also added to my distractions from school. I had a few different jobs. I started as a waiter at Chili's Grill and Bar in Greenwood on the southside of Indianapolis, which I helped open. I waited tables until one day our bartender called in sick and the manager asked me if I could tend the bar during the lunch shift. I had never done it but told them to give me the basics and I'd figure it out. They showed me how to use a jigger (a measuring device) and taught me the right amount of alcohol to pour into each drink, and a few other things behind the bar (like how to make margaritas, frozen and on the rocks, one of the staple drinks of the restaurant) and turned me loose. Once I made my first drink, I was off to the races. If I didn't know the ingredients of a particular drink, I'd ask the guests and because the fundamentals of making drinks are the same no matter what the drink is, I usually made them perfectly, even if I had never heard of the drink. I never went to bartending school but was a server and bartender after that day. I used to love getting my Tom Cruise in *Cocktail* vibe going. I discovered that bartenders are like therapists for a lot of people. Folks would bare their souls to me after a few drinks. I loved getting to know the guests who came in. Most of them. Not all the guests were cool.

The southside of Indianapolis was well-known for having racial issues and my Black friends and I experienced that hatred regularly. Some of my buddies thought I was crazy for living and working in that area but I wanted to get out of school, and that situation was what I had to go through at the time because it was what I could afford. I did what I had to do. Chili's was the only job I could find that would give me flexibility for school. After a while, work slowed down and I wasn't making much money at Chili's. So that I could have a guaranteed check of some kind, I got a job working the second shift from 2:00pm-10:00pm as a Pizza Hut pizza delivery dispatch person. I also got a third job working the graveyard shift as an attendant at a gas station on the north side of Indy, off of 82nd Street. I would work from 11:00pm-7:00am at the gas station, go home, and take a shower to be at school by 8:00am for my first class, which I was usually late for. I left school by 1:00pm and would work the pizza dispatch job until I had to be at the gas station. I did that for a couple months. I wasn't sleeping and usually fell asleep in class, or a few times, I shut the gas station down for a few hours (from about 1:45am to 4:45am) and slept there. I would put a note on the doors saying "Attention customers- The pumps are down. Please come back later. Sorry for the inconvenience." I never turned the pumps off (because I didn't know how) so people could've used their credit cards to get gas, but I don't know if they did. I would lock the doors, turn off the lights, and sleep under my jacket on the floor near the register, using my school bookbag as a pillow. I got myself up before the early morning rush at 5:00am. I always got my work done (mopping, cleaning up the lot, taking out trash, cleaning bathrooms, etc.), and no one ever said anything to me about shutting down the station. I only did it a few times because I knew I was going too far, but I was exhausted. I was trying so hard to get as much money as I could that school was last on my radar. My preliminary grades reflected as much. I was flunking every class except one. At one point, I was called to the Administration Office to discuss my grades and learned I had a .67 Grade Point Average (I was only passing Introduction to Acting). I was placed on academic probation and told that if I didn't bring up my GPA, I would be kicked out of school. I knew what was waiting if I got kicked out. I would be trapped in the same dead-end rat race that a lot of people I knew were caught in. I wanted to get out of Indianapolis to finish my education. I needed to get out. Donnie and I talked about it and since he was already in school at Ball State, I set a goal to do what I had to do to be able to join him there. I talked to the Admin Office again and they said only my credits of C or better would transfer and that I needed a minimum 2.0 GPA to be allowed to transfer. I worked my ass off for the rest of that semester and the next three semesters. I learned the hard way that if you start your academic career in a hole, it's really hard to dig yourself out of that hole. If I had been focused on my studies in high school, I would've learned that lesson earlier. At least I learned it. After working hard, I brought the .67 up and finished that first semester with a 1.5 (I only had two passing grades: a C in both Introduction to Acting and Practicum). I kept grinding and did better each semester (1.81 second semester; 2.5 third semester; 2.94 fourth semester) until I finally got my cumulative GPA above 2.0 (finished with an average of 2.12 after four semesters). But because I had done so poorly at I.U.P.U.I. (and with credit transfer restrictions from the university), I had only accumulated 18 credit hours that were able to transfer so although I should've been going to Ball State as a junior, I went there as a freshman. I was disappointed with myself and went to Ball State on a personal mission to get myself caught up and out of school. With determination and focus, I finished the rest of my college career in the next 2 ½ years. I took the maximum credit hours that BSU allowed each semester (17), plus a full load during both summer sessions, two summers in a row. I graduated with a 2.851 GPA. Truthfully, I have some really great memories from school, but most of my time as a college student felt hurried because I was so focused on getting out. I participated in different aspects of school when I could. I was in plays. Those were the times I felt most alive and free. I did several at I.U.P.U.I where I got my start and as many as I could at BSU. I even added musical theater to my repertoire when I got there. I learned an interesting lesson from that experience. I had already been established as an actor at my previous college but because no one had seen me work, I wasn't really embraced when I transferred into the department. Everyone was nice enough, but still guarded. My break through came at Ball State when I was cast by one of my former classmates (Eric Emery) as one of the supporting characters in the musical *Working* when he directed it shortly before he graduated. I played "Lovin Al" and another incidental character. When people saw me in *Working*, I felt like their eyes were opened to me as an artist and peer for the first time. I felt emotionally welcomed into the theater family. I never forgot that feeling. I understood that no matter where I went in my life, even though I possess talent, if people don't know it, then I may have to prove myself until they do. Until I don't have to. Shout out to my former classmates at I.U.P.U.I and all my theater family at Ball State University! I love you guys! Chirp Chirp!

I also did a couple of dance performances with Donnie (one competition, that we didn't win and the opening performance for the 9th Annual Phi Beta Sigma Step Show that we co-choreographed with our buddy Shawn Cowherd). Despite the different performances and things I did, what I never stressed to anyone (other than Donnie) was how much I wanted to just get done with school.

I was in such a hurry to get on with my life after college that I never fully embraced each moment I was in. I still had my love for diving and briefly joined the Ball State Diving Team under coach John Wingfield, who went on to become coach of the 2008 Olympic Diving Team. I loved Coach Wingfield, "Winger" as we used to call him, who was a terrific coach. He was giving me the fundamentals I never got in high school, the foundation for diving I always wanted. But I was always dealing with personal issues and they interfered with my training. Because of the outside distractions, I only practiced occasionally, never gave the commitment to diving that was needed so I could discover my full potential on the board. Still, I have a nice front one and a half (tuck or pike) and I was happy with myself when I learned a front 2 ½ tuck on the 3m springboard. Other than that, my highlights at Ball State were nonexistent. I told myself that maybe one day I would explore diving again and find a Master's program to participate in. I loved diving but wasn't focused on competition.

Just like at I.U.P.U.I, I needed money and became distracted with working my way through Ball State. I worked as a student assistant in the Learning Center (Mrs. Hall was my favorite faculty member) and as a waiter at Chi-Chi's Mexican Restaurant. I made it through college but although I was there, school was never my priority while I was enrolled. If I had it to do over again, even with an outside obligation, I would take the time to enjoy my college years more, day by day, moment by moment, with no underlying expectations other than learning and enjoying the process. Still, I acknowledge that college isn't for everyone and there are a lot of people who may never know what it's like. I'm very grateful for the collegiate experience I was able to have. I'm thankful that I was challenged to move beyond only wanting to know things within the 2-mile radius of where I grew up (domain specific knowledge), and that I expanded my awareness of my need for universal knowledge so I can function wherever I go around the world. I'm grateful for the lifelong friendships I made at Ball State, like my dear friends, educators Matthew Reeder (Assistant Professor of Directing and Shakespeare) and Margaret Reeder (Membership and Individual Giving Manager) and William Jenkins (Department Chairman, who took over from the terrific Chair I graduated under, Don LaCasse), who were all my classmates and have dedicated their lives to help inspire future generations as they lovingly lead legions of students. I'm proud of them and celebrate their wonderful contributions to Ball State University Theatre and Dance and the world. For me, I'm proud of myself because I achieved my degree and found a career path for my life. From a kid with no direction to a dad to a college grad. Ball State didn't have a Fine Arts Degree when I was there so I graduated in December 1994 with a Bachelor of Science Degree as a Theatre major with a concentration in Performance Studies. I became the first person in my family to graduate from a 4-year university. I learned that I can achieve any goal I set my mind on and work towards. I learned that the road may be challenging, would take time, and may not look like I thought it would along the way, but any and every goal is attainable.

After college, during my time in Chicago, I went back and forth to Indianapolis so much that one day grandma asked me if I had actually moved. I laughed and stopped going to Indy as often. I made Chicago my home. I didn't have an agent and didn't know where to start so I never auditioned or got any gigs. Other than the music group I connected with for a short time (more on that later), the highlight of my time in Chicago was bartending at Michael Jordan's Restaurant, gaining the experience of working in that fast-paced environment, and meeting MJ one day when he came in. The lowlight of my time there came because I behaved like the immature person I was in Indy. I was stuck in my old ways and habits and I didn't push myself to evolve and be better. I hurt two wonderful human beings by being a shitty roommate and stiffing them with my expenses when I moved out. I'm sorry, Jay. I'm sorry, Rachel. They were good people, incredibly kind, and didn't deserve it. I carried the shame of my irresponsible actions for years. No one knew it. I never saw Jay or Rachel again. I'll always be grateful to Rachel for being so sweet and Jay for his friendship and because he introduced me to the music of Notorious B.I.G.. I f*cked up a good friendship with Jay. I asked God for forgiveness for my actions with them. Privately, the greatest lesson I learned is to always leave a positive footprint wherever I touch down (even if it's for a short amount of time) and to always do right by others to the best of my ability. I knew that but when I was younger I let my own selfish needs and actions get in the way.

I left Chicago, moved back to Indiana, and then to California to build a life on the West Coast. When I moved to LA and wasn't booking work as an actor, I never told anyone but I started doubting my foundation. I started feeling like maybe I didn't know what I was doing to be able to work in Hollywood. I privately questioned that because my education came from the Midwest, maybe it somehow wasn't translating in LA. (Acting is universal but as actors, we often blame ourselves if what we're giving to the casting directors isn't openly received. I know I used to and I've heard the same from other actors.) Back then, I felt it was me. Being from the theater stage, I learned to be "big" on stage to project for large audiences. I questioned whether what I was doing was reading for the casting directors and their associates for film and television. I didn't know I needed to learn that for the camera "less is more," which was a principle I had heard but didn't understand how to apply to my work. I didn't learn it in college because I don't remember them offering acting for the camera classes. I took acting classes to keep searching for what I thought would be a more solid foundation to ground my craft. I checked out different ones to find the right class that fit who I was as an artist. I had heard from different actors about taking classes with famed instructors like Howard Fine or Ivana Chubbuck. I thought that's what I needed to do to get the right skills for Hollywood. I compared several classes, audited a few, and eventually took a couple of classes at Ivana Chubbuck Studios. From what I saw, I enjoyed Ivana's instruction. I've always learned by watching instructors evaluate other performers. I listen intently and apply the applicable critiques to my work. But the atmosphere felt off. I didn't know what it was at the time but looking back, it felt like many of the students in class weren't there for the acting work. It felt like they were there because they wanted to be seen by Ivana, who is a brilliant acting instructor and has worked with a lot of fantastic A-list actors. No one did anything to me personally, but after a couple of classes and being around energy that felt "thirsty" to me, I could feel it wasn't the right fit for me. I wanted to work with Ivana hoping to tap into her greatness so she could help me tap into mine, like she had done for so many others, but I don't remember working directly with her. Ivana's classes were very popular and there were so many students in the classes I attended that I didn't get a chance to perform. We talked but she probably wouldn't remember me.

During my last class there I met one of Ivana's instructors, Tasha Smith, who told me she was starting her own workshops. Tasha is a fantastic and talented actor in her own right, as well as an excellent acting coach and director. I did her workshops (along with one-on-one personal coaching) and picked up some elements to add to my acting tool belt, like learning to exude "swagger" in my performances (which I've never focused on in my work). Carrying what I learned from Stanislavski's texts and the work I had done until that point, having swagger never occurred to me, probably because I don't concern myself with having to project swagger in my regular life. Anytime I've consciously tried to be smooth for a role, it's always felt like I was "acting," I wasn't "being," and because of that, I wasn't real. I worked on it and found what my version of having swagger is for the roles I choose. I added what I learned to my continued focus on imbuing my essence into the characters while exploring the emotional truths and depths of the parts. I attended Tasha's workshops off and on for a little while. I was fortunate to take an intensive with guest instructor Eric LaSalle (who I've always been a fan of) when he taught the class for a brief time in Tasha's absence. I experimented with playing a hillbilly character who was a Vietnam veteran and maladjusted from a play called *Pvt. Wars* by James McLure. It was inspiring getting instruction from an accomplished actor (and director) with Eric's ability and industry experience.

After Tasha's workshops, I found a talented instructor who continued to challenge me as an actor. Joe Palese (Rest in Paradise, Joe) ran an ongoing class/scene study program. Joe was a former New York actor who had worked on stage and in television and film, so he instructed from a working actor's point-of-view. Joe studied under famed instructor Lee Strasberg (considered the Father of Method Acting), Milton Katselas, and the legendary Martin Landau. Joe's lessons were grounded in putting in the work and staying true to the material and the character, creating a full and rich history for each role, analyzing the scripts, and deciphering what moved the scenes after thoroughly breaking them down (meaning, learning what each moment in the scene represents and how that knowledge worked in unison with your fellow actor to move the story forward) and then each actor fighting for their objectives. His guidance always led me to honest work where I felt good about the direction my acting skills were developing. I loved Joe's classes and stayed in them for a couple of years. I left that class and looked for more instruction to keep expanding myself as an actor. I found a couple of other classes that were okay, but I didn't grow from them so I stopped attending.

The last acting class I took that gave me the final elements to help me feel secure about my craft came from Martin Barter at The Sanford Meisner Center for the Arts (formerly located in North Hollywood, now in Burbank). Marty studied directly under Sanford, assisted him for over a decade and opened the Center with him. Marty was a fantastic instructor. Once I studied the Meisner technique – a technique that teaches actors to take the focus off of themselves and to place that focus on the other actor in the scene by actively listening and authentically engaging – combined with all the other training I had received, I felt like I had at long last achieved a solid foundation for myself as an actor. I finally understood my instrument. I knew I would keep evolving and growing as an artist over my life, but I had arrived at a place of assurance for the first time. All the instruction I've obtained over the years put me on a career course for maintaining realism in my work and has given me multiple techniques that I can access to bring my roles to life. To keep my acting chops sharp, I also took an excellent Master Class at The BGB Studios, run by Risa Bramon Garcia and Steve Braun, and private coaching with Tess Kirsch. Whenever I've gotten away from the fundamentals I've learned on my artistic journey, my work has always suffered and been a pitiful representation of my abilities. Anytime I've been anxious or eager in my auditions (like in the past when I wanted or needed a job), my work sucked. And I never booked the jobs.

After taking a break from acting (which I'll get into later), when I got back into it I wanted to be able to control my career as much as I could. The only way I knew to do that was to become a writer myself. I had no interest in being a writer. I have good friends who are great writers and it's a challenging road. I didn't want to undertake that challenge, but I wasn't getting the acting opportunities I wanted so I knew I needed to change my approach. I knew I needed to write the roles I wanted to star in. Orson Welles (*Citizen Kane*), Woody Allen (*What's New Pussycat?*), Robert Townsend (*Hollywood Shuffle*), Ben Affleck/ Matt Damon (*Good Will Hunting*) and so many other creatives took a chance on themselves and it worked out. I was nervous but I knew what I needed to do. I didn't want to assume that I would be able to write a script just because I had been reading them for so many years. I wanted to gain a structural knowledge of what went into writing a successful script. As with anything, once I learn to do something, I can regurgitate the formula time and again. "Teach a man to fish…" With that mindset, I started looking around for different writing classes. I ended up taking a class taught by a UCLA writing graduate named Trevor Boelter whose class was, coincidentally, located in the same Sanford Meisner Center building that I had studied in before. I believed that was God saying I could trust the class. Trevor's instruction taught me the formula to write a complete feature film and helped me understand what it would take if I pursued being a writer as a career. I'm not sure if I'll write for other people, but I learned to write for myself. That's a liberating feeling. During my writing class I was introduced to the fantastic, game-changing book, *Save the Cat* by Blake Snyder. Blake's book series puts things into perspective that I learned about crafting scripts but had never considered from the perspective of a writer. I wrote from an actor's perspective to tell a compelling story. Blake's books filled in some blanks that I didn't know needed to be filled. I put my energy into completing my first feature film, *Price Tag*, which I will one day star in and possibly co-direct. If I direct, I want another set of eyes to see what I don't see while I'm in front of the camera. In learning how to write, I believe I'll be able to rely on that new skill as both an actor and creative person, no matter where my career takes me. I just have to develop a love for writing like I have for acting. It's not lost on me that writing this book is another step towards my writing future.

I have been blessed to gain knowledge in different ways from around the world. All the teachings don't come in a classroom, but I still learn what I need for my growth, and all the lessons contribute to the choices I make as an actor.

I've learned education comes in many forms, not just from school. I must be receptive to however knowledge is presented to me. I view things that challenge my growth as lessons, not losses. It's all perspective.

CHAPTER EIGHT
MINEFIELD

I started performing when I was in the choir as a kid, but I didn't call them performances. It was just singing in church on Sunday. But it was in front of the congregation so I'm told it qualifies. Anyway, mom was in the choir and I was in it too for a while. I liked singing. I probably loved being in the choir stands with everyone more than the singing itself. I always thought it was cool how people's voices were so different: sopranos, altos, tenors, basses. I loved watching everyone else sing. It was like being front-row at a concert every Sunday. I didn't sing solos, just the chorus. I could carry a tune (as we used to say), but I could never do all the imaginative singing and creative runs that people who can truly sing can do. We used to say those people could "sang." Marvin Gaye, Luther Vandross, Patti Labelle, Whitney Houston, Beyoncé, Jennifer Hudson, Usher, Justin Timberlake, John Legend. Geniuses of that undeniable talent level. People who breathed their first breath to move the world with their voices. I was always amazed by the dynamic voices of our choir members, awed by how they heard the songs we learned. I never heard the songs the same way. I could mimic what I heard, but I couldn't initiate the magic. I always wished I could. Choreography was swaying from side to side, clapping in time, and other moves that were not very difficult but were challenging for me at first. I would fumble singing trying to keep myself on the beat and then forget to sing when I got back on the beat. But I'm sure nobody ever noticed. If they did, I don't remember anyone saying anything. I couldn't hear myself sing, so I assumed no one else heard me. I just mouthed the words when I messed up. Eventually, I found my rhythm. Some of the best memories I have of singing, I wasn't actually in the choir. My mom was part of a choir called The Rapture and they did musical versions of the stories of creation and the rapture from the bible. Those are my earliest remembrances of loving musical theater, although I didn't know that's what it was called. I loved watching the productions. It gave me a visual representation of the things I learned in church. I was fascinated by the sets, costumes, and stage lighting. I loved watching the choir members give their all to tell the story. I had an indescribable feeling after each performance. I always wanted to see it again and again. A piece of me wished I could put on a show like they did. I had no way of knowing that over the years I would develop different aspects of my creative self as a performer.

As I got older, I quit the church choir. Around that same time, mom told me I didn't have to religiously go to church every Sunday anymore, so I quit going. I started only going when my spirit felt moved to go. I had been through enough pain in my young life to know that my connection to God was personal and didn't depend on anyone else but me, and didn't depend on how many times I did or didn't go to church. I decided as a child that I would maintain my relationship with God, regardless of where my life took me. After the church choir, I didn't perform anymore until I sang in a choir class when I got to middle school, 8th grade. That choir was different, though. It was an elective so I needed it, but I only wanted to be in it because I was infatuated with a girl named Tanisha. She didn't like me in the same way. She was the most beautiful girl I had ever seen. Beautiful brown skin, jet black hair down to the middle of her back, kind eyes, and a pearly white smile. She had me in the "friend zone" because I was silly but I didn't care and sang anyway. I didn't learn what my voice could do when I was in the choir because I clowned around most of the time. Except when I sang *Reasons* by Earth, Wind, and Fire. I loved singing that one. I could hit all the high notes Philip Bailey belts in that song. Then when my voice dropped, I couldn't hit the highs anymore. I didn't want to sing after that. I joked around even more and never seriously gave myself a chance at singing. When that semester ended, I didn't sing again for a while.

A different performer in me emerged when I learned how to dance. I found freedom on the dance floor that I didn't have anywhere else. Whether I was freestyling (which is how it started) or doing a choreographed routine with John (and later with Donnie), I felt electric on the dance floor. I got much more comfortable being in front of people. I stepped into my own and started demanding the spotlight. It was cool to share the stage, but I didn't need to play the background anymore. And I became a bit of an exhibitionist. You could usually catch me with my shirt open, if not off, dancing sexy (or what I thought was sexy anyway) with some girl. I was a handful. I was lean and my abs were on point when I was younger so I used to pop my shirt open to show them off at the drop of a dime, while I was dancing and talking shit. But I wasn't just talking on the dance floor, I could back it up. The music hit me and I was off.

Though my family's musical roots are in Jazz with my Grandpa

Wes and Great-Uncles Buddy Montgomery (pianist) and Monk Montgomery (bassist), my musical interests developed differently. I have an eclectic palate when it comes to music (I'm a huge fan of R&B, also Pop, Rock, Soul, Jazz, Country, and many other genres) but I love Hip-Hop most. I've always liked Hip-Hop but got more into it when I started rapping a little with my boys back in Nap during my teen years, Jaava and the guys. I say "a little," because my buddies were pursuing their shots in music, but I never made any real moves to get my music career off the ground. I was a fan who dabbled in it. Tupac's music spoke to me. I could feel his struggles and how he dealt with it all and associated my struggles. I listened to a lot of rappers from the south like Outkast (Andre 3000 is a wizard with words) and Geto Boys (Scarface is a lethal lyricist). I wasn't a student of the genre so I didn't know much about different emcees, but I knew my spirit felt moved when the raps had substance. I listened to whatever was popular, whatever had a beat that moved me so I could dance, with lyrics that were speaking to me. Truthfully, some of the music I used to listen to wasn't good, but as I got older and my tastes improved, my music choices improved. Just like with fashion, music in Nap wasn't caught up to the East Coast or West Coast, so I usually just vibed out to whoever was playing on the radio. I wish I had known. I can never figure out one Top Five list because I love so many lyricists, so I don't try.

Anyway, back home we used to get smoked out and spit – our version of ciphers. We weren't lyricists like out of NY. I've never been to a true cipher with real emcees. We had fun but our ciphers weren't like the ones I've seen on different shows. I wish I could say I was great, but I wasn't. Freestyling wasn't my fortè. Every once in a while I would get on a roll and go unconscious, but most of the time my timing was off. I got excited and got ahead of the count, instead of being in the pocket and riding the beat. I was in my head too much and tried to think about what I wanted to say and how I would say it, all in the instant that the words needed to be coming out of my mouth. I also tried to cram too many words in each bar, instead of letting my verses breathe. I started putting pencil to paper and discovered I was better at writing my raps. I learned I'm nice at it. I just wasn't the best at coming up with dope cadences for the songs (finding the right "flow"). One of my guys once told me my flow sounds dated, like 80s or 90s, and that I need to devote all my time to writing and perfecting my sound if I want to find my flow. First, I love Hip Hop from the '80s and '90s, so that makes sense. But I got the point because second, I agreed with him. That is what it would take. Except, I'm a grown man. I have a life and responsibilities. I don't have time to put in my 10,000 hours to become an emcee. So, I go to Plan B. As an actor who can rap, when I get a musical urge, I write songs that come to me and work with a team of guys I trust who are all like brothers (Dakari, Treez, and Myke Smith – producers) and (Flii Stylz and JNaugh-T! – lyricists), to help bring my music to life. They've each put in over ten thousand hours into their respective crafts. My team of guys has helped me find the right flows and sounds for tracks I've written, and we made some records I'm proud of.

A great opportunity came during the time of the collaborations and I put out an album internationally (more about that later), but I didn't do any real self-promotion. I had a good album but I didn't know what to do with it. I didn't have the money to do a full marketing blitz and although I'm confident in my writing and rapping skills, I didn't feel like exerting the energy to deal with what the public would say about someone my age putting out Hip Hop for the first time, especially if the music wasn't attached to a film or television project. 30 was the new 20, and I would've made 40 the new 30. But I know how people can be. I love rapping but I don't want all the bullshit that comes with people offering their opinions and talking trash about my contributions to Hip Hop. I am glad I learned to write music, though. It gives me another creative outlet that I'll revisit throughout my life. And even though some people in the Hip Hop culture may try to come for me for not being "Hip Hop enough," I'll see if I can win them over by putting out a few undeniable bangers. Hot music is hot music. More importantly for me, whatever I do in music, I'll have fun and do my best to make my Grandpa Wes, Great-Uncle Monk, and Great-Uncle Buddy proud.

I never thought about being an actor as I was growing up. The closest I ever got to acting (which wasn't acting at all) was when we read *Our Town* out loud when I was in school. I don't remember if I was any good. I probably goofed my way through it. Acting came later.

When I was in high school, I linked up with three other guys and we tried to form an R&B group. I was a back-up singer. I don't remember the name of the group or much about it (or us) other than we sang a lot of The Temptations and New Edition songs. We never had any major performances, I just remember us practicing a lot. We weren't great, but we thought we were. The truth is we were just okay and were never going to be the superstars we were hyping each other to think we would. But they were good guys and we had fun.

When I started college and needed money, before I had direction in my life (before I started acting), I tried out being an exotic dancer. I justified it because when we danced at the nightclubs, I usually ended up with my shirt off. My boy and I talked ourselves into it by saying we could be the Naptown Chippendale dancers. We got up on stage at a strip club on the Eastside of Indianapolis. I had to be sure I was in a location where no one we knew would come in and see us. We went by the names Silk and Smooth. I was Smooth. We just danced like we did at the club and took our clothes off, like at the club. I learned the actual dance formula strippers use while dancing: 1st song) Dance with clothes on; 2nd song) Take clothes off; 3rd song) Strip down to the final look. I stripped down to some boxers with animation characters on them and my boy went down to some silk boxers. The manager of the strip club said he liked our show and that the ladies liked us, but if we wanted to dance there we would need to strip down to either a G-string or T-back. I didn't know what a T-back was, but I knew I wasn't wearing a G-string. I went to a stripper shop and bought what I needed and we got on stage the next night. I went through the songs and eventually stripped down to the T-back. Even though I explained it away in my mind as "just dancing," I didn't feel like I usually felt when I danced. I hated the feeling I got being on that stage and exposed the way I was. I learned that night that stripping wasn't the life for me. I held no judgment for anyone who did it, but my exotic dancing days were over.

From my first time on stage in my first play, I felt like I was where I was supposed to be, like I finally belonged. I was already comfortable on various stages because of dancing so I wasn't thrown when I entered the new environment, I just needed to learn the rules of being on stage as an actor, including learning stage directions (upstage, downstage, center stage, etc). Once I did, I found my bliss. I was at peace when I was on stage and in the middle of performances. I didn't know what an actor's career path looked like because I had never known any actors or anyone who wanted to be one, but I assumed the road would be difficult. I didn't care. I love acting, like I love breathing. I knew what I would do for the rest of my life. My direction was confirmed when a classmate of mine at the time, Angela Northington, cast me as the lead in a play she directed called *Medal of Honor Rag* by Tom Cole. It's a one-act play about a Vietnam veteran named DJ who came home from the war and had a difficult time adjusting to life back in the United States. The psychiatrist who examines him deals with his own survivor's guilt and they do a beautiful dance as they each expose their vulnerabilities. It's a very powerful piece and when we performed it, we had a profound impact on the audience. It was my first time carrying a play and I learned a lot. I worked harder than I ever had and I learned that I'm more than capable of leading a project. The feedback I received proved to me that I made the right choice and was stepping into my calling. I was able to make people feel. I was able to make people think. Wherever the journey of connecting with my work took the audience, I knew I wanted to make them feel deeply. I felt good about myself when the audience went on an emotional journey. I was still learning about acting and although I didn't have complete control of my instrument as an actor, I was still able to tap into some solid work. It was during the run of the *Medal of Honor Rag* that my mom saw me on stage and declared, "My son is an actor." I'm paraphrasing but it was something along those lines. Mom saw what I was capable of and has supported my acting career from that moment on. I was proud to make her proud. I had been a disappointment too many times in my life, in my mom's life. It felt good to honor my mom by being my best and being a good actor. During our run, one of my professors told me I should move to LA to pursue my acting career as soon as our run was over. She told me she wasn't supposed to tell students that, but she said I had *it*. I was proud of the endorsement but I promised myself I would graduate from college. I knew if I left school to go to California, I wouldn't go back and get my degree.

Once I knew acting was my vocation, all the performance experiences that followed added to my box of colors to choose from as an artist.

Sometime during my first years of college, I started working with a terrific company called Artistic Enterprises, a local casting agency in Indianapolis, owned and run by Judy and Skip Welker with the help of their daughter Michelle. I took a class with Artistic Enterprises to keep expanding as an actor. Skip and Judy are both talented actors and had each gained performance successes in the market and they graciously shared their journeys, running a business to help other aspiring actors like myself. I soaked up as much knowledge as I could while I worked with Artistic so I could keep growing in the area. I was excited for any opportunity that gave me a chance to act. I booked a couple of regional commercials and did numerous industrial videos for a company called A.I.T. (Agency for Instructional Technology). Working in the industrials allowed me to make money doing acting work while gaining experience. I enjoyed working with the team at A.I.T. and I learned to be more and more comfortable in front of the camera. However, I felt like I could only work with them for so long, or I might get pigeonholed as the "industrial videos guy." I had talked to other actors about the subject and didn't want to take the chance. I stopped doing industrials altogether after a while.

When I was at Ball State University, a former student had gone to Hollywood and came back to talk to us about what it might be like for us in California. He gave his perspective on acting life in the LA market. He could see we were all excited about the life we were entering as thespians and what we were planning to do to take over the world as actors after college. But he looked around at all of our bright and shining faces and said, "I hate to disappoint you guys, but most of you will never work in Hollywood. Like 99% of you will never work in Hollywood." I remember looking around the room and feeling, "Damn, I feel bad for you guys." I may have even said it out loud. But I wasn't being conceited. I knew what I was going to do with my life after college. I knew what I was born to do. To be an actor. To entertain. It didn't matter to me what odds would be stacked against me, or what hurdles I would have to jump over. I knew that I was not going to fail at my life's calling. Once I knew, I knew. I know God is on my side so I didn't care what obstacles may come. The speaker gave some insight into Hollywood, but as I learned when I finally joined it, you can't prepare anyone for their journey in the industry. Everybody has their path. The best advice he gave was telling us that the process would be hard and to make sure it was really what we wanted before pursuing it. I was sure.

After college, while living in Chicago, I was part of an R&B group called A# (A Sharp). We had five members in the group and had a good sound. One of our lead singers used to sing as a backup for Patti LaBelle, and our other lead was a powerful gospel singer who sang in his father's church. The guy who put the group together was a cool guy named JJ whom I met at a nightclub when I was out dancing one night. JJ liked my dancing (and my look) and asked me if I could sing. I told him that I was alright but that it wasn't my specialty. I questioned why he was asking and he said he was putting together a singing group and wanted me to be a member. JJ then told me about himself, that he discovered a group called Subway in Chicago and signed them to Michael Bivens and his company, Biv 10 Records. JJ had the mindset that since he was able to get Subway signed, he would be able to do the same thing with us. But what "getting us signed" meant to him was us performing in the Chicago subways every day until we got discovered. That was how he got the group Subway noticed. I had already graduated from college, owed tens of thousands in student loans and was ready to get on with my life, so I was not interested in standing in a subway and hoping that someone would walk by and discover us. I've always been up for an adventure so if I thought we could make it that way, I probably would've tried it. At least for a while. I couldn't do it, though. They showed me that everybody wasn't willing to work as hard as we needed to work to make ourselves successful. They were nice guys and talked a good game, but there was no action. We rarely rehearsed, we barely got together and went over what our actual sound and look and career and everything would be. I had never done it, so I had no idea how to lead us. I was following them because they had experience in the music business. When it became clear that the group was not going to work out, I told them I was getting back to focusing on my acting career. I never saw or spoke to any of them again.

Back in Indianapolis after living in Chicago, I started doing stand-up comedy. I did my first show on January 8, 1996, at Crackers Comedy Club at Keystone at the Crossing. I only got on stage because I was goaded into getting up there. My girlfriend back then was good friends with Marshall Faulk who played for the Indianapolis Colts at the time. I got cool with Rush (his nickname) and he heard me talking with my lady about trying my hand at comedy. One night we found out Crackers Comedy Club did open-mic nights and after a bunch of shit-talking and me letting my ego get the best of me, we went there for me to give it a try. I had never actually practiced a comedy set, not even in the mirror at home. I just assumed I could do it, and people used to tell me I was funny. I was anxious. Rush brought a couple of his buddies from the Colts (I don't remember who) to support. But when we got to the comedy club, we found out there wasn't an open mic that night. The club was doing an HBO Special for a talented comic named Dave Duggan. The venue held about 300 people and being Dave's special, the room was packed to capacity. It was standing room only. Rush talked to the managers and because he was who he is, they still agreed to give me six minutes on stage. I was nervous as hell. The host was a really funny comedian named Mark Craycraft and he could tell. Mark was supportive and gave me a joke in case I bombed: "Thanks for having me, folks. Hopefully, I can come up here and suck for you guys again." I thanked him and filed it away in my mind as a "last resort." Before I hit the stage, I did two shots of tequila to calm my nerves. I had never performed as an actor under the influence of any substance so I didn't know how my body would react, but I was in a new arena. I wasn't nervous about being on stage because I was completely comfortable on stage by that time. I was uneasy because I would be on stage alone. Every time I was on stage in a play, I was with other people. Whether the show went well or not, we swam or sank together. When I was dancing I had partners but I could be on stage alone because the music moved me in such a way that I didn't need anyone else around. When I hit the stage as a comic, it was solo. I knew if I tanked, I was going to drown by myself. And I did. I was pretty bad. I got a few laughs when I talked about eating a bowl of cereal while driving to work one day, but I dragged the joke out too long and it fizzled. I only did 6-minutes but it felt like a lifetime. I didn't have an identity as a comic and saying the jokes without having a carved-out point-of-view made my performance commonplace. I never read any reviews about my set but I'm my worst critic. I know I bombed. About halfway into my set the alcohol kicked in and I loosened up, but by then it was too late. I got through the rest of the time and used Mark's joke at the end. I wanted the room to know that I wasn't blind to the fact that I sucked. I left there triumphant for having gotten on stage, defeated that I stunk up the place. I was determined to get better. I took comedy seminars taught by Mark Craycraft and Judy Carter so I could learn exactly what I was supposed to do as a comic and what goes into a quality joke. With more of an understanding of the genre, I went back to working on material and came up with a gimmick to get the audience going. I created a gay persona that I used to start my set. I was never offensive, just flamboyant (my version of what Damon Wayans and David Alan Grier did on *In Living Color*). Instead of starting my set on stage, when I was introduced I had the venue play music (the first show was Mystikal's "Here I Go," and I used other songs that hit hard at subsequent shows) and I started in the back of the room. I covered up with an oversized jacket that had a hood (always with a hood so they couldn't make out my features very well) and walked through the audience on my way to the stage. I would "mean mug" the audience (meaning, I gave them dirty looks and looked like I was ready to attack someone). Once I hit the stage, I would have the tech cut the music and I'd drop the oversized jacket revealing me in all my splendor. I wore a yellow silk shirt, a gold lamè scarf around my neck with a matching bow on my head, over a fitted black "muscle" shirt (Remember that look from the 90s? Not the gold lamè, the muscle shirts. Yeah, I rocked those a lot. Way too much.) with jeans and boots. I would say, "Hey, ya'll! How ya'll doing?" and the audience would fall out. The contrast when I transitioned from gangster to gay persona cracked them up every time. I would make a few jokes as the gay character and then come out of the character on stage. That got them even more. I took off the scarf, bow, and silk shirt and did the rest of the show in the muscle shirt, jeans, and boots. I would pick out a tough-looking guy (or any guy) in the front row and have an amazed look on my face (which was usually their reaction) while I started clapping for myself (pretending to be the guy) and would say, "This guy looking at me like – "You son-of-a-b*tch! I was starting to feel something!" The guys always got embarrassed and the audience laughed hysterically, instantly on my side. I learned that once the crowd was with me, they stayed with me for the whole show, even if some of the jokes throughout my set didn't hit as hard as I wanted them to. I had found a formula, a comedic niche. I started performing at a lot of different venues in and around the Indianapolis area. I did stand-up for months and continued to hone myself as a comic. I kept doing comedy until I moved to California. Doing stand-up is when I started using the stage name A.T. I didn't know it at the time, but making the change from using A.T to using Anthony came with a lot of resistant reactions. I only started using a stage name to do stand-up, I never planned on using that name for the duration of my time performing. I had always planned on using my full name when I was established as an actor in Hollywood (Like Sidney Poitier or Denzel Washington). So, I went to California using A.T, but when I got on *Enterprise,* I asked people to start calling me Anthony. Most people were cool and honored my request. Several people started acting weird. I wasn't doing it from a place of ego. I wasn't doing it to be arrogant, or because I was "Hollywood" (which I was called once). I was doing it because that's what I had always planned to do throughout my career. Just like Laurence Fishburne went from Larry to Laurence. I don't know if he planned it, but he still made the change. It didn't stop him from doing brilliant work as an actor. And people got used to it. I didn't think anyone would think anything of me changing my name because no one knew me. I had done a few jobs but not nearly a star. But I got pushback, even when I tried to explain that the T isn't in my name (my middle name is Dwayne). It made me laugh (and, admittedly, sometimes irked my nerves) when people felt some type of way about me or gave me odd energy because they were more attached to my made-up name than I was. I got the nickname from one of my college professors. I never knew why he called me that, but I loved him as an instructor so it didn't bother me. When prepping for my stand-up, I stood in the mirror and said the names as an announcer, "Ladies and gentlemen, coming to the stage, your next comedian, Anthony Montgomery!" Nope. Felt too lengthy. "Ladies and gentlemen, coming to the stage, your next comedian, A.D. Montgomery!" Nope. The D doesn't roll off the tongue. And what my professor used to call me popped into my head. "Ladies and gentlemen, coming to the stage, your next comedian, A.T Montgomery! Give it up for A.T, ya'll!" Yes! That was the one. It felt right. Then I could work into my set that I was a real-life ATM. I moved past caring how others felt about my name change. I knew the truth. And the name came back around when I started doing music. I knew I needed a name for Hip Hop, so I used A.T again because it worked. The irony of me going through all that only to name my album *A.T* has never been lost on me.

I was exposed to being a Master of Ceremonies when I was offered an opportunity to MC for the Indiana Film Society Festival in 1996. I was suggested for the position by Jerald Harkness, a close friend who was a Board Member of the Indiana Film Society at the time. An award-winning documentarian I had worked with on several projects, Jerald knew I was an experienced performer and that I was doing stand-up comedy, and felt I would do a solid job as an MC, despite my inexperience. That was a safe bet. Being an MC felt like a natural extension of my stage performance background. I was asked to entertain the crowd and keep the energy up so the show would keep moving. I was able to incorporate comedy and because I genuinely like most people, I just talked to the audience like they were all friends of mine. I remember folks being very kind and complimentary about the show and how "comfortable" I looked on stage. I was comfortable. I wasn't sure how it would go when I started, but I was confident I could keep a crowd engaged so I knew I would be okay. I learned that being an MC is about connecting with the audience and keeping the flow of the event. An MC has to bring energy, much like being a dancer, being in a play, or doing stand-up comedy. Being an MC gave me an essential tool for the toolbox.

What I never let anyone know was that behind all the professional work I was chasing, I was still wading through the intense painful drama of my personal life. Underneath it all, I was still in a lot of pain. I was ready to improve my circumstances and was positive I would not achieve the life I truly desired by staying in Indianapolis. I needed a new environment for my personal and emotional well-being and professional expansion. Having a job as an actor made it easier to move because I can act anywhere in the world, not just in one location. Since there was only so much acting I could do in Indy, it was time to make a move to either New York or California. If I moved to NY, I planned to continue doing theater. I knew it would be a brutal grind to achieve what I wanted in theater: to become a consistently working actor and permanent Broadway main attraction. I wanted a career that went from show to show to show until I eventually retired one day. And if I went west to Hollywood, I decided I would pursue a career in television and film and work on the stage when I got the chance. I didn't know anything about either city other than I would be working my ass off to make it as an actor, whichever coast I chose. My choice was easier because I knew it snowed in NY and not LA. I started thinking hard about the California move.

Around that time, Judy and Skip from Artistic told me a call came in that a feature film starring Christian Slater and Morgan Freeman would be filming in Jasper, Indiana, a small town about three hours outside of

Indianapolis. Judy and Skip didn't know if I would want the job because it wasn't a major role with any lines and I would only be a background person. I told them I didn't mind working as a background performer and was grateful for the opportunity. I wanted to know what it was like being on a set, an actual working Hollywood set. Taking the work was less about the job itself as background and more about me being able to soak up as much as I could from the production, cast, and crew. I worked on the feature film *The Flood* as a background person for one day and had good interactions with everyone, got to know a few members of the production team, and asked many questions. From what I was told, the 1st A.D. (assistant director), Matt Earl Beesley, noticed me and told Jason R., 2nd 2nd A.D., to tell me they would be coming back to film in that town again and asked if I would like to be a P.A. (production assistant) for the show. I didn't know what a P.A. did but as long as I would be part of the show, I didn't care and said yes. Jason R. stressed that the job wouldn't be as "glamorous" as what I was doing as a background person, that I would be hustling and given a lot of work to do. I told him something along the lines of… I wasn't worried about hard work and was ready for whatever they could throw at me. I knew being a P.A. would be a great experience for me as a performer. Since my goal was to be in front of the camera for the bulk of my career, I wanted to learn what would be happening behind the camera too, and how the other departments worked. Jason R. told me I could bring any friends who would be hard workers too. One of my close friends, JC, my brother-from-another was the first person who came to mind. I N I. JC and I went to Jasper when the production came back into town and worked with the show the whole time they filmed there for about two weeks. During the shoot, I ran and did everything that was asked of me. From getting breakfast orders for the cast to getting fresh batteries for the walkie-talkies when they died, to passing out sides to the cast and crew. No matter the task, I showed them the kind of energy that they said they looked for in all of their production assistants. A phrase I learned on the first day of working as a P.A. was "Shit rolls downhill and P.A.s sit at the bottom of the hill." I took all the shit that was dealt to me and still did my best with every duty I was assigned, and I had a positive attitude while I did it. I worked so hard that when I told Matt Earl I was planning a move to either California or New York, he told me if I moved to LA he would have a job for me as a P.A. to finish working on the production in Palmdale, California. It would be approximately 2½-3 months of work. I was in. I didn't know what job I would get to be able to support myself when I initially left Indy, so having some sort of a lead on employment was all I needed.

My decision was set. California would be my new home and a career in television and film my next goal. I didn't know what was waiting for me as I prepared to navigate the minefield of the Hollywood industry, but I was ready for the challenge.

I've learned that every opportunity that is presented adds to my overall growth as a performer. Once I found my calling in life as a performer, the universe aligned to help me towards my goals.

CHAPTER NINE
FORTUNATE SON

When we wrapped production in Jasper on *The Flood* (a title that was later changed to *Hard Rain* before the film's release), I went back to Indianapolis and immediately started making preparations to leave. I took steps to get my life in order. I gave my two-week notice at work (Mountain Jack's Restaurant, where I worked as a waiter) and let the manager of the apartment complex where I lived know that I would be breaking my lease and moving out of town for work. I told everyone close to me that I was leaving for Cali and most of them thought I was crazy. The ones who truly knew me wondered what took me so long. I had done crazy stuff before, more than my share. My decision to move wasn't crazy, it was the sanest thing in the world to me, even though I didn't put any true planning into the move. I didn't have any money saved up and only had a place to stay because Aunt Frances lived in Altadena and told me I could stay with her until I got on my feet. I took her up on it and was determined to have that time be as short as possible. Although I knew I wouldn't have much money (I had scraped together a couple hundred bucks), I was determined to make it work. On my last day in Indy, I packed up my gray 1987 Honda Accord LX with more than 100,000 miles on it with what I thought I'd need: clothes, music, snacks, and my Beretta 92F. I wasn't driving that whole way without protection. I had my gun permit, so it was legal. But I wasn't completely legal. I drove illegally because my license was suspended from getting so many speeding tickets. And because my license was suspended, I didn't have car insurance. But I was so desperate to get out of Indy, that I couldn't let that stop me. I put everything else I owned (which wasn't much, Spartan furnishings from my one-bedroom apartment) into a storage unit.

I needed to go and was excited about advancing my life, but I was also worried about leaving my family, especially my mom. Grandma talked to me outside her house and told me it was my time. I felt overwhelmed and cried on her steps. She told me Grandpa Wes had to leave his family (meaning herself and my aunts and uncle) to go on the road to play his guitar, but that's what he had to do to get where he wanted to be. He made the sacrifice. She said I had to do the same to get where *I* wanted to be. She said I needed to go live my life. A couple of my aunts told me the same thing in other conversations. I knew they were right. It didn't make leaving easier. But I had to do it. I had to choose to live my life to the fullest. I had to pursue my dreams, even though I was unsure how the process would work or what would happen to everyone when I left. Grandma reminded me that God would take care of my mom and the rest of my family, just like He would take care of me. Grandma surprised me and gifted me a few thousand dollars so I would have money when I made it to LA. I promised I would pay her back even though she wasn't asking.

With God as my co-pilot, on November 18, 1996, I drove out of Indianapolis and across the country by myself. A mixture of emotions engulfed me as I drove across the I-70W freeway. Eagerness. Enthusiasm. Curiosity. Trepidation. Guardedness, but with wide open arms. I wasn't scared, though. I didn't feel what I felt as a child, a fear of running from someone or something. As I drove, anticipation of what I was moving towards flooded me. I felt anxious but not in a bad way. My mind raced. What would California be like? How long would it take for me to book an acting job? How long would it take to make my mark and work consistently? When would I get back to Indy? Question after question swirled in my head. Even without any of the answers, the time had come for me to leave Indianapolis and go boldly to make my mark in the world of Hollywood. Whatever that meant. I didn't have any expectations, other than I would give it my all and dedicate myself to my art and craft. I believed I would make it in Hollywood, I just didn't know how. I hoped to experience a quality and inspiring career like Sidney Poitier and Denzel Washington, not trying to be either of them, but by pursuing my craft with truthfulness and integrity and creating my lane as they've done. I believed in my talents and knew I just needed one of the brilliant filmmakers (Frances Ford Coppola, Stephen Spielberg, Martin Scorsese, George Lucas, Quentin Tarantino, Spike Lee, F. Gary Gray, James Cameron, any of the greats) to believe in me and want to invest in me and my talents. I had heard that "It only takes one," meaning it only takes one great project to launch your career into the stratosphere. I wanted to be the one to get that one. I had to calm my mind. I was trying to envision my whole acting career and I hadn't even left the city limits. I watched the road in front of me and realized the next chapter of my life was officially beginning. When I checked the rearview mirror and saw all that I had ever known getting smaller and smaller in the distance, I thought a prayer to all the people I loved, that I would make them proud and I would see them as soon as I could - and looked back to the road. I smiled. I didn't know what to expect but was excited for whatever adventures lay ahead.

I drove until I got tired, about 13 hours. I only stopped for gas or when I got hungry (for real food, not snacks), and very few bathroom breaks—I wasn't stopping, unless it was an emergency. I loved being on the open road. I listened to music or drove in silence, alone with my thoughts and countless hours of conversations with God. I took in the beauty of our country, and I took in the boring and mundane parts of it as well. I planned to pull over to whichever hotel or motel was closest when I got sleepy. I didn't care what kind of place it was as long as it had a clean bed and shower. But the first motel I hit was pretty shitty and there were no other stops in the area. It looked like one of those semi-rundown motels you see in slasher films that someone was trying to keep running. The creepy room they gave me could've come from a Stephen King novel. It had a rusted water odor coming from the bathroom. The yellowish-brown carpet was blackened and worn from heavy foot traffic and years of neglect, and a dirty old RCA television with missing buttons was bolted to the dresser. The ugly beige and flower wallpaper was coming down all over, peeling in some places and bubbling in others, while cracked and chipped paint splattered the walls where the wallpaper missed. And the bed had an odd smell to it. The sheets were clean but they smelled strange. It was late, I was too exhausted to drive and the next town or city was a long distance, so I stayed. I slept for 5-6 hours, showered (used what felt like sandpaper soap and a washcloth and towel that were as coarse as a scouring pad – I may have drawn blood while drying off), and hit the road again. The trip was supposed to take me three days but I drove determined and made it to Las Vegas the next night. Aunt Frances' house was only four hours from there, but because I had heard so much about Vegas, I had to stop.

Instead of going south from Indy, then taking the 10W freeway so I could see Baton Rouge, Houston, and other cities I had heard great things about but never visited, I drove west on I70 so I could experience "Sin City." I stayed at the Tropicana. I parked my car at the hotel and checked into my room. The room was cool and simple. The bed was clean (regular hotel clean) and I could see the lights of the strip. I was good. I stood at the window and looked out in wonder. I put on my Discman headset with "California Love" (Dr. Dre and Tupac) on repeat, grabbed some other music to keep me hyped, and went exploring. I had to see the Vegas Strip up close. Before I even got to the Strip, I was amazed at how long most of the blocks were (from one intersection to the next). So. Damn. Long. And it was HOT! Indiana got hot and humid in the summer but I had never experienced a heat like Nevada heat. It was so hot I couldn't breathe. I had to step into one of the hotels to cool off. Eventually, my body adjusted. Or I just stopped thinking about it and got used to it. Vegas was an assault on my senses. I had seen wild depictions on television and in movies but I still wasn't ready for what I saw. I took it all in. Throngs of people, excitement in the air, sexual energy that seemed to be oozing from almost everyone, gorgeous women everywhere, guys trying to sell me dope on the sly, and "working" women offering their services. Shit was crazy. And I loved it. If it was nuts like that on a Wednesday, I couldn't wait to see what the weekends were like. I gambled a little bit at the MGM. Not too much because I only had so much money, but I had to see what the hype was about regarding casinos. I broke down a hundred dollars into $5 chips and played. I loved Black Jack, Craps and Roulette. I lost all my money ($200 total) but had a blast. I understood how folks can get addicted to gambling. I felt the intoxicating dopamine rush people get when you double down and hit 21 (and the dealer busts), or when your point is 10 and you have the whole table rooting you on while you're rolling the dice, or the exciting unknown as the little ball spins opposite way of the wheel itself. It feels like you're on top of the world when everybody's making money every time you roll (as long as you don't crap out) until you eventually hit the point and the table erupts in cheers. You want to feel that euphoria again and again, so you keep betting. And you crave that rush, even when you start losing (and you will lose, since casinos make money on the losers, not the winners). You just convince yourself you'll "hit on the next roll," or the next hand you're dealt, or the next spin of the roulette wheel. I'm sure other factors weigh in, but ultimately, high-rolling "sharks" who gamble all the time search for that same rush, they just bet a lot more money. Mystery solved. In one night, I understood the vicious circle people obsessed with gambling find themselves in. The rush, free drinks while you gamble, oxygen being pumped into the casinos and the energy of the environment kept me hyped. I should've been tired but I was wide awake at six in the morning. I had to make myself go back to my hotel. I never saw any windows and didn't know the sun had already come up. I knew I barely scratched the surface of Vegas. I couldn't wait to go back there with a couple of bucks in my pocket.

I got four or five hours of sleep and drove the last leg to California. I was awed by the beauty of the mountains and how picturesque everything looked. I was used to flat land in Indiana and got excited when it dawned on me that I would get to look at mountains every day. When I made it to Aunt Frances in Altadena on November 21, 1996, I remember feeling like, "Okay, I'm here. Now what?" I reached out to the *Hard Rain* production to see when I would be working but the film crew wasn't back in town yet. They were still filming on location. And the holidays were approaching. I had no idea that during the holiday seasons, the industry adjusts, work slows up and network productions go on hiatus, they take a break from all filming. I hadn't learned that there are seasons in Hollywood productions: Pilot Season (January-April) where productions cast, produce, and create new shows to be considered for series; after pilot season, generally, it's Staffing Season, where writers are assembled to be the collaborative force behind the series. Episodic Season starts around July and runs through mid-December (although things start slowing in November). Episodic Season is where shows that were picked up, start casting and go into production. After that, shows go on hiatus to end the year, and in January the process starts over again. Studio and independent feature films are cast and produced throughout the year. That's what it was like for me for the first 25 years I was in the industry. With cable television and all the shows on the internet now, there are more castings year-round and many productions can keep filming when networks go on hiatus. But back then, I was just trying to figure it out and get in where I could.

It was a rainy LA day when I arrived. Since I couldn't work with *Hard Rain*, I wanted to get to my business of acting. I went to LA with a cocky attitude about my acting ability and what I could do. I was ready to show somebody, anybody that I could be a leading man in Hollywood. But I didn't know what to do. I wasn't "connected" in any way to anyone who could help move my career forward. (For the record, no one has ever given me an acting gig because Wes Montgomery was my grandfather. It's a talking piece and people love and respect his contribution to music, but it's never equated to an acting job. I got one modeling job because of our connection, but I have built my career through my hard work and sacrifice. Just in case anyone thought otherwise.) Until I figured out how to keep going forward with acting, I knew I needed to get comfortable moving around in the new environment. I familiarized myself with my surroundings the best I could and started learning the lay of the land. LA County is spread out so I used my Thomas Guide like my life depended on it. Aunt Frances gave me a key to the house so I could come and go, and I hit the ground running. I only stayed at her place for a month (when I didn't sleep elsewhere), and after that, I just left my clothes at her house until I got my own place. I started staying with a couple of students I connected with from Ball State (Adam and Petra) and their friend Jeff, who all lived in North Hollywood. Adam, Petra, and I didn't hang together at Ball State but I knew who they were. We got to know each other when I started staying with them. They lived in a 2-bedroom place where the guys shared a room and Petra had her own room. I usually crashed on the couch or blankets on the floor. It wasn't always pretty but we were all artists and made it work. Adam and Jeff were really good guys and generous with their time and showed me around. To help me get going on my acting path they told me about the old entertainment magazines Backstage West and Drama-Logue. Each of those industry publications provided relevant information about the business and in the back, there were casting opportunities and other jobs, networking possibilities, and potential resources to keep you going in the business. I started looking for projects I was right for and submitting myself for short films and different independent features, and stayed on the lookout for any chances to meet agents. I never got any calls. That was my beginning in Hollywood. I also spent a lot of time at Samuel French Bookstore getting resources for my theatrical pursuits.

I didn't know anyone else in California so I spent a lot of time with Adam and Jeff. I quickly learned how ridiculously expensive California is versus Indiana (and how much faster the pace of life is too). I blew through the cash I brought pretty fast, within a few weeks. I was frivolous being a tourist and also paid for Adam and Jeff to do stuff with me, so I didn't have to do things alone. And I went out to a bunch of bars and spent too much money getting faded. But I had to see how they partied in LA. I knew I would be working at some point and thought I'd get more money before I ran out. The struggle got real, real fast. I ran out of money and quickly joined the ranks of other starving artists in LA. And I'm not being facetious. There were several days when I didn't eat. I didn't have food or money and I was too ashamed to tell my family how bad off I was. They may not have been able to help anyway but I never checked to find out. I dealt with it on my own. I looked for whatever jobs I could find. When I couldn't find work, I started selling the CDs I brought with me and pawning anything I had of value to get money. I found out that my Indiana gun permit wasn't valid in California and pawned my Beretta 92F at a pawn shop in Pasadena. Sometime after I hocked my weapon, I ran out of things to pawn or sell. I found a job as a bouncer at a bar in Old Town Pasadena, where I worked for a couple of months. I didn't make much and was still broke, but I was able to put gas in my car sometimes and I ate at work during my shifts.

I did an episode of *Singled Out* with Carmen Electra and Chris Hardwick. I won the show and got some free schwag, but never went on a date with the girl. I was too busy checking out Carmen Electra, who is insanely beautiful in person. I couldn't even buy myself dinner, I knew Carmen wouldn't give me the time of day. It was fun to be on the show though. Chris was a cool guy.

Film production started back up and I quit being a bouncer and kept working as a production assistant while I looked for acting work. While working on *Hard Rain*, I got my first theatrical representation, a personal manager, whom I was referred to by a talented actor who worked on the film. The manager helped me get my first agent, Honey Sanders at The Sanders Agency. I loved working with Honey and we worked together for several years until I got a different agent. My manager and I continued working together until I got the biggest job of my career. I learned that either representation can take a talent to the next level of their career or the talent can propel the representation to the next level. I was hoping to do that with my manager. I wanted to move up together. I didn't want to leave, but I wanted the rate I was paying to be competitive with what other managers were making. My management was getting 15% of my pay and I learned that when you get to a certain level in the business, most managers and agents only take 10% commission (print agents typically get 20%). After being established, actors don't always need managers or agents, they can just use an attorney to negotiate the deal and the attorney typically gets around 5% for their services. We were still building my career so I still needed representation. I was already paying 10% to my agent (meaning I was only taking home 75% of my pay, less after the IRS took their money for taxes at a rate of about 35%) and when I asked for the management fees to be reduced by 5%, the request was shot down. Because my accountant and attorney had already given me the numbers, it made financial sense to stop working together. Not just for that job, but for future work. I took the knowledge of what the pay scale should be and applied it to all future industry representation. Part of me felt awful because of our history and because I had never released a rep before, but I followed my attorney's advice and didn't let my personal feelings get in the way. "It's show *business*, Anthony. This is part of the business," he said. I appreciated all that was done to help me get moving in the industry, but I kept it about business. Just like the business decisions that my manager made that didn't benefit me. They kept it about business. I followed suit. I made an executive decision and because I had already paid my former manager 15% for three years totaling around nearly a quarter million dollars from that one job (not to mention the 15% I paid for every job before that one), I felt like I had repaid everything that had been done on my behalf from the beginning of us working together up to that point. Even when I held regret and resentment (which I released a long time ago) for taking a terrible job that didn't reflect who I was, nor who I aspired to be as an artist - a job that was presented to me by my management, a job I unwisely took because I was desperate (more about that one later). I eventually came to a place of acceptance and peace surrounding the termination of that business relationship. Representation doesn't always last forever and reps can release the talent they represent at their discretion. I've learned that's part of the nature of the game of entertainment. And sometimes the artist has to part ways with their representation. That's another part of the game. As an artist, you hope to establish long-term relationships with representation that believes in you and your talents, and you hope that they will represent you long-term. But they don't always. I've personally had a rep and agency drop me when I wasn't making them money. That's part of the game too. It's called show *business* for a reason.

But that clarity didn't come for a while.

While I was working as a P.A. on *Hard Rain* I asked Matt Earl to keep me in mind if any roles came up that he thought I'd be right for. I didn't know if it was appropriate for a production assistant to ask the First Assistant Director for a job, but I was never given the Hollywood rules of engagement, and I did move to Cali to be an actor, not a P.A., so I threw the request out hoping for the best. Matt Earl told me he would and to his word, I got a call one day to do an episode of *Dick Clark's Beyond Belief* that Matt Earl was directing. I played a State Trooper. I remember feeling eager and a little anxious about being on my first Hollywood set as a bonafide talent. I was excited to be starting on my journey, even though I may have seemed a little amateurish (I think I looked at my mark on the ground in one of the takes - a rookie actor mistake). I'll always be grateful to Matt Earl for giving me the chance.

Years before landing the role that changed my life, I auditioned as much as I could and still worked as a P.A. I started to get a good reputation as a hard worker and was able to jump from show to show. I went from *Hard Rain* to working on a film called *Suicide Kings*, and did a couple of days on the film *Amistad* (I didn't know how impactful that film would end up being when I was working on it; I didn't even know what the film was about), and ended up working on the television series *Nothing Sacred*. It was on that project that my friendships with Elimu, Sekou, and Brian were cemented, as well as other life-long bonds that were formed, like with my brother Shawn Papazian. Shawn and I were both P.A.'s and stood on the roof of Ray-Art Studios and made a pledge to each other that we would meet at the top of the mountain of Hollywood, him as a producer and director and me as an actor (and one day as a director). Doing P.A. work when I could get it was paying the bills but I had to make a firm decision about the course of my life. I talked to a few Assistant Directors and they advised me that if I kept being seen as a production assistant, that's all I would ever be seen as. Which was fine if that was the path I was taking to become a director one day, but I wasn't. I was in LA to act. I didn't plan to direct until I had firmly established myself as an actor. Much like when I stopped doing industrials, I had to decide the course my career would take. I believed that if I was going to break out as an actor, I was going to have to walk on faith and stop taking P.A. work. During the decision-making process, I was blessed to be in a good position because the person who believed in me and gave me the job as a P.A. was one of the most loving and nurturing souls I've ever worked with in Hollywood. His name was Cyrus Yavneh. Cyrus was a wonderful human being, a good person, and a successful producer who worked on some major films and series. Cyrus did something completely unprecedented and allowed me to be a Set P.A., (set production assistant, whose job is to be on or near the set at all times, unless on an errand for the set), while still pursuing my acting career. He allowed me to take off work to go do my auditions, and if I was fortunate enough to book a job, he would allow me to take off work so that I could go film and then come back to work as a P.A.. As I've heard from multiple sources, that *never* happens in the industry. The Second A.D. of the show didn't like the fact that I was given so much freedom because as a set production assistant, you need to be there more than I was available at times. But Cyrus was a man of his word. I was still able to keep pursuing my acting career until *Nothing Sacred* was eventually canceled. That was my last P.A. job. Cyrus didn't only help me with work, he also kept me doing the right thing in my personal life and was the reason I got my CA driver's license. He was always there to advise me if I needed it and I trusted him. I always told him the truth and when he found out I didn't have my license, Cyrus was worried that I would get caught driving with a suspended license and get arrested. He told me he wanted me to stop driving until I got my license situation squared away. I had so much love, respect, and gratitude for Cyrus that I agreed. I knew I wasn't supposed to be driving anyway. I parked my car and caught the bus, got rides or walked everywhere I needed to go for over three months, including work from North Hollywood to Woodland Hills. My feet hit the pavement until I paid all the fines against my license, got myself back in good standing with the DMV and got car insurance. Cyrus' influence and guidance left an immeasurable positive imprint on my life. Cyrus and I maintained a friendship and his periodic mentoring of me until his untimely death. Thank you for everything, Cyrus. I love you, my friend. Rest in Paradise.

———

Eventually, Petra moved out and I moved into her room and kept working to break into the industry. I learned the bulk of what I know about show business once I was immersed in it. Hollywood gave me on-the-job-training and I'm grateful for it. Since being in Hollywood on my own, I've learned that many parts of Hollywood aren't always what they're cracked up to be. I'm a real dude. The appeal of being part of the machine that brings joy to so many people, lost some of its luster for me when I joined that machine. I pulled back the curtain and saw the wizard. I learned some real, hard truths about some aspects of the film and television production business. Hollywood has a lot of people in it who want to be part of it, but it's a very lonely place. At least it was for me. I didn't feel like I was at home in California or at home moving through Hollywood for about a year. I had Donnie and Jeremy back home to talk to, but they're not part of the industry so our conversations could only go so far. I felt like I was by myself until I met my best friends, my Brothers, Elimu, Sekou (whom we lost in 2011), and Brian. None of us were from California and we were all making our way into the business. Elimu and I were grinding as actors (which we still do to this day), while Sekou was attacking from the writer's end and Brian was forging his way as our local teamster. We were each other's rock through the hardest times, and proudly supported each other's victories as we partied our asses off through the great times. Billiard marathons and playing pool until the pool halls closed happened as often as we could, and as much as we could afford. Having my guys, a solid circle of true support to celebrate and elevate with, and commiserate with, people I knew I could trust no matter what, made the process of pursuing a profession in Hollywood bearable. When I found authentic friends, I felt like I could conquer whatever was thrown my way in the business. I knew I wasn't alone. I love acting and all it entails but I can only deal with the rigors of pursuing a career in the arts because of the love of my amazing children and the wonderful group I surround myself with. I talk a lot (less than I used to), but I keep my circle small. People who inspire me with their everyday actions. Donnie has built a career in the hospitality industry with the odds stacked against him from a corporate structure that continually bypasses his achievements, giving his recognition and career elevation opportunities to people far less qualified than him. Despite the opposition, he's earned his way to being General Manager of one of the largest hotel chains in the world. And they still try to hold him back. But he perseveres. Elimu has taken his insane talent on the basketball court, an incredible basketball IQ (having been a true student of the game and formerly played for Syracuse University and gone overseas one summer and played in pro leagues with a team), and turned it into a great career as a private coach. All while building a career in Hollywood, being a phenomenal father to his beautiful son, and becoming a skilled writer, actually paid for his talents along the way. Another of my close friends and confidants, Shawn A., built himself up from being a sick ass dancer (I didn't know him back then), to being one of the top club promoters in Florida, then LA, and expanding to Las Vegas, until a horrible series of unfortunate events sent him to jail for a brief time. This caused him to fully embrace his true calling: to bring about change in the world as a Life Coach, Motivational Speaker, and Author while building a life with his brilliant wife and their amazing daughter and son. The love and inspiration I get from my children and close circle of friends (you know who you are) gives me the strength and support I need as I journey through my professional life.

Back to the tale.

To keep bringing in whatever money I could, I got a print agent and started doing some modeling work. I did a couple of print jobs when I was in Indy but never pursued modeling seriously. I'm not a model. But if people want to pay me to take photos in their clothes or with their products, I'm open to the opportunity. Elimu and I modeled a little for a designer named K-Bobby for a minute. We never got paid but had fun and practiced runway walking, learned modeling poses and things, and did a couple of events modeling some clothes he designed. Nothing major came from it. I did meet some great people, including my dear friend Ahyoung Kim Stobar, founder of JOAH LOVE, the fantastic kid's clothing line that she launched in 2008. I'm grateful for the new family, lifelong friendships and what I learned about modeling. At one point, I got a little inspired and wanted to see if I could get a rep to find me gigs. I worked with an agent named Robert at DZA (Deena Ziglar Associates). I did one or two small gigs and the biggest came for me when I was added to a Tommy Hilfiger campaign. Robert told me the campaign would spotlight the relatives of famous people. He didn't say I would be with entertainment royalty. In the ad I was featured in were Kate Hudson (Goldie Hawn and Kurt Russell's daughter), Kidada Jones and Quincy Jones III (QD3, Quincy Jones' kids), Jesse Wood (Ron Wood's son (Rolling Stones)), the grandson of the owner of the Baltimore Orioles and a couple of other celebrity's family members (I forget who they were because we didn't talk much). I was included because my grandfather was Wes Montgomery (the only job I've ever gotten because of my connection to Grandpa Wes). I had a blast on the shoot, but also felt out of place. The difference between me and all the others was that all of their family members were influential, around and wealthy. Grandpa Wes was incredibly influential but he wasn't around and we weren't wealthy. Far from it. I needed the money from that shoot to survive, but of course, I never let anyone know. But the deeper feeling that came up for me during the shoot was excitement for the other participants that they still had their family members and got to know and love them, but a simultaneous sadness for myself that I didn't get to meet Grandpa Wes. Grandpa Wes died three years before I was born, so I only got to know and love him through my family and other people who loved and admired him and his work. At the time, I didn't know why I felt a little off, but figured it out years later. Hoping to learn more about Grandpa Wes, I produced a documentary - *Wes Montgomery: The Price of Genius* - in which I was fortunate to interview some of the people who knew him (including grandma) and people who worked with him (like Dr. David Baker, former Distinguished Professor of Music and Chairman Emeritus of the Jazz Department at the Indiana University School of Music - Rest in Paradise, Dr. Baker). At the Hilfiger shoot, no one ever made me feel uncomfortable, though. What I felt were my own insecurities and feelings of lack and loss. Everybody was super cool, especially Kate (she was really sweet), QD3 (my guy! a down-to-earth, chill brother), and Jesse (who, along with his dad, was a big fan of Grandpa Wes'). They were all good people. Admittedly, I had to stop myself from looking/staring at Kidada because she was so beautiful. There was no way I was going to embarrass myself trying to talk to her. I wasn't on her level. I had nothing to offer her. But if I had been in a different situation when we met, I definitely would've asked her out. It was my first time in that circumstance and I hadn't become who I am now, who I will become, but I instantly knew there are levels to this thing we call celebrity. I'm grateful to have been part of that campaign. I got a small glimpse of the elite fashion world. Coming off the high of the shoot, I hoped the business wouldn't be that difficult to break into because I booked the Hilfiger ad within a couple of months of being in California. And, again, I wasn't even a model.

Wishful thinking.

I didn't book my next job for about five months. I was broker than broke. Growing up poor in Indy made me no stranger to poverty, but with the cost of living in LA, I felt like I was more destitute than I had ever been. I was behind in rent for two months, owed for utilities, and had no money to live day-to-day. My desperation caused me to take the job I regret the most in my career. I did one of those movies that aired late on what we used to call "Skinemax." I acted like I wasn't bothered and kept up the appearance that I was okay, but I was ashamed of myself for taking that job. I felt like I let down myself, my mother and my whole family. I never told my family how hard up I was for money when I took the job. Part of me hoped they would never see it, but deep down I figured they probably would. It was what it was. I wasn't selling drugs or doing anything illegal. I was in a shitty movie. I did two scenes: one where I worked at some art gallery; and one where I was part of a woman's fantasy sequence as a dancer in a dance studio where she was a ballerina. I had to wear a t-back and do a simulated sex scene with the woman. It was corny. I made the best out of the experience, but I felt dirty while I was doing it. I got paid $250 ($125/day for the two days I worked, one scene each day). I knew I would never do a film like that again. Years later, a guy I had taken an acting class with tried to change my mind because he had become a sensation doing those kinds of movies. He excitedly told me about how much money he was making and how much I stood to make. Nope. I remembered how I felt those two days. And, subconsciously, every day after (until therapy, which didn't come until years later). No amount of money was worth the low I felt. I will never allow myself to feel like that again. I was happy for my classmate who was able to find success for himself because shows like those do have a place and market for people who love them, but they're not for me. I'm grateful, though. That project let me know where my floor was in this business, the low point for myself I would never go beyond, a low I would never repeat in my career. Ever. That experience also put into perspective for me what kind of belief my manager at the time had in me as an actor. I knew a representative's job was to find work for their clients, but the level of work I aspired to was so much higher than that kind of job. My manager shouldn't have presented it as an option in the first place. No matter what job was brought to me after that one, I never forgot that's what was thought of me. I dreamt dreams that were bigger than the kid from Indiana could fathom. I dreamt of winning an Oscar one day. If my rep wasn't aligned with building my career to be Oscar-worthy, then they should never have been my representation in the first place. If a rep doesn't believe in me like I believe in me, then they shouldn't f*ck with me. Being broke and feeling desolate, I took a job I should never have taken, a job I should never have even considered. End of the day, it's my life and my career. That's an "L" I have to live with. Lessons learned.

I've had a couple of different commercial agents but have only booked four commercials in my career. Before I left the Midwest, I did a regional "Futon Shop" spot in Indiana where I just danced, a voice-over for a Finish Line spot (which got me Taft-Hartleyed, giving me thirty more days to do non-union work), then a national "Gatorade" spot in LA playing the Boxer's Friend (since it was a SAG commercial I had to join the union) and a "Miller Genuine Draft" spot that I received a holding fee for but was never featured in the actual commercial. A holding fee is the amount paid to the actor for the right to use their likeness in promotion of a company's product for a set period of time. After that time runs out, the actor must be paid again for additional cycles if the company wants to continue running the commercial. I haven't done any others. It's not easy to break into the commercial market. I didn't realize how much hard work goes into making commercials that have the mass appeal that advertisers crave. I learned from some friends that commercials can be very lucrative when you can get the work, but I've never found my groove in that medium.

Eventually, Jeff moved out of the apartment to go do missionary work. Time passed and one day Adam told me he was moving out to go live with some of his fraternity brothers from college. I loved living alone for the first time since moving to California. The best part was having my own space to go through my challenges. No one was there to see me always behind in all my bills. "Robbing Peter to pay Paul," as they say. I held out for as long as I could but LA is so costly, I got another roommate, Marc. Marc was a good guy but after he moved out, I was determined to live alone until I got married one day. I stayed in the North Hollywood apartment for nearly twenty years. The longest I have ever lived in one place. Thank God for rent-controlled buildings. I'll always be grateful to the former building owner's son (Jason) for not kicking me out over the years, even when acting work was non-existent and I fell more than four months behind with rent on multiple occasions. I always got caught up, but I was late most of the time, incurring late fees by the day. He wanted his money and he probably hated giving me the extensions, but he always did it. He was truly a Godsend. When I booked *Enterprise*, I still lived there and usually paid my rent six months in advance the whole time I was on the show. I wanted him to collect the interest that my money was earning in the bank. My small way of saying thanks for holding me down.

I got back into doing stand-up comedy for a little while when I made it to California and got up at a few different locations. I did a couple of sets at The Belly Room of the legendary The Comedy Store on Sunset, a space comics used to break new material. I just worked on the material a couple of times. I also did a 6-minute set at a place called Luna Park. It was a nice intimate setting where the crowd was right next to the stage. I loved the energy of that space. I also waited in line at The Laugh Factory one day for 12 hours to have the chance to be added to the Open Mic list. For consideration, all the comics had to sit outside the venue all day and keep their place in line to be allotted three minutes. I did it once and never again. I loved doing standup, but I didn't want to be a comedian that bad. I realized that fact that day. I was only there because I knew comedians sometimes got acting jobs. By then, I had been around so many comedians that I was tired of having to constantly "be on." It seemed like every comic I was around was always telling jokes, or their conversations were made up of set-ups and punchlines. I got tired of feeling like I needed to have a joke as a response, ready to go. I wasn't that funny all the time and it got to be too stressful. I stopped worrying about being the funniest on the block and learned from the vets around me. I was fortunate to work with some hilarious people who didn't get the comedy spotlight that others did. Like Jan Bartlett, who was the funniest and sweetest woman I met on the comedy circuit. She was the nicest person to me and everyone who knew her. And a real pro. Her timing was great, her sets were always solid and funny. I always wished a comedy Exec would give her a shot. There were so many funny, funny people like Jan who never got the call to the majors. I didn't want to pursue comedy like they did, but I did love doing it. My last show was for a set that I didn't even make it to. I had scheduled to do 20 minutes on stage at The Comedy Store. It was going to be on the Main Stage and more of a variety show with me doing a comedy set, a skit with a guy who was bringing a live chicken (yup, a *live* chicken), and ending with me doing a live performance of a hip-hop song I wrote with my guys Dakari and Southstar. It would've been a showcase for me. I had a song written called "Midwest to Wild West" specifically to end the show. But I wasn't ready for it. I had talked about doing the show but didn't write any jokes or put in enough rehearsals to get the performance solid. I wasn't ready and I knew it. From an ego point of view, I believed that because I was good with a crowd, I would be able to just "wing it." I didn't understand the enormity of the task I was taking on and I got overwhelmed by the weight of the moment. I canceled at the last minute, hours before we were supposed to be there. I'm sure the people who were working with me were pissed. I understood. I would've felt the same way. I did feel terrible about the people I let down, especially the cool guy who was bringing the chicken for our skit. I let myself down most of all. I felt bad but I didn't feel like my comedy set mattered enough for anyone to care if the show was canceled. My comic career wasn't big. I felt like I could cancel the show and do it another time since I was paying for the space. That situation revealed the magnitude of what it will mean to carry a successful brand on my back. Back then, I wasn't ready for that honor. I was still figuring out my voice and was only focused on working as an actor. I never thought about running a company like Montgomery Media or building the Anthony Montgomery Brand. I didn't understand what launching a brand even looked like. I told myself to just focus on getting acting work, giving my all for every job, letting my work speak for me and having that be the foundation of my brand building. I believed doing comedy would help that process. I'll never know. I haven't done a comedy set since then. Although, the comic is still in me somewhere.

After decades of going to appointments, I have to be honest, I hate the audition process. I'm not special in that because a lot of actors do. But it's necessary. Auditioning is typically an essential part of securing acting jobs, but it is my least favorite part and always has been. I hate it because they will never see my best, never see what I'm fully capable of from an audition tape or in the room while I'm auditioning. I love acting, but no matter how much I ground myself and tell myself that it doesn't matter, there's always a level of need or wanting to get the job on a subconscious level. Because of that, after I have already booked the job, there is a magic that happens when I'm on set and free, knowing the job is mine and all I have to do is play, which will never be achieved in an audition. That's when the magic happens. I imagine that's true for many actors. When actors are just getting started, auditioning is the only way to build fans in various casting offices. If you're fortunate and become known over time, then you could be requested and take meetings for projects, but not in the beginning. I learned that an actor has to make the casting director and their office fans of the actor's work. That happens by going in and doing good, solid work, over and over again. Sometimes you book the job, but most of the time you don't. But you've got to keep showing up. And if it's an off day, which every actor has, the process is not always indicative of an actor's ability. Some auditions I felt great about and got callbacks or booked jobs, and others I felt great and didn't hear anything. Sometimes I just stunk up the room. Those were the ones I used to sit in my car and replay over in my head. I was always the hardest on myself when I didn't do my best in the audition. I can live with not booking a job because that's part of the game. Every job isn't for everyone, as they say. As long as I knew I gave my all in the room, I walked away with my head held high. Sometimes, I would have a bad audition and still get a callback. That was always confusing. And some auditions just haunted me. Like my most embarrassing audition with Overbrook Entertainment. My rep told me Jada Pinkett Smith would be at the audition. I thought it'd be cool if I got a chance to see her. They were casting a funny new series with a security guard. I got the material and did my preparation before I went in for the audition. I felt solid about the choices I made and was ready to go in and show them what I could do. I didn't know that Jada would be sitting in the room, but when I walked in, there she was. That threw me. She's not only cool as hell, she's also fine as wine. There was also another guy of importance sitting beside Jada, who may have been the director, I'm not sure. Anyway, I didn't ground myself enough after seeing Jada and just launched into the material. It felt okay, at first, but I was never really in the moment. I delivered a line that made Jada laugh and I immediately came out of the scene and got into my head. "I made Jada laugh," I thought to myself. And at that moment I knew that the rest of the audition was lost. I went up on the material, forgot where I was in the scene, and labored my way to the end. Jada was really sweet and kept a pleasant look on her face, but never said anything. I was so bad trying to remember the dialogue that the guy next to Jada said, "You know, you can look at your sides." I dismissed the idea. "No, no, I've got it." I didn't have it. Not even close. I got it in my head that I needed to finish what I had prepared, even though that wasn't going to happen. It was awful. I was down on myself for that audition because showing up for someone like Jada Pinkett Smith could've changed my life. I didn't use the fuel of the moment to make me better. I didn't show up in that audition because I made my intention about doing the scene to impress Jada, rather than being in the scene and bringing the work to life. Had I done that, she may or may not have been impressed, but she would have been able to see the real me. Because I focused on the wrong thing, Jada never got to see what I'm capable of as an artist. I held on to that disappointment for a long time, years. I released that letdown eventually. After many years of auditions, I got to a place of acceptance and understanding about the casting process. I understood that booking a project for an actor is rarely just about an actor's skill level, or whether or not they have a great audition. Many factors go into the decision to cast someone, and the actor cannot control most of them. The only thing an actor can control is their preparation and presentation of the material. My job as the actor is to make specific, honest choices and give the most truthful representation I am capable of. Unfortunately, knowing what to do and the execution didn't always sync up for me and I botched a lot of auditions. But, like every artist out there who loves their craft, I kept going. Sometimes my auditions went well and it worked out in my favor.

To keep giving myself as many opportunities to act as I could, and because I was so broke, to see if I could get some additional money coming in, I started taking acting workshops with Steve Nave. Rest in Paradise. Steve was an actor who began and ran a successful side business connecting actors with people who needed actors (agents, managers, casting directors, etc.). At first, I was skeptical about the idea of taking a class where I paid to meet casting directors or others in the business. Truthfully, I didn't know exactly how Hollywood worked, but I assumed I would get to meet casting people for free at some point anyway, so why pay? However, I learned that workshops are a more intimate setting for casting directors and industry personnel to get to know actors, a setting that may not occur during the typical casting process. I put my doubts aside and jumped in. I had a pretty decent success rate with the workshops. I took six workshops and booked four jobs through them. One of the jobs was an infomercial (it was either for a psychic line or a dating service, I forget). Whatever it was, I thought it was cheesy but I made $500 for the shoot, a couple hours of work. $26 for the workshop made a good return on my money. The best job I got was through casting director Chemin Bernard. Chemin brought me in for the series she was casting and after auditioning for it, I booked a guest-starring role on *J.A.G.* (*Judge Advocate General*). My twenty-six-dollar investment yielded me almost $9000 when I filmed the episode. I was amazed. I had never made money like that. That one gig paid for all my other workshops combined. Bear in mind that I didn't get to keep all of it because of taxes (of course), then my manager took 15% off the top and my agent took 10% (and reps get their fees based on pretax money). I was still grateful for the job. More importantly for me with that particular gig was that it was a good role, too. It was a very powerful storyline that saw my character in the middle of a difficult situation with his military buddies. I learned a lot on that show. I enjoyed working with David James Elliot and Catherine Bell and seeing how they carried the show.

I had a good streak going but I stopped attending workshops so much because I started feeling like I was going to burn out on them. I did keep auditioning the regular way, of course. I was fortunate to book co-starring roles on *Charmed*, *Frasier*, and the Showtime original series, *Resurrection Blvd*. *Frasier* was very special to me because I got to work with Kelsey Grammer and David Hyde Pierce. I only had one line, "Here's your wine, sir," but I had a wonderful experience and learned a lot on set. Kelsey, David, and the whole cast were very warm and welcoming. One of the kindest things anyone has ever said to me on set was by Jane Leeves, who plays Daphne. One time, after hearing me deliver my line in our scene, she pulled me aside and told me I would "be a star." I smiled and said, "Why do you say that? How can you tell? I only had one line." Without missing a beat, she said, "You can tell in one line. You have *it*. And you're going to be a star." And she smiled warmly at me. I smiled and said thank you. I hoped she was right.

Sometime that same year, I filmed my first lead in a feature film. It was the fifth installment in the *Leprechaun* franchise, *Leprechaun in the Hood*. I hadn't seen the other movies but I remembered Jennifer Aniston was in the first movie, *Leprechaun*. I also remember not wanting to do that audition at all. I didn't put a lot of work into the sides and didn't care whether I got the job or not. I did the audition, I just didn't stress about it. And I booked the job. I had an indifferent attitude about it at first, but I warmed up to the idea. I was happy to get the chance to be a lead in a film. There were different production issues to deal with, but we worked through them. I met some good people and learned a lot. I also still had a lot to learn about acting. Too often I was in my head watching a scene and judging it while I was filming, instead of being fully present in the moment. Elimu and I wrote a song for it, "King of the World." I didn't know anything about placement deals or publishing rights so I just gave production the song to use in the film and they used the hook. It was a lot of fun filming opposite the man himself, Ice-T. He was the coolest guy. (Run with the pun, sorry) But he was. He dropped some knowledge about the business and his approach to it. It was great to work with a legend whose music I admired for so many years. I also enjoyed working with Warwick Davis. He was a nice guy with a beautiful family. After that experience, I learned to find something to appreciate about every acting opportunity I received.

One of my favorite jobs was when I was allowed to take over as the host of the children's show *Awesome Adventures*, when the current host at the time, J. August Richards, didn't want to do the show anymore. Initially, I was mad because I wasn't given a chance to vie for the job from the start. I learned from my producer that my manager at the time never presented me as an option to have a shot at the job. That never made sense to me because I thought managers and agents were supposed to submit all of their clients if the clients were right for a particular job. (I don't know the reason I was not included but I never forgot that. That was another instance where I felt like I was shown how I was valued. Or undervalued.) After I got hired, I stopped caring about how I got there and loved the adventures. I had a blast with my producers, Lauren and Tom, and our camera and sound guys. Our small production covered a lot of ground. That experience completely altered my myopic view of traveling. I had only been within our U.S. borders at that point. I got to go around to different locations all over the world and do incredible adventures with two young people between the ages of 12 and 17. I have run off mountains in Switzerland (paragliding), gone scuba diving in the South China Sea, walked on the Great Wall of China, ventured through a Costa Rican rainforest, enjoyed spelunking in London, as well as bungee jumping for the first time (off a bridge), made it to a jungle in Borneo, Malaysia and so much more, including getting to drive a stock car at the Pocono Raceway.

Pocono Raceway

Start your engine!

I experienced more than I ever thought I would be blessed to see in my life. The first time I left the United States, I went to Reykjavík, Iceland and hiked up a volcano and other fun activities. Another first I got to experience while doing that show was staying in Europe by myself. We filmed in Interlaken, Switzerland and I got to see the Swiss Alps firsthand: the Eiger, Mönch, and Jungfraujoch. We shot for four days in the Interlaken area. Visiting an ice cave and going dog sledding at 11,000 feet elevation were some of the highlights. I fell in love with the country and the kindness of the people. I stayed an extra eight days by myself after my crew returned to the US. I stayed five more days in Interlaken and then took a train to Amsterdam and stayed there for three days. Amsterdam was my first time staying in a hostel. I get the concept but I couldn't get a comfortable night's sleep with a bunch of strangers in the room. I haven't done it since. But I love traveling abroad.

While filming the adventure show, I was taken to Florida for an episode. I sat on an alligator, rode an air-prop boat and did other fun stuff. After work I hit the town. As a former dancer and music lover, I had a rule that I had to go out and experience the nightlife in every city I visited. One night, I went to a banging spot in Orlando that was called Baja Beach Club at the time. When I was in line, a guy who was standing to the side about to go in a VIP entrance and I struck up a conversation and he started telling me about the club and the scene. It was my guy Dakari. As we talked, he asked me where I was from and I said Indiana, now living in LA. I asked where he was from and he said Boston and that he had been living in Florida for awhile. I mentioned that one of my best friends in LA is from Boston and I've heard a lot about it, that I know he's a good dude if he's from there. He asked my friend's name, and I said Elimu. His eyes widened, "Elimu?" He said his first and last name, and not only did he know him, but they grew up in the same hometown. I called Elimu and we laughed about the degrees of separation. Elimu is one of the best human beings I know so if they came up together, I knew Dakari was a solid guy. We went inside the club and the games began. I didn't know it at the time but he was not only a cool dude, but also a dope music producer (having produced in the boy band era for groups like N-Sync, O-Town, LFO and others). He showed me around and we ended up hanging out with some cool people and having a night to remember. Dakari became like a brother to me and he encouraged me to keep rapping and produced six of the tracks on my first album, including the two with verses written by my guys Rodney Bailey (Smilez – "What You Know About") and Robert Campman (Southstar – "Midwest to Wild West").

My real Hollywood "Big Break" came when I landed a recurring role on the WB series *Popular*, created by Ryan Murphy. I'm forever grateful to Ryan, Greer Shepherd, and Michael Robbins for adding me to the *Popular* family and casting director Eric Dawson for seeing my potential and casting me. That was an incredible experience. To me, *Popular* was like an early version of *Glee*, Ryan's other fantastic award-winning series. I played high school football quarterback, George Auston, who fell in love with one of the main characters, Sam McPherson, played by the incredibly talented Carly Pope. I loved working on *Popular*. All the cast and crew were kind and embraced me as part of the show. But being that it was my first time recurring on a show, I didn't know where I fit in all the time. I had a bunch of insecurities. There's a cohesion that casts and crews form after starting a show and finding their workflow. I had never started a show or been on a show long enough to know that, but I could feel how close everyone was and how connected they were as a unit. I probably tried too hard to fit in at times, much like I did when I was a kid. No one ever said it, and everyone was great, but I know my energy can be a lot if you don't know me. The person who I probably connected the most with was Ron Lester. (Rest in Paradise, Ron) He was dealing with his own feelings of inadequacy and being accepted and he tried to help me adjust. I concentrated on doing my job. And I did. I got hired for four episodes and ended up filming eleven. I met some great people who I'm still friends with to this day. I even worked on one episode with my future *Enterprise* co-star Linda Park.

Working on *Popular*, I experienced a fun "Hollywood moment." One day, I got a call from my manager telling me that the stunningly beautiful R&B songstress Maya wanted to meet me. I was a fan of her music but had no idea she knew I was alive. Maya's reps called my reps one day and told them she saw me on *Popular* and was interested in me being her love interest in her video that was coming out at the time. We talked a few times on the phone but we stopped communicating. It ended when she asked me to fly from LA to NY and come see her the next day. I was an idiot and said I couldn't go. I wanted to go, of course. But I was broke. And she was a star. And drop-dead gorgeous. I know we would've hit it off but I couldn't afford to buy a plane ticket to see her, let alone pay for myself once I got there, not to mention treating her. I was too embarrassed to tell her that *Popular* was my first breakout gig and I didn't have the money to fly out there and ball outta control. I should've just told her the truth. But I didn't want to put my business out there and take the chance of her thinking I was a bum and blowing me off. I tried to save face and made up a lie that I had a meeting I couldn't get out of. She was sweet and understanding. I didn't learn until I had money, that when you have money and you have a meeting, almost every meeting can be rescheduled. If I had been in that financial position when she asked me to come see her, I would've been on a redeye that night and woken up in NYC, meeting her for breakfast with a rose. We stopped talking a few days later. I didn't end up being in her video, either. I blew that one. Fun memory though. She was cool on the phone. And sexy.

Acting was my main hustle but I was still doing what I had to do to make ends meet. I was also working at a market research company, recruiting people to come in, test, and report on different products. I worked as a security guard for Hilton Hotel making $35 a day on Saturdays and Sundays. I was also an emcee and DJ for Bar and Bat Mitzvahs. I had those jobs when I auditioned for *Star Trek: Enterprise*. After booking *Star Trek: Enterprise*, my world changed to a strange new world. I felt like a fortunate son. I finally didn't have to stress over money, at least not in the way I had my whole life. I made more in eight days (which was how long it took us to shoot an episode) than I had in almost a year of working random jobs. When money started coming, I had one major bill that I wanted to get rid of before anything else. Many statistics show how difficult it is for a lot of students (and former students) to erase college debts. I didn't want to join those statistics, and I was already falling behind on my payments. I didn't want my college finances hanging over my head. Once I worked enough and collected enough checks, I paid off my student loans in one lump sum. It was one of the proudest moments in my life. I paid off all my debts. I mean anyone I had ever borrowed a dollar from, or if it had taken me ten years to pay back what I owed, I made sure I didn't owe anyone on the planet. And I flew to Indy and gave grandma her $3000 back in person. For the first time in my life, I knew what it was like to be debt-free. As a man, as a Black man, it was the most liberated I have ever felt. Having my own money. I remember going to the Sherman Oaks Fashion Mall (where I had worked at a Structure clothing store at one point) and thinking, "I can buy anything in here I want." I slowly walked through Macy's and looked at everything that interested me, literally, everything. I didn't buy anything. I stood in the entrance coming from Macy's to the rest of the mall and just stared at which way to go. I walked from Macy's to Bloomingdales, from one end of the mall to the other, stopping along the way at all the stores I had always dreamed of splurging in and looked around: clothes, jewelry, gadgets (Brookstones). I looked at everything, no matter how expensive because I knew I could afford it. Once I made it to Bloomingdale's, I walked down the other side of the mall back to Macy's. Then I took the escalator to the 2nd level and did the same thing: Macy's to Bloomingdale's on one side, back to Macy's on the other side. The only thing I bought that day was a pair of socks. The knowledge that I could get my heart's desires was enough for me. All at once, I understood the true power of money. It gave me options. Options that a broke kid from Indiana never had, never knew were possible. What that moment also did for me was make me determined to keep money in my life so my family and I will always have options, and so will my family for years to come. I decided I would be the beginning of generational wealth for my family.

I kept that mindset, even though finally making money came with its own issues. I guess a lot of people thought I was suddenly rich when I got on Enterprise. I wasn't. I received paychecks. They were healthy paychecks, making more than I had ever made at one time, but still paychecks. But a lot of random people kept asking me for money. A guy contacted me out of the blue and told me he was my cousin and asked me to buy him a house. I thought it was a joke at first. I knew all the cousins I grew up with and had never heard of him, had never seen him at a family reunion. He used my grandmother's name when he called so I assumed he was legitimate, but I thought he was out of his mind for asking me to buy him a house. I made sure to help my immediate family as best I could and helped out a few friends, but then I started withdrawing and doing things alone when money requests got too overwhelming. I couldn't do too much helping anyway, since I was working to give myself stability. I stayed in the apartment and lived beneath my means so I could afford to do what I loved to do, which was to travel. And I did: Jamaica, Turks & Caicos, Canada, and any place I felt like visiting. If I was having a great time, I would always extend my stay for extra days, especially if I didn't have to get back to work.

Because my bills were paid - I was taking care of my financial responsibilities where my daughter was concerned and she was doing well, I was helping out my family and doing the right things with my money - I started living wild. I should've invested. I didn't. I went back to Vegas and the city took on a whole new meaning. I understood why people constantly fall in love with it. I took five figures and stayed in a suite at the MGM Grand Hotel, got excellent last-minute seats at Cirque du Soleil's "O" at the Bellagio (and eventually saw it again because the first time I was in the front row and didn't get to fully take in the spectacle, so I went back and watched from an optimum seat in the middle of the audience), had a ridiculously delicious and outrageously expensive steak dinner and then hit the strip clubs until the sun came up. I, unapologetically, had one of the most fabulous weekends of my life while I was in Vegas. I made my money legally and legitimately and since I had always wanted to live like the "rich and famous," I wasn't rich but I allowed myself to live like I was on those weekends. I did them a lot.

And much more.

Instead of investing, I blew over six figures the summer after my first season on *Enterprise*. I did silly, wasteful things. I would go to the airport and buy a last-minute, First-Class ticket whenever I wanted to fly. Whether I was going to Indiana to visit my daughter or a house I bought there, or meeting up with Dakari in Orlando for a wild weekend (or a week if I stayed longer). That summer I stayed with Dakari for about a month and we partied like rockstars. That's when I initially met Rodney Bailey and Robert Campman. I bought new clothes every time I needed something to wear. I never did laundry that summer. When I was ready to go back to LA, I shipped all my dirty clothes to my account and picked them up when I got back to the coast.

I gained my "legendary" status (so I'm told) one night in Miami when I paid a bar tab that was over five grand at a club called Mansion. I'm just gonna say I ended up running around with no shirt, cake everywhere, and a couple of bottles of overpriced liquor in each hand before the night was over. I got a small taste of what it must've been like for people like Jamie Foxx or Jay-Z, who have thrown some mind-blowing parties and covered tabs that were thousands more than I spent. It was an unforgettable and special feeling to bring that kind of happiness to a room of friends and strangers and a whole V.I.P. section of a bar. It was one for the books.

It was all fun until it was all done.

Please understand that I am not bragging about the money I spent. Quite the opposite. This is a cautionary revelation. Spending carelessly is also how I went several hundred thousand dollars in debt. I clawed for years to escape that hole. Between paying back everyone who believed in me and invested in me and then filing for bankruptcy when the money trouble kept piling on, I finally got back to zero debt. That was a new beginning. I'll never make those financial mistakes again. But I don't regret them, not for an instant. I do wish I was more financially responsible, but I was able to live out some real fantasies and dreams. Most people don't get a chance to live at a level like that. I also learned an inner strength I didn't know I had. I've seen too many unfortunate statistics showing a lot of people who took their own lives if they built up the kind of debt that I did. And believe me, it got dark. But since I started from the bottom and worked up to making more than two million dollars over four years, I came to the awakening and understanding that money is just money. Once I got that realization, I developed a different relationship with money. After squandering so much money, I knew I wanted to invest but I didn't want to just do traditional investments (stocks, bonds, IRAs, etc.). I didn't start an investment portfolio but looked for creative ways to diversify what I put my money towards. Going against the advice of people who didn't believe it was possible, I got it in my head that my investment for the future would be creating an IP (or multiple IPs) that would give great content, offer quality and rewarding entertainment and continually generate residual income over time, in perpetuity. I thought I could do that by taking the money I made from acting and making different investments. I knew I couldn't count on the stability of acting to amass enough wealth to pass down to my children. I thought outside the box. Because I know there are billions of dollars spent in the animation world with merchandising and other ancillary ways to make money, I made up my mind to launch an animation series and slate of intellectual properties. The biggest hurdle was, I had no idea how. And more importantly, I didn't have the money to fund an animated series. However, I was determined to not let my lack of experience and lack of funding stop me from reaching my goal. What I didn't know, I would learn along the way. Quality is quality. I believed as long as I offered a quality project with substance, an animation house or production company would see the financial possibilities and want to partner with me to get it to market. I was naïve but still pursued that course of action. It only takes one. Just like Seth MacFarlane got his one with *Family Guy*, I believed *Miles Away* would be my one.

I came up with the concept for *Miles Away* (which I originally called *M5*) back in 2001 while I was filming *Star Trek: Enterprise*. Being a huge fan of science fiction and growing up a fan of cartoons, I wanted to create an epic animated television series for our unbelievably supportive *Star Trek* fans, all the "Trekkies" around the world. Even though *Miles Away* isn't *Star Trek*, I've learned that Trekkies love quality sci-fi, even if it's not *Star Trek*-related. I wanted a cartoon I could one day turn into a live-action feature film franchise, like J.K. Rowlings has with Harry Potter. The idea for the graphic novel for *Miles Away* came later. I wanted a lot more than just a series. I wanted to create a unique animated indulgence that people around the world would fall in love with. One that would address real issues that everybody could relate to (and of course, issues that nobody could relate to). And I wanted it all to be entertaining.

I knew what I wanted but wasn't a writer at the time, so I had no idea how I would get it. I'm terrible at drawing, so with my work cut out for me, I put the idea away to develop it down the line. In 2002, I was introduced to Ugly Dolls co-creator, David Horvath. David is a terrific guy and after explaining my series idea to him, he created the first interpretation of what my animated series could look like. I thought David's drawings were excellent and fun, but felt the style didn't complement the vision I had in my head. So, again, I shelved the project until later.

Sometime between 2003 and 2004, I connected with my homie Ahyoung, who was the Vice President of Product Development for the Wayans Brothers' merchandising company. We talked about taking my I.P. (Intellectual Property) to the Wayans. Ahyoung was helping to produce Marlon Wayans' comic book at the time and their slate was too full to take on more projects.

Fast forward to 2006 when I filmed the lead role in a romantic comedy independent feature film. The Production Designer for the film was a very talented artist named Phillip Boute, Jr., who was still a student at Cal State Long Beach at the time. I talked to Phil about my series to see if he would be able to help bring my vision to life. He loved the concept and immediately started drawing. Because of his hectic school/work schedule and my having a very specific idea of how I wanted the series to look, it took more than a year for us to carve out the twenty concept characters that would be the cornerstones of my franchise.

In 2007, I contacted my friend Eric Vale (a fantastic voice artist - Trunks on *Dragon Ball Z*, Sanji on *One Piece*, Shaigaraki on *My Hero Acadamia* and so many others, who's also an excellent writer) about writing the pilot episode for my animated television series. I sent Eric material about the series and a list of some of the things I wanted in the script and he wrote the M5 spec script (a "speculative" screenplay to get the feel of a show). I did a rewrite of the pilot and was able to use it to help convey what I wanted the series to look like.

After getting all my artwork, designs, treatments, and scripts registered with the U.S. Copyrights Office and Writer's Guild of America (WGA), in 2007 I put together my version of a pitch book (a marketing tool used as a presentation of the material a person has to excite people about the idea) and began scheduling meetings with animation houses. Although I didn't have representation, based on my affiliation with *Star Trek: Enterprise*, I was able to meet with Warner Brothers Animation and Cartoon Network. Both companies thought I had a great idea and they said they liked my presentation, but neither moved forward with a development deal. WB was concentrating on the in-house properties they already owned and the Exec at CN told me my story was too similar to their existing hit show *Ben 10* (about a kid who finds an alien watch and can change into superhero alien characters). He said even the name of my show was too parallel, M5. I explained that granted, the title of my show was derived from my main character's name, Max, and an aspect of his super ability (it took 5 minutes for his power to manifest), hence, M5 - and I was willing to change the title if they wanted - but my premise was nothing like their show and that it was just coincidental that there were similarities. My hero owned a watch, of course, but he can't turn into aliens. My rebuttals didn't matter. He still passed on my series, but left the door open for me to pitch ideas in the future if I created other shows I thought would work for their network.

I didn't want too many companies saying no to my idea because in Hollywood that can spell doom for a project before it even gets off the ground, so once again I put the project aside to revisit later. But before I did, I made a significant change to the material. I changed the title from M5 to *Miles Away*. My meeting with CN made me think about the legal implications if my title was too similar to an existing IP and I didn't want any future companies to have the same feelings about my show in comparison to any others. The new title was justified: my main character is "Maxwell Miles" and since he would be traveling the universe, going light years from his home...*MILES AWAY* was born. This is also when I began thinking about *Miles Away* as a graphic novel. If I couldn't get people to see my vision of an animated series from a pitch, I figured seeing a comic might be easier to digest. I had taken a screenwriting intensive course and learned how to write feature films, so I decided to apply what I learned and write the book myself. Or at least attempt.

Several years before, I met J.Naugh-T! on the sci-fi convention circuit and we stayed in contact and eventually became friends. In 2009, I went to the San Diego Comic-Con (SDCC) to show support for an animated project he was attached to as a voice artist. J.Naugh-T! knew about my animated series and introduced me to Hollywood industry veteran, Ralph Farquhar. Ralph immediately saw my show's potential and gravitated to the story. Since I didn't have any representation at the time, Ralph agreed to introduce me to his literary agent, James Kellem. James signed me to his agency to champion my animated television series and told me, very bluntly, that he loved my idea but that I "suck at pitching." I laughed and didn't take it personally because I knew he was right. But I was passionate. And I wanted to get better. He explained the fundamental elements that go into a "good pitch" and I started practicing. For the next year, I honed my pitching skills on my own and would periodically practice with Ralph and James. I would also practice with my brother, Geoff Campbell, who was Vice President of Business Development for Sony Pictures at the time. Geoff is brilliant and helped me understand how my projects would be viewed from a financial aspect at the Executive level. His guidance helped me develop patience for how long the process could take to launch *Miles Away*.

But I wasn't deterred.

While attending Dragon Con in Atlanta in 2009, during a chance encounter, I met a professional artist named Brian Denham. After a short chat at our initial meeting, Brian and I talked the next day and following another brief conversation, exchanged contact information to keep in touch. Brian, who had worked for numerous powerhouse companies (including Image, DC, and Marvel), gave me advice on turning *Miles Away* into a graphic novel. He told me the realities of getting into the comic industry, about page rates, and a lot of general knowledge that was foreign to me regarding comics, marketing, and sales. I thanked him for his candor and we didn't talk again for a couple more years.

I attended SDCC 2010 as a guest for the first time (because of *Star Trek: Enterprise*) and as I was leaving, I met Brandon Easton who was a fan of my work, including my 2006 independent film. Brandon related to the film because he was (and is) a graphic novelist and so is my character in the film. After chatting about the film, we discussed a possible opportunity for me to participate in a graphic novel project he was planning to further develop. I loved the concept but my life was overwhelmed at the time and I knew I couldn't add more to my plate. Brandon understood but still wanted to send information about the project to my Facebook message folder. I explained that I didn't check my FB mail often, but he was welcome to shoot something there and I would get back to him. Brandon emailed me after the Comic Con but I didn't check my FB messages for nearly six months.

Once I felt I was ready, James set a meeting with Maggie Murphy, former Senior Vice President in charge of development at Cookie Jar Entertainment. I gave the best pitch of my life. Cookie Jar kept *Miles Away* for six weeks before finally passing. Ultimately, it came down to the fact that the company targeted a younger audience. Even though I got another rejection, I was encouraged because the feedback Maggie gave James was that I had given "one of the best pitches she had ever heard." With that positive momentum, we worked to set a meeting with Disney to see if Miles Away would be a good fit on one of their networks, preferably Disney XD. While we waited for the appointment, I continued to refine my pitch. I was also more determined to turn the project into a graphic novel.

Early in 2011, I checked my Facebook messages and came across the email Brandon had sent many months earlier. I replied to his message and said I was interested in talking about his project and that I wanted to talk about another possible collaboration. When we finally reconnected, Brandon told me about an awesome sci-fi adventure he had created and planned to do as a graphic novel. He wanted to base the main character on me. I said yes and questioned how far along he was with its development. He was still in the early stages of working out his concept so I suggested that we work on turning my material for *Miles Away* into a graphic novel since I was already so far along. After reviewing what I had, Brandon agreed and we became writing partners. Brandon was close to launching his first graphic novel, *Shadowlaw*, and told me about a talented artist named Jeff he had worked with and wanted me to meet about drawing *Miles Away*. Brandon, Jeff, and I met one afternoon at The Grove in Hollywood and Jeff showed me some of his artwork. I liked his work and we finalized the strategy for Jeff to draw the whole book. Brandon and I fleshed out notes about the direction for the book, and being a true graphic novelist, Brandon had great ideas about how to keep the readers engaged. Since I was new to writing and had no experience with writing comics, Brandon took our notes and went to work writing the script for the book. He sent me the draft pages and since I had learned to write scripts, I just followed Brandon's writing format and did the rewrites I felt were necessary. After the pages were sent back to Brandon to confirm that what I wrote worked in the story, I sent the pages to be drawn. We repeated this process and planned to continue until the book was complete. During that same time, we found the person to color the book: Dawnsen. Dawnsen is a talented colorist from Canada who also worked with Brandon on *Shadowlaw*. Unfortunately, the plan didn't pan out. Jeff worked on *Miles Away* for about 5 months and finished the first 25 pages of the 96 total pages, but then took other work so I was forced to search for another artist to complete the remaining pages.

The Disney meeting finally came. Ralph and I went (James was unavailable) and I gave a better pitch than the one before. However, although they agreed that I had a solid project, I was informed that Disney had just spent more than four billion dollars acquiring the Marvel Universe catalog. I was told that even though my story may be different, there were certainly some similar characters, with similar abilities, within the 5000+ characters in their new database. I had to agree. I didn't meet with an Exec, but the Executive Assistant we met gave a couple of notes to help me target my pitch even more: 1) Play up the "impending invasion" I mentioned during my presentation because it would enhance the sense of urgency for the hero to have to go to the alien world to stop the invasion before it got to his home world, and 2) It wouldn't be a bad idea to specifically target 9-12 years old boys, because all of the networks were trying to create programming to reach that demographic with minimal success. His suggestions were things that were already part of my overall package, so his notes were easy to implement. I didn't have to change what I already created, I just had to highlight particular elements differently in my presentation.

I told Brandon about my meeting with Disney and said we were going to make some adjustments to *Miles Away*. We would play up the invasion more and reach the 9-12 years old male demographic, instead of Max going on his quest with only the two alien refugees (which the representative thought was a fun element for sci-fi fans in general), we would add his best friend (who was already part of the original story) to the mix, and make it more of a "superhero buddy adventure." These adjustments were easy to make and the writing continued.

As I was looking for an artist to help finish the graphic novel, Brian Denham happened to Tweet congratulations to me for the 10th anniversary of *Star Trek: Enterprise*. So much time had passed, I didn't immediately remember him, but I checked out his web page and asked if he would be willing and able to help me complete my book. Brian reminded me of our previous correspondence and I remembered him instantly. He informed me that with his schedule and workload, he didn't have time to work on my book but that he had the perfect person to help. He made an email introduction with Jonathan Mullins (professionally known as Jey Odin), a talented artist who was in college in Savannah, Georgia. Jonathan had a great drawing style that complimented my existing pages for *Miles Away*. Since I didn't want to start over, after a lot of back and forth during the collaboration, we found a solid "Americanized" drawing style that worked perfectly. Because I needed a colorist also (having lost my previous one), Jonathan introduced me to his roommate/best friend, Rashad Doucet, who was a SCAD (Savannah College of Art and Design) graduate and who had colored for the likes of DC and Oni Press. It was divine intervention how it all came together.

I told Brandon that I planned to put together a "preview book" before my next pitch meeting. This book would also serve as an introduction to publishing houses to see if I could get them to publish my full graphic novel. I tasked my agent with getting me meetings at the publishing companies. I was hoping Image Comics would publish *Miles Away* because I loved what they had done with Robert Kirkman's *The Walking Dead* and *Invincible.* One of Image's requirements is that when a project changes artists there needs to be at least 5 pages of artwork from the new artists included with the submission. Brandon and I gave Jonathan the next round of pages to draw and had him concentrate on the first five pages so I could have my preview book generated. While the pencils, inks, and colors were being done, Brandon told me about a website to find a person to letter the book. After receiving proposals from several prospects, I was fortunate to find a terrific letterer named Adam Pruett, who had already worked professionally for many large publishing companies, including Image Comics. I was really proud of my team and our preview book when it was finished. It took me back to the fun times reading comic books as a kid. It was wild to have a book in my hands that was mine.

After several months, feeling certain I had all the elements required for my series to be embraced and with my preview book in hand, I had my agent schedule another meeting with CN. It had been more than four years since I pitched to their network and I believed I would be able to get them to take on *Miles Away*. I learned that the Exec I met with originally was still at the company, but a new person was in charge of securing properties. My agent and I met with the Manager in charge of the Action Adventure Original Series and his associate. The meeting went great. The CN Exec confirmed that the big animation houses were, indeed, trying to reach the 9-12 years old male audience and *Miles Away* could be a great fit. There was one hitch though. CN had already done an adventure series called *Generator Rex* that didn't do as well as they had hoped, so they were looking for shows that were more like *Phineas and Ferb* or *Danny Phantom*, shows that began with a scenario that sends the heroes (and audience) on an adventure that concludes by the end of the show. *Miles Away* is more of an epic adventure that will play out over a long period (three seasons), more of a series like *Star Wars: Clone Wars.* After keeping the preview book for two weeks and talking to the various decision makers at CN, the CN Exec got back to me and said they would pass but (since the animation industry is cyclical) wanted to revisit the idea in nine months to a year.

I am eternally optimistic but I was discouraged that CN had passed again. I was also frustrated that my agent wasn't able to set up any meetings with publishing companies or secure some sort of distribution deal for my graphic novel. I decided to take *Miles Away* out on my own and find a literary agent who specialized in my form of book. I thanked James for all his efforts and took my project to continue the journey by myself. I submitted to the major distributors on my own. Shortly after leaving my agency, with no representation, for my IP or theatrically, I prayed that the right opportunities for *Miles Away* would present themselves.

I continued to promote the *Miles Away* graphic novel and franchise. I already had copies of my preview book printed and wanted to keep getting the word out to the masses. I attended WonderCon in Anaheim, where I did a "soft launch" to introduce my universe to the general public. I also attended SDCC 2012, where I met a well-connected industry Exec. After seeing the potential for *Miles Away*, he offered to help me see my vision to completion. We discussed the need for me to get voice talent attached to the animated series. Planning to assemble an "All-Star" cast, I thought it would be a fun idea to have Star Trek alums from every television series represented in *Miles Away* so I reached out to former Star Trek actors to see if they wanted to be involved. Scott Bakula (*Star Trek: Enterprise*), Marina Sirtis (*Star Trek: The Next Generation*) and Garrett Wang (*Star Trek: Voyager*) were the first people to say yes. Garrett was the very first person. (Of course, I'm going to have roles for my whole *Enterprise* cast.) A few months later, I attended the Creation Entertainment run Star Trek Las Vegas convention where I sold 337 copies of the Preview Book to the 421 people we counted who came to get an autograph from me. I got fantastic feedback from core Star Trek fans who loved the book and were eager for the full book to be released. I also spoke to Robert Picardo (*Star Trek: Voyager*) about participating in *Miles Away*. Robert was on board. After getting great responses from the Star Trek alum, I decided to approach Nichelle Nichols and George Takei (*Star Trek: The Original Series*), Nichelle said yes, George said no, and Jonathan Frakes, Brent Spiner, and Michael Dorn (*Star Trek: The Next Generation*), all said yes. By the time I stopped getting actors and others interested in voicing roles in the series, I had 64 terrific talents, and not all of them Star Trek actors. We have a couple of Harry Potter actors and a variety of other creatives who agreed to join the *Miles Away* universe as voice actors. But I still needed someone to fund the animation or buy and produce the series so I could get people to work. The Exec talked about a lot of things but never produced any results, and never connected us with anyone who would greenlight the property. I got frustrated and stopped working with the Exec.

I got back to going at it on my own.

I wasn't getting any responses from the major distributors I had solicited, so I reached out to the few people I knew in the comic industry. My prayer was answered. Brian revealed to me that he worked for Antarctic Press, a small but very respected publishing company in the comic industry, and would present my preview book to his publisher. Brian also reached out to one of his contacts at IDW on my behalf and the response was that they couldn't even take a look at *Miles Away* for more than a year because they were overbooked with projects for a couple of years. After a week or so, Brian told me his publisher liked *Miles Away* and agreed to distribute it for me. Brian relayed that Antarctic Press was a rarity in comics because they could get a project on the stands within months of thinking of it. That kind of flexibility allowed them the opportunity to navigate to the impulses of the comic audiences. The only catch was that they didn't have any money to complete the book or for marketing or promotion so that would be left up to me. I didn't have the money needed to make it a huge success, but I just needed to get the book done so I could use it to promote the animation. I knew getting the word out would be a challenge because I'm known as an actor, not as a graphic novelist, but I wanted to take advantage of the blessing I had received, so I accepted the offer from Antarctic Press. In the end, including all the mistakes I made during the process and paying for things I didn't need, I ended up spending more than I should've to get the book complete. I paid a competitive rate for 96 pages of full-color story, plus the amount it cost me for all the errors (and lessons). I count the additional money as the cost of my education in comic production.

I left out a lot of information that would've made the tale even longer, but that's the story of how the *Miles Away* graphic novel came to be. It hasn't been turned into a series yet, but the book was optioned by Oscar-winning company, Lion Forge Animation. They partnered me with their Senior Development Editor and we took the foundation of what I created and based the series on a different entry point into my Miles Away Universe. Lion Forge wasn't able to turn it into an animated series or secure any sort of production deal, so I got the rights back and kept working to get the series made. I had no idea when I started the process that I would have to go down as many winding roads as I did to get the book complete. My ignorance was probably a good thing, too. If I had known I would have to deal with a lot of the issues that were coming and spend as much money as I did, I probably would not have done it. I loved and needed comics when I was younger, but as I got older I lost my connection with them. As an adult, I don't have enough of an interest in comics that I would've wanted to jump into that, oftentimes, scattered world. That said, I'm grateful I had the experience. I learned a lot about the process and now I know how to create my own if I ever get the urge to do a comic again.

After the second season of *Enterprise*, I was a little smarter and more responsible with my money. I didn't know a lot about Wall Street, but I began investing in a few stocks. Since I wasn't being used very much on *Enterprise* and I wasn't feeling creatively fulfilled, I produced and starred in a play I wanted to do in college called *Dutchman* by LeRoi Jones. I loved learning how to produce a play. It was great gaining the knowledge of how to launch a production and what goes into it. I added to the knowledge I gained from my plays in college. Producing the play was stressful, as many shows can be, but it felt like second nature bringing the production to life. I found another level for me to move through with my art.

While I was on *Enterprise,* I filmed an episode of *Half & Half,* starring Essence Atkins and Rachel True. That was my first time in a situation where I got work based on meeting the person in charge and not getting an appointment from my representative. I was at a UPN event and met and interacted with the cast of the show, along with Executive Producer and writer, Yvette Lee Bowser. Yvette was amazing and they were all the coolest, kindest, and most wonderful group of people. We laughed our butts off that night and Yvette said, "I want you on my show!" I responded that I would love to, of course. She told me she would set it up and we parted ways. That had never happened to me so I wasn't sure if she would do what she said or if she was just talking because we were at the event and in the moment. #funfact I never felt comfortable "networking" when I was placed in situations where I needed to. I didn't know how to network. I knew how to meet people and have a connection. If we could create something magical for the world and make some money together, hopefully, we would get to work on that. But I never learned the gamesmanship or art of networking. And sometimes when I'm around people who are obviously doing their version of networking, it feels like they're trying to get over on you. It's just a feeling. I didn't feel like my time with the cast of *Half & Half* was networking. I felt like I had met some wonderful people who I wanted to have a chance to work with. I felt like we had an authentic interaction and I remained hopeful. True to her word, Yvette came through. A short time later I was brought in for *"The Big Keep Your Eyes Off My Prize Episode."* I played Congressman Ron Brown. The Prize. I had an absolute blast. Every single person made me feel like I was a part of the family. (Years later, Valarie Pettiford played my mother in a project and Chico Benymon and I got cooler when we played in the Entertainment Flag Football League he co-founded.) *Half & Half* was a wonderful home-away-from-home and learning experience. I realized how hard doing sitcoms is and gained even more respect and admiration for the cast, writers, and other creatives who've mastered that area of comedy. I'll always be grateful to Yvette for giving me the opportunity.

The only other time I booked work that way (circumventing representation) was when I filmed an episode of *Boomtown* starring Donnie Wahlberg. Donnie is from Boston and knows my boy Dakari because Dakari was friends with Donnie's brothers. Dakari told Donnie about me as an actor and Donnie got me the audition. I prepared well, went in and felt comfortable in the room. I booked the job. When I saw Donnie on set, I thanked him for the opportunity and he made it a point to tell me that although he got the audition, I was the one who booked the job. He said I did a great job in the audition and earned it myself. With my feelings about auditions, I've always appreciated him for saying that.

When *Star Trek: Enterprise* ended, I was optimistic that I would work right away, but I didn't. The Writer's strike made all the work dry up. The next opportunity I received for consistent acting work didn't come for a couple of years when I tested against Flex Alexander for *Nice Girls Don't Get the Corner Office*. I felt great about my audition but the studios went with Flex. It had been two years since I landed a job and when I didn't book the series, my agent dropped me. I was pissed. I felt discarded. I had never been dropped because I didn't make money. I couldn't wait to book something to make them regret giving up on me. But I didn't have a rep to find me work opportunities and I didn't book any acting work again for several years.

During the downtime, I got married and had my prince. I kept doing what I needed to do to provide for my family. I got to a low point when I couldn't find any work. I was stifled creatively and financially everything was gone. My savings, my stock options, everything. I had used my resources to maintain the life I had built. That was a very costly mistake, to say the least. A lack of money was the root of almost every argument in my home. To prove to my ex-wife that I would do whatever I had to for my family, I started waiting tables again at Chili's in Encino. (During that time, I considered going into the restaurant management program.) I rode my motorcycle to work to save on gas. Going back to Chili's, I felt like I wasn't good enough. Especially when I would get recognized for being on *Enterprise*. It didn't happen all the time, but it happened enough. The guests would look confused at who they were seeing, wondering if I was really who they thought I was, then get excited about meeting me, "You're Travis Mayweather!" I tried to keep a poker face and not let them see how I was feeling. I'd respond, "Welcome to Chili's. What would you like to drink?" It tore me up inside. It shouldn't have bothered me, especially with all the people out there who can't find jobs. But it did bother me. I was embarrassed to be waiting tables again. To save face, I made up a lie that I was doing research for a role I was about to do. People believed it and would usually not ask me any more questions. I would feel like shit at night, though. On top of every other feeling of inadequacy, I felt pathetic for feeling the need to lie to people I would never see again, just because I hated where I was in my life. I didn't sleep most nights. While waiting tables again, I had a major setback at the beginning of April when I was in a motorcycle accident. I was fortunate to only come away with a few scars, but my bike was totaled. That forced us down to one car and I had to take the bus to get to work at Chili's so my ex-wife could drive the SUV. I felt worthless. I thought about the course of my life riding on those buses. I went from being broke as a child to always living paycheck to paycheck with a bunch of random jobs (waiting tables being the one I spent the most time doing), to making more money by getting on television (still living check to check but the checks were a little bigger), to making the most I had ever made in my life while on *Star Trek: Enterprise*, making over two million dollars over four years and still living paycheck to not having to live paycheck to paycheck for the first time, to frivolously spending (and not growing my business), until I found myself living off my savings, until the savings ran out, to having to get another "regular job" (working at Chili's waiting tables again) to bring money in and make ends meet, which still weren't meeting, all while still pursuing my acting career. Because I felt alone in the marriage, I always carried the weight of the world with me. I knew all the trials I survived made me stronger, and were making me stronger, but I still felt completely defeated and insignificant. I knew I was not being my best. And my need for artistic expression kept me moving forward.

I've had different agents and managers over the years.

I had a terrific personal manager Adam W. at Thruline Entertainment. I should have stayed with them and followed the plan that Adam and I laid out, but it was taking time for us to build my acting career and I got impatient. The biggest career mistake I made was leaving that management company because I was enticed by the idea of doing music again and working with Jackie Chan. And I handled the situation terribly. I just walked into Adam one day and told him I was interested in doing something else and I was going to leave to go work on music. Adam was surprised and tried to get me to pause and think about what I was doing. But I had my heart and mind set that I wanted to do music (and I was led to believe I would work with Jackie). But I'm not sure Jackie even knew about it. My next rep, David, had a partnership with Jackie at the time because of a successful music venture they had launched together. David presented a lot of grand possibilities to me like I would be able to become an international talent in the Chinese film market and globally because of the relationship he had already established with Jackie. He knew I had an album and loved making music, so we talked about me doing a similar music venture to the one he did with Jackie, as well as me being in a Jackie Chan film and *that* being the bridge to introduce me to the Asian market and the rest of the world. I was lured away from Thruline because I saw how partnering with Jackie Chan launched Chris Tucker's career. I wanted that. I wasn't a comedian like Chris, but I'm an actor and a true martial artist. Granted, I wasn't close to being on Jackie's level, but I knew Jackie and I would make a great franchise of films, whatever we came up with. It sounded like a good strategy, so I went with it. Ultimately, David was a good guy and he had good intentions, but he didn't have any real artist management experience, and none of the opportunities he proposed to me ever manifested into any kind of job. And I never met Jackie Chan. When no jobs were produced, I stopped working with David. I took the lesson to stay on my course. Like Adam once told me, F.O.C.U.S. – Follow One Course Until Success (I don't know where he heard that but I loved it and never forgot.) After that pivot, I got my focus back on my acting.

But, again, I couldn't find any representation for a long time.

After some time away from the industry, I returned to acting. I landed the lead role of Jay Brooks in the independent feature film, *I'm Through with White Girls*, written by Courtney Lilly. The project was led by an intelligent, skilled, and driven up-and-coming director named Jennifer Sharp, whose vision was to make sure the film had more depth than typical urban projects. I wanted my character to have more levels than what we usually saw in those types of films and Jennifer agreed. Jennifer and I worked many nights to massage the script and work out moments for nuance. I really enjoyed finding Jay's quirks and moments of growth. It was a fun Rom-Com with heart. My only real problem with the whole project was the title. Courtney is a fantastic writer and I loved the script, but I hated the title of the film. I felt like it was racially divisive, even if it did make people laugh. I know how some people can be and I never wanted to be put in any uncomfortable situations if someone couldn't separate a film from reality. Maybe no one would have seen it and no one would have cared. I didn't know. And I didn't want to take the chance. I felt so strongly that I told production I wouldn't be in the film unless the title was changed. I was virtually a nobody in Hollywood and they may have felt like "Who the f*ck does he think he is?" but no one ever said anything. They came up with different title ideas and changed it. But even though the new title was more reflective of the film itself, it was not better than the original title. It wasn't funny. I was hoping for a title that was funny, but non-race-related. They couldn't come up with one. I didn't want to make the film suffer in any way, so I talked with Courtney about it and he explained that he came up with the title at a concert he attended. He thought it would be a funny title for a film. That's it. Our straight conversation helped me put my concerns aside. I didn't know Courtney, but from what I learned of him, he was a wonderful person with a beautiful family. So when we talked, I was okay to change the title back to the original. I prepared myself to deal with any issues if they came up. I just hoped the public would give the film a chance to see its merit. It was a shocking title that got your attention, yes, but when you break the film down, it's not about race. It's about a quirky, neurotic guy who was figuring out how to evolve and be a better person. He kept breaking up with girls he dated before they had a chance to break up with him. And he was black. He blamed his serial breakup history on the race differences because all the girls were White. He had to grow up. That's not about race, that's about maturity. Everybody can relate to that. That was my thinking, anyway. Working with producer Lia Johnson, who was also my co-star and championed the film along with her twin sister, Phyllis, we were able to create a special film. Lamman Rucker and Ryan Alosio played my best friends in the film and became my brothers in real life. Our Romantic Comedy received ten awards on the film festival circuit, including seven Audience Awards for Best Narrative Feature Film, before being acquired by Image Entertainment for national distribution. I hoped to show people I had range as an actor because of the atypical character I created, but the momentum from that project didn't move the industry needle for me. Still, I'm proud to have been a part of a quality indie film.

At some point, I auditioned for *Criminal Minds*. I loved the show but wasn't in a good space to audition. I had been going through with the divorce for years, splitting time between California and Texas, and was emotionally spent. It broke my spirit every time I had to get on a plane and leave my prince. I would have to stay in California so I could be available for opportunities because I couldn't afford to fly back very often. Sometimes two or three months at a time. At first, I stayed in Texas for months at a time, but my agents made sure I knew that as an actor, if you're "out of the loop," as they say, for long periods, you're quickly forgotten. It hurt but I stayed in LA more than Texas. The day of my audition, my prince was in Texas with his mom and I found out earlier that day that he had his first performance in front of people and I couldn't be there. It broke me down to not be able to support him. I took the pain I was going through and channeled it into the scene between a man and his family member. I don't remember if it was a brother, father, or son but they had a powerful exchange and I got emotional as I confronted the situation. I didn't book the job but that appointment stayed with me. I remember it because Joe Montegna was in the room. I was surprised because when I finished, Joe stood up, shook my hand and complimented the work I had just done. A sincere compliment. I could feel his appreciation and respect for my talent. That had never happened before, or since. I love and admire Joe's terrific body of work and I felt honored that he took the time to recognize me for mine. I felt like I had been acknowledged by a peer in a peer group I was still aspiring to reach. I was bummed when I didn't book the job but the exchange with Joe has never left me. His encouragement added fuel to the fire for acting that burned inside me. I may not have gotten that role, but I knew I was on my course and believed the right job would show up for me sooner or later.

While making my way back to acting, I pursued a different artistic interest and released my debut Hip Hop album, *"A.T"*. I learned a lot of really important lessons from people in the music business. Music can be cutthroat. Music can be underhanded. I got cheated out of $4500 by being too nice and paying a producer for beats upfront. He said he needed payment for the beats and because I was working to build a good reputation for myself as an upstanding businessman, I paid him all the money in advance. He let me hear some tracks that he already had (like a lot of producers do) but when I wasn't feeling any of them, he said he would craft some beats for me to check out. At first, he would call and give me updates on when the beats would be ready for me to get them, but then I heard from him less and less. He stopped all communication and I never heard from him again. He never gave me the beats or my money back. I was pissed at myself for getting beat out of forty-five hundred bucks. I only trusted him because he was a friend and business partner of someone else I knew, someone I was close to like a brother. That's one of the hard lessons I had to go through learning about the music industry. I loved recording songs in the studio, actually making the music, writing songs, and collaborating with other artists and engineers. But all the extra garbage that goes with it? You can miss me with all of it. While doing music, I missed dealing with the simplicity of being an actor: auditioning, negotiating, signing a contract, putting in work on my script, going to work, and doing my job. With music, there always seemed to be all of these different elements added to the production that weren't presented initially, but I was still forced to deal with them. It was draining. And sitting in meetings with guys who spent most of the time having ego contests about what they had done in the music business, became monotonous, and for me, very boring. I was only in the rooms because I brought a degree of celebrity in the rooms with me (that's what I was told once). Even if none of the attendees had seen our series or were fans of Star Trek (and there were usually at least two or three who were), they all still knew what Star Trek is and what it represents, so I was embraced. I appreciated the love and getting to know the people, but I could've done without a lot of the theatrics during their presentations. However, I'm grateful for those meetings. Because I love music and love performing, I soaked up what I could use and decided to ignore the things that bothered me about the music business. I'll focus on making the best music I can every time I get a chance to create. Completing my album was a private accomplishment that I was happy to have achieved. It was interesting to learn that my album makes me the first actor in the Star Trek franchise to release music in the Hip Hop genre. I wish that #funfact came with a check or some sort of monetary compensation, but it's a cute piece of useless information. *A.T* was distributed internationally through Universal Music Group, via my German-based record label, AGR Television Records. That was an interesting period. The representative from the company was a nice guy and reached out to me to see if I was interested in them distributing my album internationally. I was. I've always wanted to tour and perform overseas, but I didn't know how to do that. They said they would plug me into their existing pipeline and I would start promoting the album. I said yes, I was in. I wasn't crazy about the deal because they weren't offering to pay to complete the album, I had to do that. They essentially wanted to put it out once it was finished. It would've been nice if they had helped produce the album, but looking on the bright side, with me paying, I got to maintain ownership of all my original music. I heard about artists fighting to own their masters for years. I never had to worry about that.

I own all my masters. I paid for beats from different music producers, paid everyone for their time and services, paid for all my studio time to record, and paid to get it mixed and mastered. Combined with what I spent for the original demo EP, I ended up spending a lot to complete the first album. As an artist who had no track record and no sales, no label would have spent that on me. I'm glad I invested in myself. AGR pressed up copies of the album and told me they were promoting it internationally. I have no reason to doubt them, but I don't know what they did and didn't do regarding promotion because I was never overseas to verify anything. The report they gave me was that I got a grade of "B" from the outlets where they promoted it. As much as I wanted to, I never got to Germany or anywhere internationally to promote my album, (other than performing my tracks at conventions sometimes, and that was mostly in the US). I did get some favorable reviews from a couple of German publicity outlets. I'm not sure but I believe the label got turned off to me when I asked them to fly me First Class to promote the album. I was told by some people who had record deals that I should ask for what I wanted and be open to negotiating down. Ultimately, I just wanted them to set up a lot of shows for me to perform and promote the album, and build a Hip Hop career for me internationally. Then bring the success home to the U.S. I would've taken a coach seat on Virgin Airlines as long as they were booking venues. Instead of talking with me about anything, they eventually stopped communicating. The album never got a real promotion and didn't do anything more. I never promoted *A.T* in the U.S. because I thought we were going to do it as a unit with me as part of the Universal machine. I was enlightened to the fact that Universal Music Group's domestic division is not the same as its international counterpart. I wasn't part of Universal Music Group. I was disappointed because I believed if Universal had heard my music, seen what I have to offer and put their marketing and publicity network behind me, we would've made an impact together. As it was, I paid for the experience I gained working in music. I learned much later that I didn't have to spend the kind of money I originally spent for beats and other services to finish my album. Some of the people I dealt with charged me higher prices because they knew I had some celebrity. I didn't know I was being charged extra until the album was done. It was an expensive lesson but I wouldn't call it a waste of money. I never got my return on that investment, but I got something much more. I got an education in the music business and didn't have to impact anyone other than myself and the people I chose to deal with on my musical journey. The knowledge I gained was worth what I spent. I learned how to make records and make an album. I learned to maneuver in rooms with powerful people where I was previously uncomfortable. I used to talk with my guys about doing an album back in the day, but I never knew how I would get one done. But I got it done.

I got back to acting and over a few years, I landed guest starring roles on *NCIS*, *House*, and *The Client List* and had a great time filming with Eric McCormack and Tom Cavanagh on the TNT original series, *Trust Me*. Those few yeses came years apart but kept giving me periodic fuel with confirmations that I was still on the right path. I persevered through the nos.

A major break burst through the walls of rejection as a cloud of opportunity when I landed a role in the Queen Latifah-produced, Made-for-Television Movie, *Single Ladies*. The project was done as a pilot presentation and aired on VH1. *Single Ladies* was the first scripted programming for the VH1 network. It was also the first job I had landed in years. And we were expecting our son, so the pressures at home were at their highest. I took the job because the due date was months away, I wasn't supposed to be gone filming in Atlanta very long and I was going to make okay money that we needed. I'm grateful for the opportunity but I wish I hadn't taken it. My prince came two months early and I wasn't able to be there because of filming. I was absent at our child's birth causing a deep rift with my ex-wife. Productions can replace actors if the actors affect the shooting process and filming costs. I never told production because I needed the work to hopefully help reignite my career. Stacy Littlejohn, series creator, and showrunner, who is an awesome human being, brilliant creative mind, and cool-ass person, and who will always have my gratitude, brought me back when *Single Ladies* was ordered to series. I reprised my role of Darryl Jenkins as a recurring character, playing opposite Charity Shea, Lisa Raye McCoy, and Stacey Dash. During the series, I heard the music supervisor talking about them needing music for the show so I got with my guys and recorded a club banger, *Stimulation*. It was my first real placement. I heard it playing behind one of the scenes and it felt great. I had never done a video of my own but I wanted something to accompany the song. So, we shot a video and it debuted on VH1.com. Doing *Stimulation* gave me a chance to do music and just have some fun. I produced the video with Darryl "Treez" Turner, who also produced the beat. Treez knew I wanted something to move the crowd and went to work, and came up with some heat. I was directed by Life Garland, who also edited my video. (Life won a VMA for editing Chamillionaire's *Ridin' Dirty* video; also edited *Get Low* by Yin Yang Twins. He's a BEAST!) Life is one of my close friends, so it was a blast getting to work with him. I shared the stage and spotlight with J. Naugh-T!, who's a prolific lyricist and singer in his own right (treat yourself to his joint *Hair Down* feat. Phantom Boss. It's a banger! He's also a new member of the group AZ Yet!). J. Naugh-T! helped me arrange my lyrics on the song and showed me how to use my full voice on the track. I was fortunate to have his voice and support. Recording *Stimulation* with, and having it engineered by, my brother Myke Smith was the perfect environment for me to get back in the music flow. Myke is a mastermind engineer with an excellent ear for music who works behind the scenes for American Idol. But he's also produced over 200 albums. His production abilities, engineering expertise and vast knowledge of the business part of music allow me to be completely comfortable and relaxed when I record with him. We always have fun and make magic.

Sometime in 2011, I landed a role on *General Hospital*. I had fun. It was a one-day role as a guy brought on to help get one of the characters off the show so she could go shoot a feature film. I don't remember much about my character though. I think he was an ex-boyfriend or something who came back into the picture.

A couple more years passed and I wanted to take my career into my own hands. I felt it was time to produce a project of my own. Easier said than done with no money and no investors, but I looked at it logically. To show I can be a box office draw and that I can carry a film, then I have to actually be given the opportunity to be a lead. But the Hollywood Execs who have the final say don't usually give actors the lead if they haven't been proven as a bankable commodity. But how can I prove to you I'm a bankable commodity if you don't give me the chance to do it? Catch 22. I knew that if I want the decision makers to recognize me and truly consider me a leading man, then I have to show them. My friend Eric Vale had written a suspense thriller called *Chariot*, about seven people who wake up aboard a moving airplane with no idea how they got there or where they are going. When Eric told me about the script, I told him I wanted us to produce it together and for me to star as the lead, Cole Weathers. Eric had already been working with his friend Brad Osborne, who was our other producing partner and director. We didn't have any money but we were fortunate to fund our film through crowdfunding with Indiegogo. Thank you to all the contributors, with a special shout out to Simon M. who showed up as the last donor. Without his sizable contribution, we wouldn't have made it over the finish line just before time ran out on our campaign. Thank you, Simon! Although our film was a high concept and we were independent filmmakers, other elements were already aligned for the project to move forward once production money was in place. Brad worked for a company that had part of a plane (fuselage and cockpit area) on its back lot and they were about to have it removed. He got permission from his bosses for us to shoot our film before it was carted away. Since our location was already locked, once we had funding, each of us got to work with our respective responsibilities. I became laser focused on bringing the role to life and leading our cast. I enjoyed transforming myself into a different character for that part. Cole was a truck driver from Beaumont, Texas. I'm not known for doing accents in my work but I've practiced with a couple of them. A long time ago, I came up with my version of a southern/country twang and adapted that for Cole. I grew out my hair and beard for about four months and kept dropping into the character until I found where he lived. Eric also worked as producer and handled all the day-to-day production activities with the rest of our team. Brad had to come up with creative ways to film in one location and make it look like we had a full, functioning plane. And he did it. We did it. We had a wonderful cast and crew who all gave their hearts to make *Chariot* a success. We dealt with some issues while filming (all productions encounter their own sets of challenges), but despite the problems we faced, we had the best time shooting our movie in Texas. We finished our film and were then forced to tackle our biggest grievance, a distribution company who stole our money. Our film was distributed but to get what we were owed, we had to weather the storm of their lies and deceit, plus hire a lawyer - and we still never received the full compensation they stole from us. Besides the distribution nightmare, as a creative, I am grateful I learned how to produce films. Along with our team, I've proven that as long as I can get the financing secured, I will always be able to bring an idea from conception to completion.

To keep building interest in *Miles Away*, and to keep making money to supplement my income while I was looking for more acting work, I used my appearances at different sci-fi conventions as a book tour to visit multiple cities around the United States and globally in places like England, Australia, Germany, and Spain. I called it the Miles Away World Tour. As a person doing it by myself, I was able to sell about 1200 graphic novels and build awareness. That's not a lot for most investors, but I was building a grassroots effort. And since I paid for everything, I was happy. Fans were excited and receptive to supporting a fun new franchise. But I couldn't find anyone who would invest. Most of the possible investors would say they loved the idea but they were always working on three or four ventures of their own, "low-hanging fruit" as they called them, so they didn't have any free capital to invest in *Miles Away*. Which I understood, even though I hated hearing it. Each of those rejections hurt but they energized me to keep pushing to find the right partnership for *Miles Away*. If J.K. Rowling could do it, so could I.

After months of no work and no auditions, I booked a job on the ABC Family series *Baby Daddy* where I guest-starred opposite comedy veteran Melissa Peterman. What a fantastic experience. Melissa is BRILLIANT and such an amazing person. Her comedic timing is incredible. It was so much fun being a part of the magic they made on the show. The entire cast was incredibly kind and welcoming.

Experiences like that don't happen all the time. Too often, it's just a grind.

There came a time when I hit my breaking point in dealing with the bullshit of the industry. I had already struggled through the business for more than ten years, part of that time dealing with a divorce without letting anyone know. I had already paid my dues. I was already known around the world, not superstar level but I was much more than a novice to the game. It didn't matter. I auditioned for a role and was led to believe the job was mine - I didn't assume, I was told by the show's writer/creator that I got the part and my reps began negotiating the contract - but the role was still given to another actor. I learned a painful truth about the industry. I learned that even if you're told a job is yours, it's not real and the work is not secured until you've signed the contract and you're on set filming. Anything prior to that is just talk. Without paperwork and actually making it to set and working, no actor "has a job." I wanted that one. Bad. I needed it. Losing that one made me sick, and made me want to walk away from acting for good. When I originally auditioned for the role, I believed it would be a game-changer for me. I felt it when I read the script. I didn't remember there ever having been a show like it before. I wasn't thinking about awards or any accolades. I could see the potential to have a long run with a successful and impactful representation on screen. The writer/creator is a great writer and with all the source material at his disposal, I believed the series would find a really supportive fan base. I knew the fans would love it. I could see the possibilities. But I didn't want to get ahead of myself. I had to get the job first. I focused on carving out my character so he was undeniable when I was in the room for the audition. Part of the casting team was a producing partner who helped with the audition session, and who is a seasoned acting coach. Also in the room was the writer/ creator. I had a great connection with everyone and a solid audition. I felt it. I did my job. I won the room and felt like I gave myself a real chance to win the part. My feelings were confirmed when the writer/creator told me I booked the role. I was very proud of myself because when the time came, I met my moment during the audition and delivered. And it was a job that I truly desired. I could tell the show would be big. I was most excited about the opportunity because I had never been allowed to carry a series before. I was already established before auditioning and had already been a series regular on *Star Trek: Enterprise*, but our Trek series focused more on other characters. I was ecstatic to get my shot at having a more prominent leading role. I was looking forward to doing solid work and creating a compelling character with a great cast, and finally showing Execs, filmmakers and decision-makers in the industry that not only do I have quality acting chops, but I'm also a bankable commodity. I felt like I would finally be seen. I had already prepared and I was ready for the chance to do what I do.

But before the contract was completed and we were able to get started, I was informed by the writer/creator that the project was being put on hold while business elements were worked out behind the scenes. In the meantime, they wanted to get something filmed by the end of that year, so I was given a supporting role in a different project based on successful source material. We filmed the movie and I portrayed a character that I had never gotten a chance to play. I'm grateful I got to expand myself as an actor. I enjoyed the work, but because I was holding onto the possibilities of the other show, I was still looking forward to bringing my role in the postponed project to life. I was already breaking down the script, considering choices to approach each scene, and getting inside my creative process. I planned to be ready when the call came to film. Time moved on and while the production kept dealing with whatever was going on behind the scenes, I went on to find other work. Acting opportunities were slow again for a long time. The production team for the postponed project hadn't come back about that project yet, but they contacted me again for a supporting role in a different independent feature film they were doing, based on other established source material. I had a blast filming the new movie and working with the production team again. We finished filming the new project and, still being hopeful, I waited again for the postponed project to go into production. I continued auditioning. The fact is because there was no contractual deal in place, I should never have believed that the job in the postponed project was mine. That said, up until that point in my career, I had never been told by the creator of a show (who was also one of the people funding the project) that the job was mine. I optimistically believed, and based my anticipation on what I was told.

Another turn on the Daytime television landscape was presented when, after a series of auditions, I went back to *General Hospital* playing a different character than my previous time on the show. I landed a Contract Role as Dr. Andre Maddox, an expert psychiatrist and government profiler. (Read Chapter 12 – "Damage" – to learn about my experiences on the Soap Opera.) During part of my time on *GH*, I was feeling creatively stifled because I wasn't being used very much. I also wasn't making enough money. So I kept auditioning to see if I could find other work on my off days. Although I didn't have a contract, I was still patiently waiting for the postponed project to come back around. One day, I saw something on social media that stopped me cold. I read a post from an actor who posted about being happy to be filming his new project in New York City, and he named the postponed project I was waiting to start production and hashtagged the character I believed I had booked and had been waiting on. I called my agent and asked what was going on, if she had heard anything, if anyone from the production had contacted her. What my agent thinks might have happened is that the production called checking my availability, but didn't name the specific project. My agent told production that I was on *GH* at the time. When I called my agent, and asked specifically about the postponed project, she may have just not put the two inquiries together. My agent told me agents don't typically notify the talent about availability checks (since they don't always pan out). I wasn't aware of that at the time. Back then, I was completely confused. And started to resent an industry and process that I couldn't seem to overcome, even when I gave my best and was led to believe my best was good enough. Because I was already working, it lessened the pain a little but it still hurt. I was thinking beyond the project I was on. Actors never know how long a show will last or how long they will be on a show. Once I was taken off contract from *GH,* after having received an

Emmy nomination with them (more about that in "Damage"), having to get back auditioning again, I thought about not getting the role in the postponed project and my mind started filling with frustrating thoughts of my place in Hollywood, or lack thereof. I was the most disappointed because during my time on *GH* I had more than enough available time to film something else. A studio or network can make allowances for actors to work on multiple shows if they choose to, but there are factors to consider. Most importantly, it's at the discretion of the studio or network and Exec Producer if they want to let an actor work on anything outside of their production. Contractually, they have the right to say no if the material, tone of show or role is too similar, even if the actor has availability in their schedule. Granted, it does present scheduling complications, but it is possible. Because the two shows were not remotely similar and Dr. Maddox was nothing like the postponed character, coupled with the fact that I had a great working relationship with our Exec Producer Frank Valentini, I believe he may have allowed me to film the other show, especially since my participation would never have interfered with my time on *GH*. Unfortunately, I wasn't given the opportunity to find out. When I found out the postponed project was in production without me, I felt overlooked again. The team at the production company are good people and I have a great relationship with all of them, so I didn't believe they excluded me intentionally. When I finally asked why the show moved on without me, I wasn't told about scheduling conflicts. I was told it was the network that made them replace me. I figured that was possibly the case. I know how the game goes. The other actor they went with is already established with their core fans and has a higher social media presence (which matters in the new climate of the business), and for their own reasons the distributors liked the other actor better for their bottom line. Honestly, the reason why the role was given to someone else didn't matter to me, because the fact remained - the role was given to someone else. The artist at my core was shattered. I had done the right thing, given my all and that still wasn't enough. And my spirit was tired of being skipped over. I contemplated walking away from it all. I sat quietly and thought about quitting the industry for good. I had some career-examining conversations with God. Grateful for everything I had experienced and accomplished, I told God if I was supposed to keep acting, I needed Him to let me know. But I didn't quiet my spirit to hear God's answer. I stayed in my head and tried to work through it myself. I thought maybe it was time to build a different career in another state and move on to the next chapter.

Until I got God's answer, I kept going. Parts of my mind wondered...

Following more long stretches of not getting work, I landed a recurring role as attorney Elliot Garner on the OWN (Oprah Winfrey Network) drama *Greenleaf*. I loved being reunited with my Brother Keith David, as well as my Brother Lamman Rucker. Keith, Lamman, fabulous

Merle Dandridge, remarkable Lynn Whitfield, and the rest of the cast and crew were awesome and made me feel welcome, like I was part of the family and had worked with them the whole time. It was a great homecoming, even though I had never been on their sets. But, just like with many gigs in Hollywood, the job was short-lived. My character was not written back into the show before the series ended. I was fine with that, it happens. But I hoped to finally be on Oprah's radar to establish a relationship with her and work with her and Harpo Productions. Part of me was hoping Oprah would recognize my work and put the word out about me as "one to watch," and maybe name me as one of her "Favorite Things." Or people. I just want to be one of her favorites. But not so I can receive, so we can give. There are some fun Reading Initiatives I want to launch in conjunction with my animation projects, once the animation gets moving. I haven't heard from anyone at Harpo Productions, yet. Maybe they didn't see the episodes.

Back to auditioning.

After a long time of trying hard but not booking, an opportunity was presented for me to put my energy and talent behind a very worthy cause. I was at a point in my life where I was tired of being thought of as secondary. I felt like I didn't matter and I started asking myself why I persisted if I knew I might never get the kind of opportunity I hoped I would. Why? An independent feature film that I was a part of, one that didn't get a lot of fanfare, put everything into perspective for me. It answered the why. That film was *Lost Girls: Angie's Story*, the story of a young girl lured away from her family and sex-trafficked, directed by filmmaker Julia Verdin. I portrayed Detective Chase Dawson, a cop who fights to save young girls who have been trafficked. Think Benson and Stabler from *Law & Order: SVU*. I was brought on the project when my buddy and fellow actor Amin Joseph had a scheduling conflict and wasn't available to play the role of Detective Dawson. I learned what the film was about and met the director. I was inspired by her passion for wanting to use her gift of storytelling to help girls and women in trouble. Understanding the importance of the subject matter, I was proud to add my voice to bring awareness to the need to end child sex trafficking. Being the father of a daughter and son myself, empathizing with victims of the horrendous things happening to girls and boys, women and men all over our country and all over the globe, was a stark reminder that there are problems in the world bigger than what I was worried about. That project showed me why I persevere. I believe it was God giving me the answers I was looking for. Even when I have periods when I feel low, He was showing me that the work I do as an artist is *necessary*, and that I do matter. It reminded me that my artistic purpose is greater than just being part of a project simply because I like the role, or hoping for financial freedom, career advancement, or whatever other reasons I gave meaning to. I'm using my artistry to make a difference and to help bring positive change in the world. It reminded me that my work is not done. I am an actor. I am an artist. I am an entertainer. I am creative. I love what I do. I do my best to make this world a little better by doing what I love. I can't fix everything, but I'll do what I can. I have faith that God will bring the perfect opportunities to me, perfect acting roles, perfect projects, and perfect partnerships to help me on my quest to help others. The different situations will be mine and God will elevate my visibility to where it needs to be. And no one will take away what He has for me. It all became clear to me and I had to keep walking in my purpose. I had to keep acting.

So, I pressed on.

Another chance to be on Oprah's radar came when I got an opportunity to film my first holiday movie, *Carole's Christmas*, about an overworked businesswoman (Carole Jordan, played by the phenomenal woman, wonderful human being and fiercely talented leading lady Kimberly Elise) who gets more than she bargained for when she wishes she had an alternate life. I play Marcus Jordan, Kimberly's husband in the film. The film aired on OWN during the 2019 holiday season as part of their festive yuletide line-up. The crew and cast, including the incredibly hilarious Jackeè Harry (who I had a crush on for years) were an absolute blast to work with. We were shepherded by director Dave Costa, who was gracious and gave me some directorial insights into his process for making a holiday movie in a short period. I'm grateful to have learned a few new skills to add to my filmmaking knowledge. I look forward to making another holiday movie someday, even making my own one day.

No, I have not met Oprah. Yet.

Out of the blue, the postponed project came back around and offered me a different role. Because I understand that in this business (just like in life) nothing is guaranteed or promised, I appreciated being remembered and accepted the offer. Work begets work. I'm grateful to writer/creator Carl Weber for birthing the novel and creating such an exciting world for us to play in with his New York Times Best Selling Series *The Family Business*. I'm grateful to ND Brown, Trey Haley, Veronica Nichols and the rest of my Tri Destined family (including all the fantastic crew!) for continually making it a wonderful filming experience and always creating a loving and supportive environment. I'm also grateful to Carl and his former producing partner, Tracey Moore, for giving me a chance to be seen. Even though things didn't work out for me to be there in the beginning, Carl and Tracey initially saw my potential and wanted to cast me. Without them seeing my value, I would never have been blessed with the opportunity to join *Carl Weber's The Family Business* as Brother Elijah.

Continuing the grind, I drove Uber when I had to bring in money. For it to be a job that wasn't acting, I enjoyed the freedom of driving my car, setting my schedule, and being my boss. I did it sparingly at first because I was concerned that someone would see me and have something to say. (I was recognized a few times, but most people were so in their own world that they never gave me a second thought.) But I worried about it for a long time. Yup, I was in my ego. But I needed money so ego be damned, I worked when I needed to work. I based my driving time on what bill I needed to pay and when I needed to pay it. I worked as little as a couple of hours a day, to the most I ever worked, which was 11.5 hours in one day. They only let you work 12 hours before making the drivers take a break (for safety reasons). I made okay money but not enough to fully cover my expenses, and I got tired of being in my car all day. My ass hurt after a while. I would get out, stretch, grab food, and keep working until I hit my goal for the day. It supplemented my income so I was grateful for the opportunity. I knew that even if I didn't like it, I could be anywhere and get a job driving Uber to support myself and my family.

I revealed this little glimpse into my acting journey because some fans wanted to know about the business and my contributions to it. I have a unique perspective because I'm in the industry, not the industry. I wanted to show that the road has not been easy. But I love it and have found my purpose. It requires commitment and sacrifice. It doesn't matter if it's easy or not. The difference we make will make all the difference. We are going to make a real difference in the world. All things considered, I still thank God for the ultimate joy I get in knowing I beat the odds and that I am a working actor in Hollywood. My job is to act. That's pretty awesome.

My Hollywood journey continues.

I've come to many realizations about the business over the years. I've heard the adage "It's harder to get in than to stay in." Well, for me in Hollywood, it's been harder to stay in than it was to get in (and yes, it was unbelievably hard to get in). It's gaming. Masqueraded gaming on another level. Despite the outward appearances, I find that many in Hollywood don't always stand together unless it benefits them. A lot of people talk unity, but don't walk unity. They preach togetherness, but it's usually lip service or sound bites for social media. Unless you're embraced into the fold, most people have to spectate and hope to get a chance. A good friend of mine has been trying for years to get me cast in different productions she's worked on that I've auditioned for as their lead actor, or even as a costar, roles I was perfect for, roles I was better suited for than the choice they went with. None of that mattered and none of those jobs ever materialized. And it's not because of my lack of talent. My friend has discovered some pretty terrific talents, so if she gave me her seal of approval, the decision-makers only needed to listen to her suggestion, as they had with those other great careers she helped launch. I'm not naïve about how it works. As I touched on, Execs make productions go with their "proven" actors, or actors whose careers they want to make skyrocket. From a business side, I get it (to a degree). But from an artist's standpoint, it f*cking sucks. That formula bugs the hell out of me because it feels like it doesn't always factor in the untapped and undiscovered raw and refined talent that's out there. I know I'm talented and I work hard at my craft. I believe I meet the Hollywood criteria, I have the physical attributes and as people have told me for years, "The camera loves you." Yet, I'm not elevated to be *the* guy, not given a shot to take pole position. Not even in the Black community. It doesn't matter how many times my reps are told that I was "close" to booking the job, if they don't choose me to be the guy, close doesn't matter. I don't know what it's going to take for the Execs to greenlight me. All I can do is be me, keep doing solid work and stay ready in case they want to rock with the brand I'm building. In truth, in the past I've struggled with knowing what my brand should be. The bottom line is that my brand will be based on substance and truth: truth of character and truth of intent. When people see me, I want them to see my artistry and quality work as an artist, no matter what genre or format I play in.

But success in Hollywood isn't just defined by the art. I've found the best way to express industry success is with financial stability. Artistry will always be most important to me, but artistry isn't a priority in business. And it's not about color, even though it can feel like it most of the time. As with any business, Hollywood is about money. For a creative person, Hollywood is about selling something: your talent, your knowledge, your idea, your script, your collaboration, yourself. For a decision-maker like an Executive, it's about finding the least-risk/greatest-reward financial asset that has the possibility of making the most money. I figured out the key for me to thrive in the industry game is to maintain my integrity and sell myself and quality products, without selling my soul. I have strived to let my work and work ethic speak for me. In doing that, I will fulfill my personal goal to be a quality addition to every set I'm on, always put out a top tier product and make a positive impact in the world. And importantly for those who value the bottom line, the people I work with will make a lot of money.

I've learned everyone's road to Hollywood is different. At the end of the day, it's up to each of us to decide who we are and who we want to be. I define who I am. If I don't, others will try to define me for me. Never let someone else define you.

CHAPTER TEN
UNEXPECTED

Anthony Montgomery - Ensign Travis Mayweather
(Photo appears courtesy of Paramount Pictures)

I discovered *Star Trek* as a kid during the reruns of *The Original Series*. I didn't always understand the episodes, but I always enjoyed them when I saw them. I could always feel there was something special about the series. When I got older, I understood what it is about *Star Trek* that I love, but as a kid I just knew I liked the show. It was interesting and fun. It sparked different things in my imagination. Captain Kirk and Mr. Spock were my favorites.

While a man of great emotion, Kirk usually had everything under control. Spock was the voice of reason—always calm and collected when things got hectic. I absolutely loved that Lt. Uhura was a constant presence as a bridge officer, and she could communicate with the aliens. The idea that a Black woman could be assigned such a position was always fascinating to me—nevermind the fact that I also had a crush on her. She was stunningly beautiful, smart, strong and the crew relied on her. I loved that Dr. McCoy was gruff but also dedicated to the crew. Left on their own, Sulu and Chekov could always handle the situation. Finally, Scotty could get their ship out of almost any predicament.

One of the biggest things that stuck with me the most was the characters' reaction to Uhura. Everyone on the show, human or alien, always treated Uhura with respect. The color of her skin didn't matter—she just belonged and was judged on her own merits alone. They never treated her the way I was treated as a black person in Indianapolis, or the way I saw a lot of other black people treated. I didn't fully comprehend what I was seeing on Star Trek but there was something inside me that questioned why I and the black people I saw day-to-day in Indy couldn't be treated with the same care and love that I saw on *Star Trek*.

Watching *Star Trek,* the alien species fascinated me, especially the green girls (that I later learned are called Orions). I used to wonder if there really are green aliens, blue aliens or half-black/half-white aliens out there across the galaxy, or if I would ever get to meet a real alien.

I never had anyone I could ask so I just wondered to myself and asked God. When there was no immediate answer forthcoming, I looked at the stars and decided that if God had created life elsewhere, and if there could be Black and White people on Earth, maybe there could be different colored aliens somewhere in the universe.

Despite the silent questioning, I always loved how *Star Trek* made me feel. So it was unexpected but I was beyond happy when my pursuit of an acting career took me where few men and women had gone before.

My acting journey into the Star Trek universe began when I auditioned with casting director Ron Surma for a role on *Star Trek: Voyager*. I didn't get the part but that started a relationship with Ron's casting office. Sometime later, they brought me back in for another role on *Voyager*. The second role wasn't a physical character but I would've been playing a transmission of Tuvok's son Sek (I don't remember what the episode was, I think *Hunters*). I didn't get that role because I was told I "didn't look alien enough." I wasn't sure what they meant by that, but I felt good about my acting choices for the audition. Fast forward to maybe a year or so after that and I was called to audition for a new "Untitled Star Trek" series (which eventually became *Star Trek: Enterprise*). I was told they had been trying to cast the role for a long time, they had already seen at least 50 actors. I was told that Ron remembered me from my earlier auditions for *Voyager* and reached out to my representation to get me to come in for an audition for the new series. I was getting ready to shoot an episode of *Awesome Adventures* in northern California when I was told by my manager that Casting wanted to see me. I auditioned with Ron and felt solid about the work I did in the room. I got a call-back to meet the director, James Conway, and producers. After a second audition, I left to go shoot my show. While I was in the Bay Area, I got a call that Trek wanted to test me for the role. My agent at the time negotiated my deal and when I returned from filming a few days later, I went to Paramount Studios to do my test. When I got to the lot, I remember feeling a sense of calm. I was ready. I looked around the lot as I drove in and smiled. I thought to myself, "This is going to be my new home." I said a prayer, asked for God's strength, thanked Him for blessing me with the opportunity. I thanked my grandpa Wes and my ancestors for paving the way for me to be in the position I was in. I thanked Paul Robeson, Sidney Poitier, Harry Belafonte, Levar Burton, Ben Vereen, Denzel Washington and all the other brilliant Black actors whose shoulders I stood on walking into that anointing. I felt profound peace and headed in to meet my moment. I met with the series creators and Executive Producers, Rick Berman and Brannon Braga. Rick and Brannon walked me to the test location.

As we walked, looking straight ahead towards our destination, Rick said, "You see you're the only one we're bringing back. Don't f*ck this up." He never smiled, never said anything else. I looked over at Brannon who had a slight smile on his face. I smiled and said, "I'll do what I do." If I hadn't grounded myself before going in, I would've let Rick's statement throw me and I would've started thinking about not messing up. I was in a different space so I looked into what his statement really meant. He wanted me to have the job. He didn't want me to sabotage myself. I knew I had done the work so I wasn't worried about that. When we got to the test location, Rick and Brannon left me by myself. After a little while, I was brought into a room that had about thirteen Paramount Execs, men and women (Rick and Brannon were among them) sitting in chairs awaiting my arrival. I walked in, waved and said hello to the room and walked over to Ron, who was already seated at a chair in front of everyone. Ron and I launched into the material. The scene was feeling good but at one point I messed up, dropped a line. But I didn't get nervous, I didn't stress out. I did what I do when I'm on set and something happens. I took a moment and refocused myself, then reconnected with Ron and we finished the scene. I got up and thanked Ron and those in attendance as I walked out the door. Although I didn't let the mistake affect me, I was still upset with myself that I dropped the line. I wanted to have a test with no mistakes. I didn't want to give them any reason to say no. But mistakes are a part of life, mistakes happen on every set. I didn't feel like my slipup was enough to disqualify me so I stayed positive that things would work out in my favor and headed over to my agent's (Karen Forman) office at Metropolitan Talent Agency.

Metropolitan was only about seven minutes or so from Paramount. I was sitting and reading a low budget feature script (my next audition) when a call came into Karen's phone. She excused herself to answer the phone while I kept looking over the script. I wasn't excited about the material but I was in a nice groove with auditions so I planned to put in the work and go see if I could book the next job. "Work begets work," as Brion James said. As I was reading, Karen said out loud, "Would you repeat that? You're calling to do a pick-up for Anthony Montgomery (I looked up from my script) who just booked the role of Travis Mayweather in the new Star Trek series..." I didn't hear anything else because I threw the script in the air and screamed. I don't think I had smiled that big since I got to California. Karen congratulated me. After sitting there for a minute to process what I just heard, I got some information about what would happen next and left the office. I pulled out of the agency parking lot and drove down the street until I found a place to pull over. I laughed and cried. The happiest tears in my life. I thanked God for his Grace and blessing me when I finally showed up in my moment. All of my sacrifices, hard work and perseverance had paid off.

All the times I was told No over the years while working my ass off were worth it for that one "Yes." I had fulfilled my promise to Meghan, myself and my family. I had finally done something significant with my life. I wasn't the only one who believed it. Because of the success of the Star Trek franchise and its longevity, most recently with *Voyager* and *Deep Space Nine* going seven years each, random people used to say I "hit the lottery" when I booked *Enterprise*. I didn't know about that but I knew my life had just changed forever. I may be wrong, but I believe everyone in the world knows about *Star Trek*, even if they don't watch any of the television shows or movies, everyone knows what the franchise is. *Star Trek* helps make this world better. I knew that no matter what happened with the rest of my life or my career, in my small way I would also be a part of helping to make this world better. That knowledge gave me a sense of fulfillment and purpose that I can't explain. I was overjoyed at what the possibilities meant on a global scale. After sitting in silence and letting the waves of emotion run over me, I called my mom and told her the great news, then my grandma and then hit up Donnie and Elimu.

I had prepared and was ready for whatever was coming.

I had no idea what was in store.

My first day on set was incredible. And unnerving. I was eager to step through the Lift Doors for the first time. I loved how cool our set was. It felt like those old submarines I had seen in movies. With more technology. There were a lot of people watching, I mean A LOT. Maybe fifty to a hundred people. I took it all in. Filled with anticipation and pride, I couldn't stop smiling. I was excited and nervous. I was also in the wrong headspace. I should've been focused on the work but deep down I wanted to "get it right." Looking at my helm, I knew there were some outstanding and talented people who held the position before me, including George Takei (Hikaru Sulu) and Robbie Duncan McNeill (Tom Paris), who are two of my favorite helmsmen - George because he was fantastic as the originator and Robbie because his character was so layered and so much fun. But more than my respect and admiration for my predecessors, I was carrying a torch so much greater than that of a helmsman. I carried with me the legacy of the Black culture as the next African American in space within the *Star Trek* lore, behind the iconic Nichelle Nichols, Alfre Woodard, Avery Brooks, Cirroc Lofton, Whoopi Goldberg, Levar Burton, Michael Dorn, Tim Russ, (Michael and Tim played aliens, but you get the point) and so many more. The legacy of a people constantly fighting for their right to simply exist. I didn't have anyone there to speak to me about the importance of what I was about to do like Nichelle Nichols had when Dr. Martin Luther King Jr. talked her out of quitting *The Original Series*, but I understood the significance all the same. Nichelle made a stand for Blacks of the time and for generations to come and every Black actor after her carries that same responsibility. I didn't talk to anyone about it, and I never behaved in a way that made me come off like I was bearing a heavy burden, but I still carried that truth with me. I did it with love and joy in my heart. I was honored to take on that mantle. I really appreciated Tim Russ (and Garrett Wang, who was the very first person from the franchise to embrace me) for reaching out to me when I got started on *Enterprise*. Tim and Garrett had finished their run on *Voyager* and both offered wonderful words of support and encouragement, and welcomed me to the Trek family. I was able to pass the torch as well. I was thankful when I got a chance to bond with Sonequa Martin-Green at the CBS and Creation Entertainment official Star Trek convention in Las Vegas and wish her a heartfelt congratulations on *Star Trek: Discovery*. She had already stepped into the role of the next African American in space but we had never been able to connect before that day. Sonequa is a phenomenal spirit, magnificent woman, brilliant artist and extraordinary human being, wife and mother. With the addition of exceptional and outstanding people like Wilson Cruz, David Ajala, Tawny Newsome, Dawnn Lewis, Michelle Hurd and Celia Rose Gooding to our Trek family, I know the Star Trek franchise is in great hands. Similarly, with the addition of insanely talented people like Melissa Navia, and all the crew who come after, I know the helmsman (helmsperson) position will be solid for generations to come.

I did my best to honor Gene Roddenberry and make my contribution to his legacy meaningful. I gave my all every time I walked onto the sound stages. Despite the fact that my character was born and raised in space, I made a decision to play Travis as someone who was still excited about the adventures that he embarked on as a member of Starfleet. I didn't want him to be a "perfect" human. I wanted to show his experience but still show his flaws to keep him relatable. That was one of the things I loved about *Enterprise:* we got to show how all the things that society has grown to know and love about Star Trek came to be, yet still be close enough to humanity of the time (2001 when we first aired) to be relevant to the masses. When I sat down at my helm I looked around and started making choices as an actor. The very first thing I worked out was the joystick. I thought if I used it too much it would look like I was playing a video game every time I touched it. I decided to only use the joystick when doing precision maneuvers with the ship. I designated areas around the console to guide the ship on normal missions. Once I knew what would happen at my helm, I worked out all the other actions as the series progressed. One of the things I always loved was when we had to coordinate our "shaking" together. It was almost like stunt training. We learned that each of the other series had a scale from 1 to 7 that determined the amount of shaking the ship and crew needed to do when they were under attack or experiencing turbulence. Level one was just a slight rocking, but if you got to seven, it knocked you out of your seat and on your ass. It was so much fun. I loved working on our show so much that I even wrote and recorded a Hip Hop track for it called *What You Know About.*[LYRICS 3] I felt like it could be a great way for us to bring in a new and energized group of fans by relating to them from a scientific perspective in a way that they could identify with. I thought it could work because I took some of the great parts of the show and flipped them in a Hip Hop way. I had my guy Rodney Bailey (Smilez) watch our show and write a verse about my character from my character's perspective. I told Smilez to give me some "space swag." We've got the hottest sci-fi banger most people have never heard.

Once the track was done, I recorded two more songs that were based on what my character had gone through on a couple of different episodes. I wanted to make sure the Execs in charge would get a full idea of what I wanted to do. I took one of the tracks to the legal team at Paramount to see if they would help me promote it and held on to the other two (until they were interested in hearing more). But they didn't want to hear more. They didn't want to entertain the idea of expanding the base. My concept was shot down and I never pursued it any further. I always felt like we missed a great opportunity to do something special with Hip Hop and *Star Trek*. I wanted us to collaborate on a cool and otherworldly project with mega-producer and hitmaker Pharrell who's a fan of the franchise. Congratulations to Kid Cudi, who was able to build a partnership with decision makers showcasing that Hip Hop and Star Trek are a beautiful fusion with great potential.

Our cast was like a family. I learned so much on that show. I learned the most from our inspiring leader and Captain, Scott Bakula. My Captain. Having a successful series with *Quantum Leap*, Scott knew what I was experiencing when I got on *Enterprise*. He was always a voice of clarity and understanding when I needed to talk. Scott wasn't just my brother and mentor-like figure at times, he was an encouraging shepherd who guided all of us with love, care and compassion. I learned how to be a number 1 on a call-sheet watching Scott. I watched as he made sure our sets were handled with kindness, nurturing and ultimate professionalism. Scott made all of us better (cast and crew alike) and led us in making the best series we were capable of creating. Our cast - Scott, Jolene, Connor, John, Dominic, Linda, and myself - was a family and became more so as the years went on. We each brought our own unique gifts to the collective to round out our Command Crew. Of course, like with any family, there were times with drama, but that wasn't all the time. Some of my greatest memories were when we got to have our entire cast on set together. It was usually on the bridge and didn't happen very often, but it was always the best energy when we were gathered together. We laughed a lot. We grew together.

And we worked hard.

CHAPTER ELEVEN
PROVING GROUND

Star Trek: Enterprise Command Crew (Clockwise from center)
Scott Bakula, Jolene Blalock, Linda Park, Dominic Keating,
Anthony Montgomery, John Billingsley, Connor Trinneer
(Photo appears courtesy of Paramount Pictures)

I don't usually watch the shows I perform in—after living a script, an actor doesn't always want to revisit the experience. For this book, however, I wanted to catch a glimpse of what went on during production—and doing a rewatch was the best way to jog those memories. It reminded me that I gained my confidence as an actor to be able to carry a franchise going through my time on Enterprise. This series was my proving ground.

WEIRD PLANET: S01E04: Strange New World

Watching the Star Trek: Enterprise episode Strange New World brought a fun recollection to the surface. I was excited to be working with

Connor because it was the first time our characters were written to have any lengthy storyline together. When I was hired, I was told Commander Charles "Trip" Tucker and Ensign Travis Mayweather were going to be good friends but until that episode, we had never filmed anything showing their friendship. Shooting was a blast. Connor is insanely talented and we had the best time filming. One of our shoot days, we were off the bridge set and filmed Trip and Travis in a tent. I love working on sound stages because a fantastic advantage is that production has complete control of the environment. In the script, there was a pending storm outside the tent and it was a lot of fun learning how the FX guys create the storm using giant fans and other special effects equipment. While the weather churned outside, part of the scene called for us to react to an alien bug that Trip felt crawling on him.

When I did my work on the script at home, I thought the scene could feel like an Abbott and Costello skit while the two of us searched in vain for the alien creature. The comedy would be heightened by escalating the problem—Trip was to pull out his phase pistol and want to shoot it.

As the alien bug would be added in post-production, I had asked the visual effects guys how big the creature would be. I was still learning about Travis and still forming his world. I wanted to get some sort of reference so I could decide how Travis would respond to what he saw. Being raised on a cargo ship in space and having been to numerous alien worlds, if he saw something small, then it wouldn't warrant the same response as if he saw a bigger, fiercer looking alien bug.

I was told the bug would be between 6-12 inches long—a pretty damn big bug. When we shot the scene, I had a reaction worthy of the stated size of the imaginary alien insect—Travis was scared out of his sleeping bag. The fans were blowing fierce, the tent was coming down around us, and we were searching for the alien bug.

When I watched the episode much later, I was in for a shock. As it turned out, the alien bug that they added was only about 2 inches long. Travis' reaction was way over the top. At first, the artist in me was bothered because Travis looked so frantic. Then I just laughed it off. This was my first time seeing something we filmed over twenty years ago. The bug just didn't bug me anymore. My only regret is that the series never explored Travis and Trip's friendship after that episode. A lot of good stories were never told.

NEW EARTH: S01E05: Terra Nova

A few episodes in, Enterprise began to feel like it was already shaping up to be about the captain, the Vulcan first officer, and the engineer (much like they had a trifecta in The Original Series, with Captain Kirk, Mr. Spock and Dr. McCoy). With the writers having seven main characters to write for, getting an episode focused on a character was a big deal. As it was, I had been feeling like Travis was already taking a backseat to all the other main characters—despite flying the ship.

Then the news came down that the episode Terra Nova was to heavily feature Travis. I was beyond happy that I would get a chance to dig into Travis and get to stretch my acting chops. Better yet, Travis finally wouldn't just be sitting behind the helm. I was excited about Travis being more involved with the overall story arc, but I was also nervous about it. What would it mean if the episode didn't go well?

Going from excitement to full-on stress wasn't at all how I thought I would feel at that moment. It wasn't the usual kind of stress an actor puts themselves through during the process of getting a performance ready. No, this was true worry. Worry that it really fell on me to make sure Rick Berman and Brannon Braga saw I could carry an episode. Worry that if Rick and Brannon didn't find that confidence in me, they might use Travis less if the episode didn't go well. Worry that if that happened, Travis' screen time would be relegated to sitting at the helm and giving the occasional "Aye Captain" —and that that would be the extent for him as far as my involvement in the episodes would go.

I had landed the coveted role of a series regular on a *Star Trek* show—the dream of so many—and I was terrified I might blow that opportunity if I did not make the episode go smoothly.

On *Enterprise*, I learned to be very precise with my dialogue. Some projects allow actors to adlib lines, but not so much in the *Star Trek* world. That's more than fine—I wouldn't know how to talk my way through Trek's so called "techno-babble" anyway. On *Trek*, in most cases the directors want their actors to say the exact lines that the writers provided. Because there was so much history that preceded everything that was recorded, what we captured on film needed to be precise, very specific. Whenever we would come off script, even for the slightest thing, our wonderful script supervisor, Jan, would come over and give us the correction and we would get back to it. That process helped me develop a skill of being word perfect on the projects I work on.

As an actor who must always be able to emote on cue or deliver lines in a wholly believable manner, adhering to this state of being in your own head is problematic. While shooting *Terra Nova*, it only worsened when I learned that the episode Travis was to play a pivotal role in was going to be directed by none other than Levar Burton! *Reading Rainbow* Levar Burton. *Star Trek: The Next Generation's* Lt. Commander Geordi La Forge.

Levar's acting on *Roots* was incredible, not to mention the road he paved for actors like myself in Hollywood and in the Star Trek universe. I wanted him to see what I was capable of as an actor. I wanted to convey all the respect and admiration that a young actor should and although I didn't know him at all, I wanted to impress him.

Now the more seasoned—that's a nice way of saying older—actor I have become would know that I shouldn't have been concerned about these things. That same seasoned actor would tell my young actor self that it wasn't on me to carry an episode. It was only on me to do the best I could with the skills I had and the script I was given. That wiser version of me would have said that I should just focus on the work and let the rest happen organically. Instead, I was fully in my head. I was feeling the imagined phantom weight of the world on my shoulders—and when Levar Burton called "Action," I sabotaged myself.

Our crew was on an alien planet, and Captain Archer, T'Pol and Travis were being chased and shot at. The three of us had to jump in the shuttle pod and I had to say my line quickly—something about how aliens had killed the planet's colonists and they might do the same to Enterprise's missing tactical officer, Malcolm.

It was set up for me to do a fun move with the camera, where I rotated my helm seat from right to left after delivering my line. This move would draw the camera's focus towards T'Pol and then to Archer for the final image of the scene. It was a great shot that Levar had planned, I just had to get it right. Things didn't go as planned.

I jumped into the shuttle and blanked on my line. Over and over, it was the same—run, jump in, and blow the line.

"If Malcom killed the aliens, they could kill the colonists, too!"

"If the colonists killed Malcolm, he could kill the aliens, too!"

If Malcom was a colonist, he could be an alien, too!"

I can't remember how many takes it took—just that I was embarrassed and pissed at myself. The more pissed I got, the more I messed up and got even further in my head.

I had to stand on the side by myself and keep saying the line over and over. Both Scott and Jolene were encouraging and supportive-they never made me feel bad, gave me shit or anything. I felt like garbage on my own. It wasn't just me missing the line, every time I messed up, I knew I was costing the production money. I shouldn't have been thinking about that, but I couldn't help it. We had to reset the cameras, reset the squibs that are used to represent the bullets hitting our ship, and reset everybody's energy. There was a lot weighing on me saying that simple line and I kept f*cking it up. But eventually, I got it.

Finally, either through the grace of God, sheer luck, or serendipity, we got at least one take where I managed to say my line right.

"If those aliens killed the colonists, they could kill Malcolm, too!"

Cut and print. Applause, please! I had never been happier to move on after shooting a scene. After recently rewatching the episode, I was really happy to see how smooth things looked. None of my internal struggles at the time appeared in my performance of Travis—and for that I am grateful. All actors have scenes they will never forget, I just wish that one was remembered for better reasons.

ROLLERBALL: S01E08: Breaking the Ice

As someone who grew up both loving and hating snow, I really enjoyed shooting Enterprise episode 08, Breaking the Ice. First—a frame of reference. In this episode, the crew of the Enterprise discovers an unknown comet and decides to explore it. Reed and Mayweather were tasked with taking a shuttle pod to land on the surface and study it up close—and chaos soon ensues.

Back home in Indiana, I always loved the feeling I got from the first snowfall. It was always majestic to me. The blanket of snow transformed the landscape and all its surroundings into something serene, pristine, and immaculate. I used to have fun building snowmen, making snow angels and having snowball fights. Snowfall on the morning of Christmas was the BEST time to see snow. Even when Christmases weren't the happiest, a new snowfall seemed to brighten my spirit.

But then the novelty wore off. After months and months of snow, annoyance set in. Wet clothes, freezing, not being able to walk around, having to shovel the sidewalk, and having to clean off the car (when my mom had one) all made life miserable after the newness of the snow was gone. When we shot Breaking the Ice, I remembered all the wonderful things I used to love about experiencing snow and made sure that was the driving force for

Travis.

It was easy to be in that headspace because the writers set it up that Travis had only encountered snow a couple of times. I drew on the excitement I always felt when snow began falling in Indianapolis and layered Travis' experience from there. The "kid in a candy shop" feeling definitely came through.

In watching the episode, I was reminded of Dominic's fantastic performance as Malcolm. It made me recall just how much I loved working with him, and how much I hated working with him when we had to wear those EV suits, which were very problematic.

On away missions to hostile environments, we would have to wear environmental suits that were made of some rubberlike material that just did not breathe. It was like walking around in a rubber sauna. As if that wasn't uncomfortable enough, production had to put small air conditioning units in our helmets to cool the inside of the suit. The issue? The battery pack that powered the AC units was heavy. Stuck in the suits for several shots, Dominic and I would sit with the battery backpacks propped up by an apple box in order to ease some of the strain off our shoulders, necks and backs.

Wearing the EV suits was a challenge for all of us. From the first day we put them on, Dominic started complaining about it—and he continued complaining every time we wore them until our series ended. To his point, they were incredibly difficult to be in, but I knew how blessed we were to be on our show and working, so I made the best of it.

I knew that one day we would all look back and remember how much we loved working on Enterprise, even during the times we wore the EV suits. I would usually try to get Dominic to see the glass as half full, but eventually ended up yelling at him to stop complaining when I couldn't listen to his griping any longer.

The EV suits were unpleasant but they looked great on camera. Since we were pretending anyway, I pretended that the unpleasantness didn't bother me. I focused on the positive and tuned Dominic out when his protests persisted. After some time, Scott talked to production about the suits and adjustments were made.

LUCKY BOY: S01E10: Fortune Son

Even after nine episodes, I was still dubious of my abilities on set. I was still finding my way through the character of Travis. Then came Fortunate

Son—an episode about Travis and his family of spacers. All my insecurities and waxing and waning confidence aside, I was eager to have another opportunity to be featured in an episode. I was even more excited because this particular episode gave more insight into Travis's backstory of being raised as a "boomer," since he was born and raised aboard a space freighter.

Like many in my profession—I have a process of coming up with specific details of the backstory for the characters I play. This process helps me inhabit a character and I hope, better portray them. Using as much pre-existing information that is available as possible, I write out all the other aspects of a character's past, starting with childbirth. I write what kind of pregnancy the mother had, how the character went from being a baby through adulthood. I create what the character's life is up until we meet him in the script. I integrate all the supplied info about the character as I'm setting up his world. I make sure to be specific about the details that I include in his life. The more specific, the more substance I'll have to draw from when we're filming the actual scene—even though none of the pre-work I do is ever seen. I immerse myself in the character's world and backstory for hours and hours leading up to filming.

While that's my usual process, I had limited knowledge of what Rick and Brannon created as part of Travis' past. I could only come up with minimal history. I assumed that since Travis was part of Star Trek lore, that there would be some sort of guide to what his life was like prior, during, and after he joined Starfleet. With that in mind, I just needed the production to tell me his story when they were ready. But they never did, and I never asked.

Because of my insecurities over being part of a big franchise, I didn't want anyone to know how lacking my level of confidence was on set —so I just went with what little information I got from the series bible—an earlier version of which is reproduced here. While not the final draft (this one dates back to when Travis was named Joe), the information is essentially the same:

LIEUTENANT TRAVIS MAYWEATHER

African American. Helmsman. Mid-twenties. A unique product of 22nd century life, Mayweather was raised on a long range transport vessel. "I was born and conceived during a two year run somewhere between Alpha Centuri and Arcturus Prime." As a result, Travis is more "interstellar" than even the Captain. He's traveled to dozens of planets and met many different alien species. He even had a Terrelian girlfriend at one point, which fascinates Tucker to no end.

Mayweather know the best place on a ship to watch

the stars rush by, or feel the vibrations from a passing pulsar. He prefers to sleep in a "zero-g" environment. Every night before he goes to bed, he deactivates the gravity plating in his quarters, and his cocoon-like hammock floats up on its tether.

Mayweather will prove to be a valued member of the crew, a talented pilot with an "instinct" for space-travel that few humans possess. This will help Captain Archer through situations where intellect and protocol alone won't suffice.

While touching on some key elements, the write up left much open to interpretation. Luckily, the Fortunate Son episode answered some of the questions I had about Travis's life in a big way. I learned that Travis has a sister. They didn't go into much detail about his relationship with her but they did reference that she exists. There was a subtle exploration of how Travis's family felt about him joining Starfleet and leaving the family business, but the story didn't reveal much. It was my job to fill in the blanks of the story pieces I was given. I enjoyed how in the episode I got to play Travis's special affinity for his family's vessel—a space freighter that had been attacked by pirates—and its crew. I loved how the experience reminded Travis of being on his home ship. This storyline let me discover the nostalgia and nuances of Travis. The entire episode became an emotional journey for me.

The arc started with Travis being excited and enthusiastic about encountering people who were similar to his upbringing. Then to Travis trying to establish a genuine connection with the First Officer, then to feeling insulted at the judgment he was receiving for choosing his life path joining Starfleet. Then shifting to Travis sorting through his feelings about the Enterprise's involvement in a situation that wasn't their concern. Transitioning from not caring about what happened in the situation, to finally finding his emotional footing and fighting to convince the freighter's commander to see the error of his ways, all in an effort to try and prevent future pain and suffering.

There were many times I felt Travis was undervalued as part of the command crew, but not in this episode. The emotional arc here was a fun and rewarding journey for both the character and for me as an actor.

Levar was directing again and I was excited to have a chance to improve on my previous problematic performance from the Terra Nova episode. This time turned out so much better. I was more relaxed, acted with increased confidence, and it came through in my performance. Fortunate Son was not only formative for Travis, but for younger me as well.

A NEW DAWN: S02E20: Horizon

The most in-depth and artistically fulfilling episode that I got to work on came during season two when we filmed the episode Horizon. After 40 episodes and the trials and tribulations of more than a year and a half worth of shows, I eventually settled into my routine for approaching my role as Travis. Concerns aside, I felt good about the work I was doing. The truth is, I shouldn't have thought about the scope of what my playing Travis Mayweather meant on the vast landscape of all things Star Trek, but I did. I knew that what I was doing mattered to people around the world. I knew the work I was doing and what we were collectively doing as part of the Enterprise production, would be analyzed and scrutinized for all time.

I shouldn't have worried myself about it but I did because we worked hard and I cared about what people thought of our show. I cared about what people thought of me. It was a lot for my younger actor self to process. I just did my best to concentrate on the work. I gave everything I had every time I filmed and trusted that I was making a positive contribution to the Star Trek universe and Gene Roddenberry's legacy.

Eventually I adopted the mindset that even if I did doubt myself at times, what I was doing must be working. I was sure Rick and Brannon would tell me if I needed to change anything in my portrayal of Travis, and they never did. I focused on the character and continued to grow over time.

That attitude didn't get rid of all of my anxieties—because I had already been hearing that Enterprise could be canceled. I never knew the details behind the rumors of our possible cancellation, but the talk started in the first season. It continued through the second and third, and kept going until we were officially canceled during our fourth season. The looming thought of cancelation was something palpable on the set. Other than maybe a quick quip in passing, I never talked about it with anyone from the cast—but I did feel the pressure.

I assumed there were Executive-level factors that weighed in on the decision to pull the plug on our show. I didn't believe the failure was completely on us, but as part of the cast, I still felt like I was contributing to letting down both the fans and the franchise. I vowed to keep doing everything in my power to help make Enterprise the best it could be, canceled or not.

By the time we got to filming Horizon—which again focused on Travis—I was ready to take on the responsibility that came with that episode despite all of the outside noise. Horizon is the first time that I (and the audience) get to meet Travis's family. I was excited to finally come face to face with Travis's past and give fans a deeper look into his life. His sister was referenced in a previous episode, but we never got to meet her. It was thrilling to know that we would actually interact with Travis's mother 'Rianna Mayweather' (played by Joan Pringle) and his brother 'Paul Mayweather' (played by Corey Mendell Parker). I didn't even know what Travis's mom's name was before I got the episode, nor his brother's. Having more family history that I could really hold onto made me want even more to ensure Travis's family life was portrayed correctly.

The story arc follows Travis as he goes back to visit his home ship, Horizon. The stakes are raised because just before the reunion, Travis finds out his father has died. Travis carries a lot of grief because of unresolved issues with his father. After getting home and settling in, Travis learns that his younger brother, who's now the acting captain of Horizon, holds deep resentment for him leaving to join Starfleet. As a brother myself in real life, it was a fun exploration diving into the sibling conflict dynamic on the show. Unfortunately, I wasn't able to get in full rehearsals with Corey prior to filming (which is the case with most productions), but we did talk about the relationship between the brothers. We found the drive that motivated Travis and Paul and caused their division, stemming back to when they were kids. When we filmed, Corey and I were able to find some really special moments. I loved being able to play the kind of vulnerability and uncertainty that Travis displayed. Those feelings were amplified as I worked with Joan and we established the mother/son relationship between Rianna and Travis. I loved working on the Horizon episode. I was so inspired that I wrote and recorded a song called *Gotta Believe* that is an homage to the episode.[LYRICS 4]

HELD UP: S02E21: Detained

Written by Mike Sussman and Phyllis Strong, Detained was the first episode where Travis was in a solo storyline with Captain Archer. I loved working with Scott any chance I got, especially since it didn't happen often. I learned many different lessons from him. The experience was enhanced on Detained, because we also worked with Dean Stockwell, who starred alongside Scott for many years on their hit sci-fi series *Quantum Leap*. It was really wonderful being in the presence of these two actors because I could see the years of camaraderie and friendship in their interactions and work. I could feel the love, respect and trust they have for one another.

It was fun being a proverbial "fly on the wall" as they periodically recounted stories of their old filming days. After only one day of working with them both, it was easy to tell why *Quantum Leap* was so successful and had such a long run. I already knew how fantastic Scott is, both as a human being, an actor and leader on set, and after getting to know Dean for the brief time I did, I could feel that their chemistry translated into a positive dynamic that made going to work a joy. That type of environment is always going to produce a quality product and a successful venture.

More than my enthusiasm for working with Scott and Dean, I was also extremely proud to work on an episode that spotlighted the ignorance of preconceptions and racial biases. The story follows Archer and Mayweather as they were imprisoned in a detainment camp after curiously exploring an area of space and unintentionally violating some unknown military boundaries. The detainment camp housed innocent aliens who were being held against their will simply because they resembled a group of aliens who were at war with other species. My character's consciousness expanded and evolved over the episode. Travis arrived in the situation with his own fears and prejudices, judging the alien species based on the actions of others in their species. The prejudices presented in the episode aptly mirrored the way that Black people and other minorities of color are often judged and misjudged by others' fears and prejudices. Once he got to interact and connect with the beings on a level that was deeper than the surface, once he got to truly know them and understand them, Mayweather realized that his thoughts about the aliens were skewed, misguided, and flat-out wrong. He chose to grow from his encounters and eventually ended up helping Archer liberate the captive aliens.

Travis was not alone in his thinking. Some of the aliens also had their own prejudices against him and Archer because of past trauma that they suffered at the hands of people who looked like them. They, too, chose to grow and shift their ideals after getting to know the Enterprise crew members. I was grateful to be part of a story that actually showed people (and aliens) dealing with biases and working past those presumptions. I've always felt that our portrayals in that particular episode are a perfect mirror to how we as people in regular society can (and should) deal with ethnicities other than our own. By getting to know other human beings without judgment and basing our decisions about their characters on our interactions, not on appearances.

I enjoyed working on the episode so much that when I did my Hip Hop album, *A.T*, I did a record called *Yes They Are* LYRICS 5 that was influenced by the work we did on "Detained."

THINGS TO COME: ES03E15: Harbinger

Episode fifteen of the third season, "Harbinger" showed that Travis could handle himself in a fight.

194

A little backstory about the episode: The "A" story (the main story) was surrounding the crew of Enterprise who came upon an enigmatic space pod carrying an alien that seemed to be in distress. The "B" story was a terrific showcasing of Dominic's excellent acting chops. This storyline pitted Lieutenant Reed against Major Hayes (played by Stephen Culp), leader of the starfleet military force known as Macos. The gist is that Reed felt threatened that Hayes was trying to steal his job, when in fact, Hayes was just trying to make sure the entire crew was prepared with extra military training in case they encountered hostile alien forces. The "C" story involved T'Pol and Trip in an exploration of their personal relationship.

In addition to what I learned in Ninjutsu, I started training in Hapkido during season one of the show because I always planned to give myself a more formal foundation in martial arts. Since I had a lot of time off work when Travis wasn't in the storylines, I took advantage of it. I trained for more than a year before the Harbinger episode was filmed. I hadn't achieved my Black Belt at the time, but was confident in what I could do and was excited when I got the script and saw there was an opportunity to do fight sequences. I learned Stage Combat in college so I already knew how to "fight" in a scene without hurting my scene partner or myself. I worked with our fantastic Enterprise Stunt Coordinator, Vince, and he taught me the correct way to throw a punch for the camera, to throw a kick so it looks good in the shot. Most importantly, how to do it all safely.

During one of the scenes of Harbinger, we're in a training sequence and Hayes wants the crew to spar so he has an Enterprise crew member pair off with one of the Macos. Travis pairs with the biggest guy. As an actor and martial artist, I was hyped. We practiced a combination where he throws a kick and follows with two punches, Travis blocks the attacks and counter-attacks with a right jab (which Hayes calls a right cross). Then my sparring partner throws a spin-kick, which Travis ducks and counters with a right-cross followed by a sidekick. For Travis' final combination, my sparring partner throws a left punch that Travis blocks, while simultaneously trapping the opponent's wrist, then Travis delivers a gut punch with his left fist and moves immediately into a throwing technique using his right hand. I was especially proud of that move because I had practiced it at the Hapkido dojo and was eager to use the technique. The throw is not only effective but looks great on camera. During the sparring session, the camera cuts back and forth to Reed watching and feeling proud that Travis was representing well.

Then the dynamic switches. The Maco has a sequence of his own. He gets irked and goes after Travis, a little. He throws a one-two punch combination with his left and right, then a right kick, then left kick followed by a right punch. While Travis was doubled over, the Maco throws a round kick to Travis' gut that drops him to the ground. As Travis gets up to recover, the Maco grabs his right wrist, traps his right shoulder, takes out Travis' foundation with a leg sweep and slams his face into the ground. Travis' mouth gets bloodied. Reed is visibly irritated by what he sees and as Hayes prepares to move on to the next lesson, Reed abruptly ends the session. The scene continues but you'll have to go watch the episode to see how it turns out. Unless you've already seen it, of course.

Why am I recounting all of this? Because I love doing my own stunts. I had a blast filming all of it. I remember my sparring partner and I had to give each other small indicators that the punch or kick was coming, something that the other person saw but that the camera wouldn't catch. It was so much fun doing the dance with the camera and making sure everything looked precise from a technical standpoint, but also ensuring it was engaging on screen. We did each of the stunts multiple times from multiple angles.

I'm proud of what we filmed that day, although at the time, I was irritated that our fight sequences ended with Travis having a bloody lip. In truth, I didn't care about the lip or the blood. I know that in a real fight, everyone gets hit. I was actually glad the episode showed that Travis could take a punch. I was annoyed at where it was placed in the story. I wanted to have Travis lose the first set of sparring bouts and then win at the end, showing that he can overcome adversity and still be triumphant. But doing it that way would have messed up the storyline the way it was written. Reed needs to see Travis get bested so Reed can then reprimand Hayes, which continues to heighten the tension between the two of them. I understood it, but I still didn't like it. But I knew Travis would have appreciation for the sparring opportunity, even if he didn't appear to come out victorious, so I played it that way. The scene turned out great. Having gained a lot more Hapkido knowledge since Harbinger was filmed, I know what things I'll do differently the next time I get to spar in a scene. What that experience did for me as an actor was to ignite a fire that makes me look forward to being able to do more martial arts/action projects. I hope to have the chance to work with greats like Jackie Chan, who I've always respected and feel a kinsmanship to because as well as other disciplines he trains in, he's also a Hapkido practitioner, Donnie Yen, who I loved in the IP Man series, Wesley Snipes, who I've admired since the first Blade film and Michael Jai White, an exceptional martial artist.

After seeing the final result of Harbinger, I'm grateful Travis got to be the representative spotlighted to demonstrate some of the hand-to-hand combat tactics that Starfleet personnel learned. I'm proud that Hapkido techniques I learned from Grandmaster Song and Ninjutsu techniques I learned from Grandmaster Seika are now part of the Star Trek universe.

THE LONG ROAD

I joyfully piloted *Enterprise's* NX01 into adventure after adventure for ninety-eight episodes, until our series came to an end. It was a great honor to eventually meet many of the Star Trek alumni who had come before me. Like the first time I met James Doohan, Scottie. He was the kindest person. He was up in age and his health wasn't very good but he still showed so much love and grace when he was on set. He was the first actor I met from *The Original Series*. I was in awe. He was frail so I didn't want to bother him for a photo of us (though I was able to get a photo when I saw him after that at a convention). At our initial meeting, I quietly watched him being bombarded with people showering him with love and wanting pics. I felt overwhelmed for him but he was very gracious and kind to everyone. When we were introduced, he congratulated me and said three words that I've never forgotten: "Carry the torch." I said I would do my best. He smiled proudly and said, "You'll be great. Welcome to the family." I thanked him. I found it very cool that the series made me family with many of the actors I had grown up admiring.

As much as I love connecting with my Trek family, my greatest honors in being part of such a famed franchise come when I hear from military service men and women about how much our series means to them and how instrumental it has been in getting them through rough times at war, or just being stationed away from their families. It was my greatest privilege to be able to bring some sense of comfort to all the people who gave their time, dedication and/or lives to allow me and all of us the freedoms we get to experience being citizens of the United States. And because the massive appeal of Star Trek goes beyond the borders of the U.S., I feel a special connection with all the Trekkies around the world.

No matter where I've traveled around the world, the one thing I never felt being part of the Star Trek universe was racism. In years past, many people have had something mocking to say about Star Trek and the fans associated with it, but no one can ever say that the fans or the Trek universe promotes hate or racist beliefs. In fact, that is probably the single biggest reason I'm so honored to be part of Star Trek. They don't just talk about making the world better, they inspire change to make the world better. I'm forever grateful to Rick Berman and Brannon Braga for believing in me, as well as all the Execs at Paramount Pictures for adding me to the Star Trek canon, Ron Surma for casting me and our awesome crew who always kept us uplifted.

CHAPTER TWELVE
DAMAGE

Hollywood has definitely changed in a post-COVID-19 world. I've been in California for more than two decades and when I came out here things were different, mindsets were different, people believed they were better than other people. I didn't know that I wasn't just coming out to California as an actor, but that I had to be classified to be taken seriously. I quickly learned that the goal to strive for was to be a movie actor, which was different from being a television actor, which was different from being a commercial actor, which was different from being an Equity actor on a theater stage. I had no idea there were so many levels to being an actor in Hollywood. I learned how different people in different groups felt about the other categories. Many people used to talk badly to me about Soap Operas, and the actors on them. I didn't know much about Soaps other than my mom and grandma used to watch them. They called them *stories* back in Indiana and you could NOT bother them or talk to them in any way while they were watching their shows. If you did interrupt, they went off. Every time. I quickly learned to shut up or stay away while the stories were on. I started watching too. I watched all of them: *General Hospital*, *All My Children*, *One Life to Live*... But my mom and grandma only watched theirs: *General Hospital* for Mom and Grandma and whichever other stories were on that same channel (ABC). I don't remember them watching anything else. When I moved to LA, I carried those memories of watching stories with my family with me. After a while of hearing all the soap-bashing, I started to form my own negative opinions about soaps and whether I wanted to work on them based on information I was getting from everyone else, without having any experience of my own in that medium. I approached most of my auditions for soaps with a cavalier attitude, not caring whether I got the jobs or not. Of course, I would take the work if it came, but I wasn't stressed if I didn't book one. I worked on a couple of shows (*Passions* and once on *General Hospital*) and had that mentality as my inner story while I worked. They were just jobs. But, because I wanted to be better on soaps, I took a workshop with Marnie Saitta, longtime casting director for *The Young and the Restless*, so that I could get more of a feel for what the melodrama genre required. I didn't get a lot of soap auditions and after a while, I stopped getting callbacks for those auditions. So, I never put a lot of thought into working on a soap beyond what I already had. When I got the initial audition for *General Hospital*, I was certain that I wouldn't get it anyway so I just treated it as an acting exercise. I committed to the character, and my choices, went in, and just had fun. Surprisingly, my agent told me that they wanted to see me again. I went in again, and again I just treated it as an acting exercise. The next thing I know, my agent tells me that they want to test me for the show. I was excited about the possibility of being on the show, being a part of the *GH* legacy and my mom and grandma getting to see me on the show. But a bigger part of me felt like they weren't going to hire me anyway so I didn't let myself get too excited. I tested opposite Finola Hughes and Vinessa Antoine, whom I later fell in love with and had a four-year relationship with.

After being placed on contract with *GH* in late 2015, my entire perception about soaps changed.

I had no idea how much hard, hard work goes into making daytime television, specifically soap operas, look so seamless. I didn't know that the work done by actors on those shows is like being put through an actor's Boot Camp, and if you can survive it there and make the transition, you can make it in mainstream Hollywood. The sheer volume of pages they shoot in a day dwarfs any Prime-Time show I've ever been a part of. I worked absurd amounts of pages per day with extensive lines of dialogue that you get one take to get done, one take to get it right. One take. The only times additional takes were allowed was when someone made a mistake in the scene, something was caught by Frank Valentini (Executive Producer) or one of the other people in charge, or if the director needed us to go again. Otherwise, it was one-and-done. I also made sure I was on top of my material because the directors hired for the show are there to get the shots and keep the day moving along. And the process moves so quickly. They are an incredibly well-oiled machine. When I got there, I worked hard. I worked my ass off.

And I LOVED the challenge. I was in bliss the day I sat at my living room coffee table and had five scripts to learn. It was during the court trial when my character had to testify. I had to learn eight pages of dialogue that flowed like a monologue (with occasional input from others in the court). I felt like my head would explode at one point, as I worked to break down the text and commit the scenes to memory. But I was determined to meet my moment when it came. And I did. During those scenes, and the ones where I had to be clinical or technical, I was in my element. The areas I knew I came up short were the intimacy scenes. Soap Operas (and Hollywood) are about selling sex appeal. I don't know how to be sexy. When I have done scenes and been in a zone that I believed to be sexy, I've been told "There's no chemistry." When I don't try to "be sexy" in any way, fans have reacted that our chemistry was jumping off the screen. I don't know how to exude sex appeal. That's probably why I don't always get cast as a love interest. There are times I've been told that "they loved my work" and I was going to be the love interest of a character on a show, and it didn't happen. After that happened a couple times, and the feedback some of the fans gave on *GH*, I knew it was me. I'm not worried. I'll find the "sex appeal" switch.

_____

I loved being on *GH* so much and was so invested in the work and giving my character more dimensions that I hooked up with my guy Flii Stylz - an insane Hip Hop lyricist, and also a monster as a choreographer having worked with heavyweights like Michael Jackson, Chris Brown and many others - and wrote a Hip Hop joint called *General* LYRICS 6 for my character that I pitched to Frank. I wanted to see if the Execs at ABC would allow Andre to perform at the infamous Nurse's Ball. We wrote the song from the point-of-view of my character, Dr. Andre Maddox, and incorporated the love triangle between him, Jordan, and Curtis. I was excited about the possibilities of what we could do. I'm a performer and I love the stage so I knew we would give the fans something they had never seen before. Even though he needed to discuss it with other Execs, Frank seemed open to the idea and asked me to tweak the song to see if it could play better for our fanbase (it was a little too grimy at first). I made the adjustments and the song came out great (although I liked the grit of the first version better). Ultimately, they had other storylines to follow and the song didn't make the show. I'm still proud of it though. It came out dope.

I recorded the song but never released it because music had changed so much, and continues to do so. I'd have to rerecord and change it to make it feel current. That's too much work. I might put it out one day for fun. If I don't, the song being complete was a great way for me to scratch a musical itch. I missed it.

I genuinely loved my time at *General Hospital*. I loved it. And I love every time I get to play in Port Charles.

But like with any family, everything wasn't always great.

At times, it felt like a toxic environment. It resembled the very "clique-ish" atmosphere found in many school settings - on many different levels. More importantly than that for me, there was also a major darkness hovering. The ugly darkness of racism. I could feel it in the energy around the building and because I grew up with racism in Indiana, I know that feeling. I'm no expert, but I've had enough experience with that situation to be very sensitive to it. It didn't come from everyone, though. Most of the people are wonderful, hard-working, loving individuals. But I felt it from enough people that many times I dreaded going to set. I would have to put on my "energetic armor" before I walked into the building. And those racial dynamics weren't just confined to being at work.

My intense desire to walk freely from underneath that racist cloud fueled me to make an impetuous decision, one day. I regret that decision. It was a dumb career move. The result was something I caused on my own. I believe it did real damage to my career path. I went to the head writers at the time, Jean and Shelly, when they were still the people in charge and asked them what they were planning to do with my storylines with Jordan and Anna. Foolishly, I asked them to not write my character as the love interest for Anna DeVane, even though I did want them to keep Andre and Anna working together as a dynamic crime-fighting team in Port Charles. That was incredibly stupid of me, I know. The reason I talked to them was not because I didn't want Andre to play Anna's love interest. I truly love Finola Hughes. In the real world. I love that woman. Finola is one of the most phenomenal women I have ever met on the planet. I would marry her in real life. I loved making magic opposite her every time we were given the opportunity. But with the possibility of our romantic pairing, initially, I wasn't sure how it would work because of how beloved Finola is. I was worried that her die-hard fans would object to our on-screen coupling. But after being around Finola and connecting with her, I stopped caring about what anyone would potentially say. I knew we would be a powerful couple together, a "Power Couple," as it were and we would light the Daytime world on FIRE. But I asked the writers not to pursue the storyline they hinted at when I first got on the show. That was because my concerns were realized when I started receiving hateful, racial messages on social media from different lifelong GH fans who were pissed about the possibility of having a Black man as Anna's lover. The fact that that same Black man was an accomplished psychiatrist with other extensively impressive credentials was neither here nor there to them. I would see things on my feeds like "F.H. fans don't want her mixing with that colored," and other kinds of ignorant hate that people with that outlook spew. I shouldn't have let it bother me. Since I dated White girls growing up, I had always dealt with even more racism than just due to the color of my skin, so I knew what that ugliness looked like. I should've chalked it up to their ignorance. But it did bother me. Racism in this country has plagued me my whole life (just like every other Black person) and I didn't want to have to accept it because of a story point. I never wanted them to write me off the show. I simply didn't want to become the target of racial attacks for going to work and doing my job. I didn't speak up so I would sound like a racist myself (and I'm not saying they felt that way but my intention was not to come off as racist myself). I was just tired of having to deal with the suffocating pressure of being Black and "tolerated" by so many in society at large. I spoke up out of a sense of survival and self-preservation. I have a vivid imagination and started having thoughts of what I would do if racist fans took their fanaticism to extremes and came after me or, God forbid, my family. It may seem like an exaggerated idea, but what the world is witnessing, I've known my whole life: racists will stop at nothing to hurt people they deem as opposition. I didn't want my career choice to make me an unintentional target for bigots and racial extremists. I also didn't want any of Finola's fans to start treating her differently because she was paired with me. I was secretly hoping the writing team would maintain a continuous storyline where Andre would keep working with Anna but be part of a dynamic set of Black power couples like shows had back in the day with Jessie and Angie on *All My Children* or Shemar Moore, Victoria Rowell and Kristoff St. John (Rest in Paradise) on *The Young and the Restless*. Vinessa is a fantastic actor and incredibly talented and Donnell was crushing it and doing really solid work, so I just needed a pairing for me to complete the group. It became obvious to me that the writers were moving towards having their characters (Jordan and Curtis) stay together, even though no one would tell me. And they also wouldn't tell me that they were planning to put Andre with Anna. I would not have cared and would have dealt with outside racial attacks if I had felt supported, but honestly, I didn't always feel valued or like I truly mattered while I was at *GH*. Most times, I felt like I was just there to serve the other characters. Which is great and a blessing. I love the opportunity. But I still wanted to feel like I mattered. Not from a place of ego, but just as a human being. I didn't want to have to put up with racial bigotry from some of the public at large given how I felt I was treated by some who were putting me in that position. Because I do know my worth as an actor, what I was secretly hoping was that they would bring in another terrific Black female who is extremely talented and pair me with her to give *GH* a really strong set of storylines (Jordan/Curtis and Andre/????) on the show that represented for the Black *General Hospital* fans out there. There are minimal story arcs with Blacks being featured on the show (and as far as I know, have ever been) and I felt like the wonderful Black women all across the US who have loved, supported, and followed the show for decades (like my mom and grandma) deserved to see them. That way we would all be able to do great work that would excite the fans and I wouldn't have to deal with the avoidable racial backlash from any disgruntled fans around the country. I just wanted to go to work and make the best show that we could. I did the best job I could. But that wasn't to be. And to be clear, I don't believe that I was written off the show because of racism. I'm sure I put the Execs in a bad position when I asked them not to write Andre as Anna's love interest. If they hired me for that purpose and I asked them not to do what I was hired to do, then they had to figure out a way to get me out of there since they had so many other actors to write for. It was idiotic for me to make that request in the first place and smart business for them to write me off.

That said, dealing with prejudice from the fans wasn't the only time I experienced racism working on *GH*. I was the recipient of an awful experience from one of my coworkers. We were shooting a scene and there were only a few of us in the scene during one of the rehearsals I walked up behind the actor (which is what I was directed to do) and before I could say my line prompting a response, he pulled out his wallet and said, "Please don't hurt us!" as he pretended to cower. You know, the White man fearing for his life from the Black assailant? That old trope. He thought it was funny. It wasn't. It hurt. It hurt me to my core. I was one of two Black people on set that day, including a crewmember, which was typically the case when we filmed, but no one had ever treated me that way. I never did anything to warrant him making a "joke" at my expense. I never treated him that way and had only given him respect. So, why did he feel the need to make me the recipient of his cruel action? What did he gain from it? And before anyone says, "It was just a joke," I ask, "What was funny about that "joke?"" Is it funny that some part of him perceives Black men as criminals who should be feared? Is it funny that some part of him looks at a man, a Black man, as less than a man? As a man who fights against the negative stigmas associated with Black men as much as I can, I can say, unequivocally, no, it's not. It's not f*cking funny. Is it funny that somewhere in him he's filled with so much cowardice and is so defenseless that he knows he wouldn't be able to stop a perpetrator, Black or otherwise, from violating him? That he couldn't protect those around him? I used to be a coward. I would never presume to speak on his behalf but if I was him, I wouldn't think that was funny. None of those situations is funny to me, but maybe I understand humor differently. I will say again, what he said hurt. It hurt worse because the incident happened at my job, a place where I was supposed to feel safe. But I didn't feel safe. Just like the feeling I got being a kid in Indiana walking down the street and getting called a nigger by an old White man in the car as he drove by. Only in the present, he wasn't dealing with a child. He was dealing with someone who knew how to handle bigots. That aside, for an instant, the Indiana in me kicked in, and – even though I have a black belt in martial arts and have discipline – part of me wanted to bust him in the back of his head and show him how his joke would play out where I'm from. But I didn't. Because I do have discipline. I never let him know it affected me. It's not my job to join in racist jokes. All I said was, "Really?" and walked away so we could rehearse again. His back was to me so he couldn't see the pain I was in, the hurt that was simmering.

The mentality of him making that "joke" and people like him who have that same mindset and worse is exactly why I asked the writers not to write my character as Anna's love interest. My point was proven while on the set of my job. Imagine how I or my family could be treated by some fanatic out there because they don't want me kissing Finola, or her laying in my arms in bed. Nah, I'm good. And before you ask, no, I didn't go tell Frank or the Execs. I didn't call my agent or manager and raise hell. I didn't call SAG and file a grievance. I didn't call a lawyer and go after ABC. I didn't retaliate. I didn't do anything. What good would it have done? I've seen several actors, Black actors, file grievances over the years when they were put in situations where they felt like they were being racially targeted. The complaints were never resolved in favor of the person who was wronged. Just the opposite. From what I remember, everyone made it seem like it was the innocent person's fault and somehow they brought on the racist act by something they did. I knew I had not done anything to him. I was doing the job I was hired to do, the job I was instructed to do, and he decided to be "funny"/racist. That had nothing to do with me. I wasn't going to let society at large somehow make it seem like any of it was my fault. And how would the show or the network be able to make it up to me anyway? What could they do to make it right? Other than some photo ops apologizing, and the actor saying they went to "Cultural Sensitivity Training" or something, and then posting all over social media about how they "learned from their mistakes." Well, I never said anything and the actor has never posted about going to Cultural Sensitivity Training or anything else. So, if I had said something, any of those photo ops or social media posts would have been bullshit.

Here's the truth: The one thing an actor wants in this industry is stability, employment and financial stability. That's it. I don't care about pretend public apologies, or optics for the camera. The network, Frank and any of the Execs in charge were not going to give me a lifetime contract as compensation. Nor would I expect them to. But since the emotional scar will be there for the rest of my life, my job should too. That was never going to happen. So, what really would've come from me saying something? The answer is...nothing. Checkmate. I just focused on my job and did the work. But that incident was another example of the racism I didn't want to endure. And it was most regrettable because I didn't know him very well but had (and have) immense respect for him, both as an artist and as a man. We had always had pleasant interactions and conversations up to that point, never a cross word between us.

The next day, the actor came up to me and apologized, having reflected on what he had done after talking it over with a family member, who pointed out how inappropriate and appalling his action and comment were. I accepted his apology. And I let it go. As I've gotten older and matured, I strive to see situations from more than my point of view. He's a good man and sometimes people aren't aware how something that could be perceived as innocent or harmless to them, could have such a powerful impact on another individual. Unfortunately, I still carry the pain of that experience stored in my subconscious. His apology notwithstanding, despite his incredible intellect, he will never comprehend how badly his "joke" wounded me and imprinted on my life. I hope he truly learned a lesson from our encounter and never treats another person like that.

That wasn't the only racial instance I experienced at *GH*. I just didn't talk about times that made me uncomfortable to anyone. I've said dumb things in my past and I know how much some words can hurt, even as a joke, so as an adult I am consciously aware not to engage in those disgusting behaviors. I won't tell anyone else how to live, but it's not my responsibility to make sure that an actor… or anyone who feels the urge to make a joke at a Black person's expense… it's not my responsibility to make sure those people don't feel awkward when I don't participate in their meanness. As an artist, my job is to be the best actor I can be. As a man, I strive to be the best person I can be. If others don't want to do that, that's on them.

It really threw me when *GH* took me off contract as a regular. At first, I thought it was because of my request to the writers but I was told that wasn't the case. I assumed it was a business decision. I wasn't bringing in the numbers (viewership didn't increase when I was on screen). They didn't tell me that, but I know how the game works. I did my part. I worked incredibly hard to help us make a great show, was a good castmate and person to my fellow actors, and was always respectful and pleasant to our awesome crew. I carried myself as a professional. A stark contrast and polar opposite to the times I witnessed multiple actors going off on set, yelling, cursing, and being rude and disrespectful about different things they hated or what their characters were doing. Actors who were disruptive with negative energy, and yet those behaviors were rewarded with contract extensions and increased wages, people bending over backwards for them.

After doing my job and doing right by everyone to the best of my abilities, and still being taken off contract, I questioned everything I had done for the two years I was there. I questioned my capabilities. I was down on myself for a long time for not knowing how to exude sexiness on screen. I was in a relationship with Vinessa (former Jordan on *GH*) at the time but many fans frequently commented that we "didn't have chemistry" on the show (we laughed at the paradox from time to time). I never showed it, but it bothered me a lot. I knew *I* was the reason our connection wasn't being felt by the audience. I believe it was because my acting choice made it look like Andre was too into Jordan, which had the opposite effect. I say that because I played it that he wasn't into Anna and the fans said our chemistry was crazy. Go figure. I felt that if I had been more of *something*, then the fans would've embraced my character more and the writers would've kept writing for my character on the show. I felt like I wasn't good enough. I had learned to act from a place of truth and honesty, not to be sexy. For the first time in years, I questioned if my acting was where it needed to be to compete in the soap arena. However, after some time, I realized my insecurities were unfounded. I recognized that I had accomplished something I never imagined as a possibility when I got the job. I received the second-highest honor I could be bestowed for working on a soap opera as an actor. I earned an Emmy nomination. The highest honor would've been to have won the Emmy, but I never expected to be nominated in the first place. In my eyes, I already won the moment I became one of five men to vie for Outstanding Supporting Actor in a Drama Series in 2016. I didn't take home the trophy, but I still won because I became "Emmy nominated Anthony Montgomery" for the rest of my life. The trophy would've been icing but no matter what else happens throughout my career, I proved to myself that I can excel at the highest level in a genre I wasn't sure I fit in. No one can take that from me. But, this is also a business, and it's Hollywood, and sex sells, so I will be adding the "sexy" tool to my utility belt and embracing those roles. Ironically, I was kept in the dark about the expanse of my character's backstory. The writers either didn't know or they wanted to keep the actors in the dark. Not judging, at all. It's their business, their right. But if I had known that my character had such a shady past, I would've played him differently. I would've played him more like an intellectual bad boy, especially with Jordan, who he was the love interest of and who was also the chief of police, which may have given them more on-screen chemistry, maybe even making me come off sexier. Knowledge of that story point would've affected my character's interactions with everyone on the show, including Anna, and may have made their interactions even more special. That's my theory anyway. C'est la vie.

There will always be a pang in my heart feeling like I would still be on *GH* if I had "played the game" more. But I didn't. Regardless of my flaws, and I have many, none of them were displayed at work. I am much more than my shortcomings. I am a man of integrity with an upstanding moral character. I can say that because I wasn't always. I deal with people fairly. I treat people right. I'm also a talented actor and I work hard at my profession. I don't feel like I should have to play games with anyone for them to treat me right or deal with me in the way I deserve. I'll take the lessons I learned at *GH* and apply them to my craft for the future. Maybe I do another soap, maybe I don't. Maybe they'll write my return to *GH*, maybe they won't. Regardless, the skills I walked away with have aided my growth as an actor and person. I will always be grateful to my guy Frank Valentini for believing in me and guiding me (Love you, Frank!), casting director Mark Teschner for casting me (Thank you for seeing me, Mark!), *GH* and my *GH* family, especially our camera operators Barbara, Dale, Dean and Craig (Love you guys!) and ABC Network for taking a chance on me.

From it all I've learned when I'm blessed with a gift, don't talk myself out of an opportunity hoping for "the right situation." If I'm in it, it *is* the right situation. Work through any turbulence, learn the lessons, and grow from the challenges.

CHAPTER THIRTEEN
HORIZON

As I wrote this book, I overcame extremely difficult and scary times. I'm not talking about Covid. I started this book years ago, long before COVID-19. On top of life being life and throwing things at me, times were grueling as I went through a divorce. If you've ever been through one or know someone who has, you know how painful the process can be. And the pain lasts…until one day it doesn't. Times were scary because the debt I carried was a frightening and crazy burden to bear. But I kept it in perspective the best I could. There have been many people, who made lots of money and lost it, and then bounced back stronger than they were before, having learned some great, albeit costly, lessons along the way. That's my story. My lessons showed up when I needed them and kept showing up until I learned the lesson. My path in life has been the "road less traveled," yet, traveled by many. I have grown over my time in this world.

From a challenging start in my early years at Home, to surmounting the impact of how the Stigma of violence sculpted me, I found Fight or Flight was often the only choice as I walked through a Civilization that saw me Detained whether I controlled my Impulse or not. Instead of being The Communicator I knew how to be, my dumb decisions kept me Bound to cross a Minefield of setbacks, unintentionally stifling the growth of a Fortunate Son. When my preparation met my greatest opportunity, my life took an Unexpected turn to solid ground that became my Proving Ground. I learned and grew from missteps that caused Damage to my trajectory. Now I patiently wait and eagerly embrace all the experiences coming on the Horizon. My journey has made me known (but still unknown), while it made my responsibility greater, so I work to create balance on my life trek.

After I quit being lazy and making excuses, I have pushed beyond my perceived limitations. I still have goals to achieve, but I love the journey. I got out of my own way. I've learned a lot. Richard Feynman quotes, "I'm smart enough to know that I'm dumb." I'm about growth so my variation to that is "I'm smarter because I realized I was dumber." I'm not dumb anymore. I finally have stability in my life. I control what I can, and accept what I cannot control. I understand that with the way the world has changed, I don't have to follow any traditional path in the pursuit of my goals in production. I can create the positive change in the world that I want to see, and that I want to be, through ventures that I'm passionate about. My journey may not make sense to everyone, but it doesn't have to. It's my journey. I live right and strive to do right. I don't owe anyone an explanation about the moves I make. God will judge my actions. For all the chasing I used to do to get the things I thought I wanted, things I thought would validate me, I don't do that anymore. I've learned over the years that money is not the end-all-be-all. Money is necessary to have options in life, without question, but money is not a definitive way to know the true worth of a person. I started at the bottom, so I know how to maneuver with nothing and still make it, not live extravagantly but I can always work hard and survive wherever I am in the world. I have also been fortunate to meet a lot of people who have a lot of money, and some of them are some of the most miserable people I've ever been around. I've met some people who only validate other people's worth by the wealth they possess. Through them, I learned that even though our financial portfolios were worlds apart, I was elevated to the playing field because of my "celebrity," because celebrity has value. Celebrity is an equalizer.

I've learned that there are many people with wealth who secretly crave the spotlight, while celebrities (speaking specifically about actors in entertainment) are immersed in their craft and sometimes glean the spotlight, but are usually on the hunt to build wealth. The Hollywood conundrum. However, I wasn't built in Hollywood. I'm going to keep pushing myself to discover my full potential. It's been a pretty interesting road so far, even when I fell way off track. I'm excited to see what my life will be like now that I've stopped holding myself back. I'm curious where the next chapter will take me. I'm just getting started. I want to help heal the world for everyone. I don't solely define myself by my pigment. That's not to say that I don't love being Black, because I do. I love being Black. I love my people—we can be wild as f*ck sometimes, and we can also be as regal and noble as the kings and queens who are our ancestors. That's who we are. Regardless of what I have had to go through, or will ever have to go through because of the color of my skin, I love my beautiful Black skin I'm in. <u>And</u> on a much deeper level, beneath the pigment, beyond the depths of my heart, to the core of my soul,

I love all people. Because I'm a child of God and that's what I'm supposed to do. As one of God's children, it's my spiritual duty to love all of God's other children, so that's what I work to do. And I don't feel burdened by the act. All of God's children are not Black or White, so how can I only love and embrace and celebrate the Black or White ones? All of God's children are not Hispanic or Asian, so how can I only love and embrace and celebrate the Hispanic or Asian ones? You get the point. No matter where someone is from in the world, all of God's children are ALL of us. All of humanity. So, the answer is simple: I can't. I can't, so I don't try. I do my best to love everyone, even if I have never met them and have never been exposed to their way of life or their culture. I meet them as a regular human being, embrace the cultural exchange, and enjoy the moments. I get to know them and allow them to get to know me. When we part ways, hopefully, I have felt the love of the person – which will give me the love of their culture – they have felt the love of mine and we've each grown from our interaction. And it won't feel forced. It will feel normal, for no other reason than because we are both children of God and our interactions should be filled with love. That's what God wants. My life flows better when I do what God wants. I'm not a preacher and I don't tell anyone how to live their lives (other than my son, and that's my job so I can keep guiding him to become the best version of himself, despite the obstacles and pitfalls he will face; my daughter is grown and already living a wonderful life of purpose). I will, however, always speak my truth to God's presence in my life. (But that does not mean I want to get into conversations all day, every day about God's presence in my life.) I live with love. And the concept of loving others, with no ulterior motives, not pretending to love others for the sake of sounding good or to look good for social media platforms, but to genuinely and authentically love others is not that hard of a concept to understand, accept, embrace, and employ. And for me, extending God's love is not a subject that's up for debate. Of course, there will be people who want to debate, those who don't believe in God and want to convince me why He doesn't exist, or challenge my beliefs because they feel justified in their position. No, thank you. I don't have time for that. Except for seven years of my life - four years while on *Star Trek: Enterprise* and one year after, and my two years on *General Hospital* - almost every single day has been a struggle, grinding behind the 8-ball. But I'm still here. No one will ever convince me that God doesn't exist. Period. End of discussion. Convincing others that God does exist is not my mission in life. My mission is to inspire through entertainment. I don't have to convince anyone of the existence of God to inspire and walk in my purpose. I just have to continue being who I am. And I give credit where due. When anyone asks the secrets of my success, the answer will always be…God. Hard work, determination, sacrifice, perseverance, focus, assistance from others…and God.

I've learned life is filled with valleys and peaks as it ebbs and flows. God has gotten me through it all. Once I got comfortable in my own skin and found my lane, life has become enjoyable. I've learned to embrace life experiences and be happy. I don't know what fascinating and fun adventures are on the horizon, but I'm ready for them.

ACKNOWLEDGMENTS

To my children, Meghan and Aiden, my
sources of inspiration, my loves, and two
most precious gifts in this world – Thank you
for being my motivation and for showing me
the meaning of unconditional love. I'm not
like other dads and I'm far from perfect, but
I love you both with all that I am.

To my mother, Sandra, who helped make me
the man I am - Thank you for your love and
all the lessons. I'll never forget them. I love
you, mom.

To my grandmother, Serene, who was always
there for me - Thank you for your love,
guidance and for just being you. I love you,
grandma. Rest in Paradise. I'll miss you until
we meet again.

To my son's mother and my ex-wife,
Adrienne - Thank you for your love and our
time. Thank you for blessing us with Aiden
and for being a wonderful mother to our
prince. I'm grateful we found each other and
brought Aiden's bright light into the world.
Keep shining your light. May God always
bless you abundantly with love, happiness
and peace. I love and appreciate you.

To my daughter's mother, Shannon – Thank
you for blessing us with Meghan and raising
her to be the amazing woman she is. I pray
you're blessed with happiness, love and
peace in all you do. I love and appreciate
you.

To my family, Nikki, Gayla, Keith, Dymond, Matthew, Kei'Nashia, Keith, Jr., Kaleah, Myracle and Q'Mara who I love more than you will ever know - Thank ya'll for your love and support. I love you all.

To my People, my Squad (including the ones I've lost touch with): D. Payne, E. Nelson, C. Lahmon, R. Nally, J. Ping, W. Langston (R.I.P), B. Jelloe, S. Hamilton (R.I.P.), K. Miller, M. Reeder, K. Ellsworth, C. Carlo, L. Garland, D. Turner, F. Brown, K. Brown, S. Papazian, J. St. Aimee, S. Antonio, J. Harkness, D. A. Wright, J. Wright, G. Campbell, A. Ballard, G. Wang, T. Winfrey, A. Kim, M. Wylie, J. Collins, J. Resnover, J. Nelson, T. Beard, R. Weatherford and S. Robertson, I couldn't have made it this far without you all...literally, ha-ha. But we made it. Thank you. I love every one of you.

To my attorneys, Ronald E. Elberger (R.I.P.), Craig E. Pinkus, Michael A. Aczon, Jamal C. Wright and LuAnne Morrow, my "wolfpack," thank you all for your direction and always having my back. I love and appreciate you for everything you have done and continue to do for me.

To John Billingsley, thank you for your brilliance and crafting a superb introduction to my journey. I'm grateful we get to Trek through life together. I appreciate you. Love you, Brother.

To Judith and Garfield Reeves-Stevens, thank you for your kind words and beautiful

endorsement of my work. I have the utmost
respect for you two and your literary
accomplishments. I am humbled that you
think so highly of my work. I love and
appreciate you both.

To Rod Roddenberry, Geoff Campbell, and
Joe Balsarotti, thank you for believing in
me and supporting my creative endeavors.
Thank you for investing in me. Thank you
for your trust. I love and appreciate you. I
wish you happiness, prosperity and success
in all you do.

To everyone else who has ever influenced
my life: family, friends, acquaintances,
chance encounters, and even enemies - and
all those who paved the way for me to pursue
my dreams, including people I've never met
but have inspired me - By your actions... or
inactions... you've all contributed to my life
experiences in one way or another. Whether
positively or negatively, each circumstance
has added to my overall make-up. Thank
you. Family and friends, I love ya'll... to
the rest of the world, I love ya'll too, but
different. I wish happiness and blessings to
you and yours.

AUTHOR'S NOTE: A Final Word

Thank you all for going on this journey with me. Thank you for wanting to get to know me. Now you do. To a degree. Of course, there's more to me than just what's contained in these pages. This is a curated peek into my world. Please know that I am not a tormented, suffering soul reliving the traumas of my past. I worked through my emotional scarring years ago and healed my wounded inner child. I'm a work-in-progress with everyone and everything. I say all of this to say, please respect the privacy of my family because although I chose a life in the public eye, they did not. I'm happy to talk about my life, but I don't speak from the space of a broken man. My life can't break me. I am surviving my life.

Thank you for reading. I appreciate you.

Anthony Montgomery

LIFETREK SOUNDTRACK & LYRICS

These songs are more than just music—they're snapshots of my journey, reflections of the different seasons I've lived through. Some came out of joy, others from pain, but all of them capture the man I was becoming in that moment. Like the stories in this book, they each carry a piece of my truth. When I got serious about music and wrote "What You Know About," (my first full song) my confidence grew—I realized I'm actually good at writing songs. I'm proud to share some of that work with you here.

My album "A.T" was released in 2007 via my international record label AGR Television Records and Universal Music Group.

LYRICS 1

"Kick Back" (A. Montgomery)

I need y'all to do me a favor / yeah / one favor / all y'all…kick back

Verse 1
(hey hey) too many / be mad an fussin'/ stop the madness y'all / stop cussin'/ let's have a easy / open discussion/ wit' no fear o'repercussion/ no bustin'/ o' angry rushin'/ I wanna embrace / celebrate life / 'cause it's on and crackin' / so we gotta do it right / no ice-grillin' (nope) / no mean muggin' (nah) / no fights/ just relaxin' and keepin' it tight / 'cause it's / such a frenzy in the world we live / gots to change da game / for da kids / not only that / as we grow / we deal wit' it / so I had to adjust the thinkin' cap and make a hit / Kick Back / I'm givin' you sumpin' to ride wit' / ease up the flow just a little / for you to vibe this / I'm doin' this for the masses / that's the way it is / I'm comin' at you like Oprah / gotta give big

Hook
Let's max (hey) / relax (hey) / everybody kick back / (what we doin'?) kick / kick / kick back / (what we doin'?) kick / kick / kick back / Let's max (hey) / relax (hey) / everybody kick back / (what we doin'?) kick / kick / kick back / (what we doin'?) kick / kick / kick back

Verse 2
This beat is where ya just slow down ya groove/ where you chill and just do you / there's drink / there's food / hot people too / hard liquor an brew / it's cool / let ya brain release / it holds the clues / all things ya used to do / right now we'll make time freeze fo' you / just keep on doin' you / Will gave us a jam for the "Summertime" (summertime) / that song's gonna be around for a lifetime / we was kickin' it to L.L's "Loungin'" (who do you love?)/ that

was hittin' / he was battin' a thousand / Outkast brought "Elevators" all day (me and you) / Soul II Soul, "Back to Life" on replay / the sense o' Common showed us what "Love Is" (testify) / so I'ma show ya mine / cause the mood's right

Hook
Verse 3
This journey / can end in hurry / the cycle speeds up / the more we worry / the situations presented / come in a flurry / but ain't nuttin' we can't handle / wit' vision blurry / most scurry around / in such a rush / take a second / get back in touch / wit' the source in us all / the love an' such / make a moment for 'self / that's the real stuff / we all need a minute o' two / quiet alone / no place to be / no telephone / necessity / solitude ain't gon' / we get / blinded by life / fall in like drones / on a quest to express / we do get tested / don't like to confess it / but hate to get bested / just / like real estate / time's invested / but on the 7th day / God rested / so
Hook x2

LYRICS 2

"Strongest Ever" feat. Dakari (A. Montgomery)

This song is dedicated to my mother…and all the strong women out there. Any of you that have ever had to struggle…you're still loved.

Verse 1
Women are strong/ my mother/ the strongest ever/ wherever I go mom / naw / I'll never sever my love / I'll love my mom forever / straight talk / no beatin' around bushes / o' tryna be clever / being the strongest woman that I've ever known / never been to Africa / but she needs a throne / her own / she did her best / four kids / tough love shown / her foot stayed in my butt / til' I was grown / one marriage / but she shoulda stayed on her own / for real / we woulda been better off alone / the coward / he beat my momma like a punchin' bag / I used to pray to be stronger so I could get him back/ but you don't want me to hate / so I let it ride / not a choice / gotta wait / you can't rush time / wait made hate dissipate / mom you had it right / the way I made it relate / I live a longer life

Hook
You made me strong / 'cause you was strong / now I'm the strongest ever / you made me strong / 'cause you was strong / now I'm the strongest ever / you made me strong / 'cause you was strong / now I'm the strongest ever / ever / ever / ever / (yeah)

Verse 2
I wanted to make his head crack / peel the dude's cap / break his arms and

legs / snap his neck back / though it hurt momma to know that I felt that way / "Just forgive him and pray / that's what the Bible say" / I try / that ain't easy for me to do mom / I give my life for you mom / that's where we from / you say forgive him / and momma I promise I try / but at night / closed eyes / I saw you cry / I'm sorry momma / that he hurt you / when he act that way / he never gave you a voice / an' let you have a say / was he drunk? / was he high? / crazy? / insane? / I thought we was made to protect / not cause you pain / but you don't want me to hate / so I let it ride / not a choice / gotta wait / you can't rush time / wait made hate dissipate / mom you had it right / the way I made it relate / I live a longer life

Hook
Verse 3
Before that drama / a different drama would unfold / her father died / she was 13 years old / in summer school / June 15 / '68 I'm told / a precious young soul / she lost a foothold / 2 years later / no paternal influence / a daughter born / a year later / a son saw a new dawn / the next year / on time / yeah she graduated / she didn't have a choice / (nah) grandma don't play it/ she had another couple kids by another 2 / what I learn from them clowns? / what not to do / she did her best / no plan / Pac said it / "It ain't easy tryna raise a man" / but mom did it / and she don't want me to hate / so I let it ride / not a choice / gotta wait / you can't rush time / wait made hate dissipate / my mom you had it right / the way I made it relate / I live a better life
Hook

LYRICS 3

"What You Know About" feat. Mr. Smilez, Dakari & Melodie Joy (A. Montgomery, R. Bailey, Dakari)

Hook
What you think? / what you think? / what you know about? / what you think? / what you think? / what you know about? / what you think? / what you think? / what you know about? / what you think? / what you know about Trek? / what you think? / what you think? / what you know about? / what you think? / what you think? / what you know about? / what you think? / what you think? / what you know about? / what you think? / what you know about Trek?

Verse 1
Yo, what chu know about Trek? / the universe / gazin' at the star charts 'til it's rehearsed / warp drive on line got ill speed / the energy crystals got what cha need / night's not so bright when you surpass light / no seatbelt so ya betta hold tight / what chu know about / the warrior race? / oversize brude mon / wit da screw face / rude boi screamin' tinkin' he superia / over mankind? / is he crazy bruh? / get him home / no delay / man need da journey / leave

218

'em on his feet / neva on a gurney / what chu know about alion givin' chase / genetical enhancement / no mutant case / what chu know about a mission tryna stop my crew? / try as hard's you want guy / we comin' through…you

Hook
Verse 2
Smilez, chea, look, unh
let me show you how I do this thing / how I fly past stars / at light speed through space / dodgin' them enemy and hata fleets / that don't like da fact I'm at the helm holdin' my seat / yeah / they just mad I'm here takin they freaks / but I got da red beam / on dey face and cheek / see I get around / 22 worlds / 18 weeks / you know I love dem butterfly girls / have ta send you a subspace postcard / so you can see / what chu think? / I'm da first space P. I. M. P. / I'm wit' a star fleet / you see my blue suit / up here / that's ya ice / da starship da coup / you can catch me on playback / hittin' every 36 levels / of any trade complex / we got lightyears to run dese capers / next stop fa me and crew / da decon chamba / dismissed (oh)

Hook
Verse 3
(Listen close) what chu know about a pilot navigatin' planets? / confusin' to you but he understands it / what chu know about a doc from anotha system? / interspecies exchange / bet they gonna miss him / what chu know about a weapon man full o' pride / when it's life o' deaf dog he's on ya side / what chu really think you know about communicatin'? / linguist on call always educatin' / what chu know about a engineer in da mix / stave off time no stress it's fixed / what chu know about a fem from da high command? / logical, emotions in / you understand / what chu know about a captain wit' a life missin'? / set to boldly go / sick and tired o' wishin' / thru a new era / peace beara / mankind/preconceptions behind / wit' a open mind

Hook
Sci-fi is an evolution / it's been around for so, so long / all you have to do / is allow yourself to / have an open mind / and you could experience things you / never thought possible / you could never have imagined / yeah / we should all dream / dream for a better life / for a better future

LYRICS 4

"Gotta Believe" feat. Honey B (A. Montgomery)

Got to believe / got to believe

Hook

Gotta believe in ya little brother / you both came up outta the same mother / gotta believe that he'll be okay / HE'll make a way when you see now way / gotta believe that before it's through / there'll be a pride inside o' you / watch ya' baby boy learn how to stand / no longer child now brotha man

Verse 1
It's hard goin' home / a tragedy on ya' dome / ya grown gotta be strong / ya been on ya own / come on / a family feud / façade was blown / attitude was to reconcile / nothin' left but to mourn / parent friend / thick and thin / startin' the day you was born / figured he be there foreva / but from ya' life he was torn / gotta a lot o' contained emotions / neva shown / it's on / journey to depths o' ya' soul / neva known / father preparin' command skills needed to hone / now that father is gone / finish trainin' alone / but more than missin' him is not copacetic / somewhat prophetic / that ya need his permission or the notion is thrown / crave the science his belief in you neva gave way / you heard thangs was said / you didn't hear him say / eternal pride inside when you got his praise / but not receivin' the words mean sleepless days / since sis' is on anotha ship / wit' her own life / she couldn't sit back and baby-sit and become a wife / mother's getting' older / yeah, she's still strong / that empty chair is proof / we don't live long / all that's left / a brother / love him like no other / always tried to protect him / keep him safe and under cover / did ya' best to shield him but he's gotta grow / the youngin took the reigns but can he keep hold? / will he be able to deal wit' the pain / cope wit' the strain on his brain? / no further tutelage / can he maintain? / uh, tell me / believe me

Hook
Verse 2
Extended visit / ya' brother showed crazy tension / seem he got some aggression that he forgot to mention / several sta'dates later / he's holdin' real resentment / sibling rivalry shouldn't be a life commitment / no matter how mad at 'em ya get / they still ya blood / they on ya nerves / they make ya sick / that's real love / so get cha feelin's in order / villains approachin' the border / they want cha cargo if you resist 'em they want cha lives / don't back down / don't ever give in / imperative / make a stance to win / so ya dropped a load got maneuverability / enemy stunned / statis pop / super agility / not passin' fo' fun / triangulation begun / precision blast / insure the battle is done / captain gave him an ultimatum to captivate 'em / Don't come back / next time eradicate 'em / overwhelmin' admiration it's comin' true / brotha was a captain / now a leader too (yeah, yeah / believe me)

Hook
Got to believe/ Got to believe/ (laughter) Got to believe/ that was fun
* Additional vocals by M. De La Rosa and A. De La Rosa

LYRICS 5

"Yes They Are" feat. Dakari (A. Montgomery)

It's not right to judge based on the actions of others
People, all people, are individuals
Determine your compatibility on a case-by-case basis
You'll never know what treasures you'll unearth when you get past the
surface

Verse 1
Got my man in cell / dawg / what the hell? / gonna need some help to make
the bail / checkin' energy readin's / from the other side o' da moon / a shuttle
attack / coulda spelled they doom / didn't know who it was / that got 'em
from the cosmos / gettin' got like that / coulda left 'em both comatose /
banged, bruised / thoroughly confused / let's work baby / time to pay dues/
colonel in charge / said the boys were in a "zone" / and shouldna been / it
was military owned / he can't be serious / they just curious / this precarious
situation's mysterious / I remember an adage about a cat / these two cats got
friends that got they back / they ain't dyin' / know ya lyin' / and if you don't
let 'em go / ya set's fryin'

Hook
Are they in it / to go to the limit / until the job is finished / and help you out? /
yes they are / are they able / to turn all the tables / so y'all are stable / to break
the chains? / yes they are / are they free / to help you to see / just what you
can be / outside the sect? / yes they are / are they here / cause their thoughts
are clear / for you to follow them and demand respect? / yes they are

Verse 2
(you know what they did?) they tried to beat him to break him / but his
resilience ain't shaken / they gotta find out the information anotha way / the
retribution is comin' / like a million gunners gunnin' / and when it finds 'em I
promise you they're gonna pay / they're gonna shake up the scene / and if you
don't know I mean / that when they done wit' the planet it / won't be the same
/ they gotta get 'em they freedom / they been trapped for no reason / if they
brave and they strong enough / there'll be a change / forty some yards away /
lies the ship dockin' bay / and when the wall explodes in / there'll be a play /
might be a suicide run / so grab ya particle gun / if you can't use it right / get
/ behind someone / see they blastin' up outta there / captive audience far and
near / they did this for y'all / so just get it clear / they coulda transported out /
but that's not what they about / you questioned their loyalty / but now there's
no doubt / right?

Hook
Verse 3
Dude had negative images in his mind set / but bein' in there made the
concept suspect / not all bad / in fact most good / but evil abroad / make good
misunderstood / run the fleet / cap don't condone violence / but he can't let
people be / persecuted in silence / wanted a call / nah, strict regulations / no
contact outside but magistration / that won't fly / you know why my guy? /
they got the fire to blow ya sky high / manipulate / frequency / secure the line
/ they 'bout to circumvent the legal this time / them boys / underrated / system
infiltrated / had the chance to spring 'em / but he hesitated / now he gotta pay
/ done talkin' today / they settin' off charges / ignitin' his way
Hook x2

LYRICS 6

"General" feat. Flii Stylz (A. Montgomery, A. Burton)

Hook
I'm speaking just in general (just in general) / I run it like a general (like a
general) / I'm just speaking in general (just in general) / I run it like a general
/I walk like a... I talk like a... General / I move like a... Smoove like a...
General (yeh, yeh, yeah) / Catch me on the General / but don't fly off the
deep end / I'm speakin' just in general / Walk like a... I talk like a... General
/ I move like a... Smoove like a... General (yeh, yeh, yeah) Catch me on the
general / but don't fly off the deep end / I'm speakin' just in general

Verse 1
Ya, ya, ya, ya / here's ya level / Tried not to lose my patience / after I lost my
patient Mentally it's bendin' me, I'm feeling some frustration / Not to mention
the tension meter is ran up / my heart has been torn apart / if ya feelin' me,
throw ya hand up / stand up / I'ma stand up / for what I believe in cause I'm
evolvin' / I think I even need a shrink to do this problem solvin' / I'm ballin' /
how do you do? I'm well do to / Or should I say well off / neva fell off / cause
it cool / True this ain't the verbiage that I usually use / But it's the Doc, let it
rock, I ain't the usual dude / You gotta face it / they only know me for healing
da patients / So this whole thought is just a generalization

Hook
Verse 2
I made it to the Port / played a sport / had to cut it short / lotta awkward
angles in this love triangle boy / more like a square box / four corners four
walls / I've been known to get inside your head when I'm on call / Chi-town
was my town / a block that didn't glisten / all I could do was listen / that was
my opposition / Curt knocked me out position / Jordan I'm really missin'/
sorta sick how I be having silly visions of 'em kissin'/ but I could never PH /

that's a coward-ly way / rise above it cause it's just anotha game dat we play (yeh) just anotha game dat we play / rise above it cause it's just anotha game dat we play

Hook

THANK YOU!!

To all the wonderful people who supported and pre-ordered the book:

Amanda Harber	Crystal Baker	Aaron Ray
Adeena Mignogn	Richard Dickens	Janet Harlow
Constantin von Campe	Jean DeBellis	Ben Lucas
Marisela Lorray	Cassandra Girard	Laura Moose
Carrie Schwent	Peter Borreggine	Sharon Meyer
Mary Jo Schrabasz	Kimberly Wilson	Fazia Rizvi
David Toledano	Samantha Fraser	Kristen Costa
David Loconto	Scott Williams	Alita Reed
Christopher Arzberger	Lori Queirolo	Mark Bird
David Gregory	Chef Lovejoy Cole	Marc Wade
Rodney Simmons	Kimberly Ferrell	Lisa Pellam
Sunday Sabbath	Benjamin Crook	Morgan Kiser
Joshua Ostrovsky	Kasey Shafsky	Bill Erickson
KarenLynn Robinson	Marjorie Munoz	Anton Lents
Finn Solterbeck	Margit Baldauf	Esther Silva
Mike Oxbrown	Malcolm Goldiner	Alain Bloch

THANK YOU ALL FOR YOUR LOVE AND SUPPORT!!

I APPRECIATE YOU!!

www.ingramcontent.com/pod-product-compliance
Lightning Source LLC
Chambersburg PA
CBHW060417130626
46555CB00005B/2103